Mila and Mervusya

Mila and Mervusya

A Russian Wedding

Mervyn Matthews

seren

seren
is the book imprint of
Poetry Wales Press Ltd
2 Wyndham Street, Bridgend,
Wales CF31 1EF

ISBN 1-85411-259-7

A CIP record for this title is available from
the British Library

The publisher works with the financial assistance of the
Arts Council of Wales

Printed in Plantin by WBC Book Manufacturers, Bridgend

CONTENTS

Introduction

Perhaps the plaintive numbers flow
For old, unhappy, far-off things,
And battles long ago:

(William Wordsworth, 'The Reaper')

The events which make up my story took place some thirty to forty years ago, which in human terms is a vast amount of time. The curious reader may well ask why (if the story is so interesting!) I have not told it before. The ending, after all, is a happy one: the marriage did eventually take place, and there were even a few amusing moments. The answer to the question is easy: the anguish and pain involved were so great, after my Moscow marriage plans went awry, that I could rarely bring myself to think about them, let alone write. So the story was not told, and hardly mentioned even in the family. When friends referred to it I would sometimes, in a jocular fashion, question whether the events occurred at all. Our children knew nothing of them, either. It was only recently, as old age approached, that I decided to recount the tale. Many of the events in it were unique and dramatic.

Another fair question is how can one resurrect so distant a past, and indeed write a whole book about it. This is, after all, autobiography and not fiction. The explanation is again simple. The main events have lain firmly embedded in my mind, even though I have not talked about them, and could easily be shaken out when I came to write these pages. Some episodes have been preserved in the memories of other people who played a part, and are still alive. The reader may be surprised to learn that I have scarcely drawn my wife into this work: she has, it seems, jettisoned many memories, perhaps by way of self-protection. The work is almost entirely my own.

Memory may be rich, but it is not enough, and I have relied heavily on piles of yellowing paper. Fortunately, while in Russia, I kept an occasional diary of events which seemed important to me, and most of this has survived. Within a year or so of dealing directly with the KGB (that is, from the autumn of 1959), I made another forty pages of notes, including an account of events for MI5: I also kept dozens of photographs, vouchers and tickets dating from that time.

After I left Russia in 1964 I gradually filled a trunk with document-ation – official letters, appeals, travel receipts for journeys to Europe and the USSR, articles in the national press. In addition there were some three thousand letters, nearly all in Russian, which passed between myself and Mila during our long wait to get married. Nevertheless, I would be the first to agree that there has been an inevitable slippage of recollection. Detail has been lost, and the sequence of some minor events as related here may not be quite correct. The problem of the conversations involved a great mental tussle: should I set down the gist of what was said, as noted or remembered, or should I 'reconstitute' it as accurately as possible? Following editorial advice I have reconstituted a few key sentences in each case: this at least makes more interesting reading.

One or two important documents have been lost, a few events have been left out in deference to other people's wishes, or because I could not remember them well enough. A few names have been changed. There are doubtless factual blemishes, but enough has been saved, in one way or another, to support the story without imagination or embellishment. I have tried to be honest throughout and have not added any dubious detail which might (with hindsight) idealise, or enhance the tale. And since it is always interesting to ponder other people's fates, I have added a final chapter containing events which took place later, but which illuminate earlier years. The marriage itself has remained uncommented.

I am grateful to friends whose names appear in the text for occasional assistance. Mr. Harry Willetts and Mrs. Pat Utechin corrected various minor errors, and Mr. Mick Felton provided much valuable editorial comment. The spellings of Russian words have in some instances been simplified to accord with common usage in the West, and the earlier Soviet place names have been retained.

Mervyn Matthews

One. A New Friend

The adventure which was to take up several years of my life began quietly enough in Moscow on the 15th May, 1959. It was a cold spring day (summer comes late in Moscow) and I had the morning off from my translating job at the British Embassy to visit the Soviet Ministry of Higher Education. This might not seem a very exciting prospect for a young man of twenty-seven, especially as the object was to collect material for an exceedingly boring dissertation on Soviet youth employment. But I was quite delighted, because it offered a welcome contact with the real world of Russia, outside the isolated embassy compound.

I had taken the embassy job because it was a rare opportunity to live in that mysterious land, something which I greatly wanted to do after spending years learning the language at Manchester University and studying Russian affairs at St. Antony's College, Oxford. The visit to the Ministry, I was sure, would reveal another little piece of the Russian jigsaw. But it involved an element of risk, too: for although the horrors of Stalinism were over, and Khrushchev was in power, the KGB (the much-feared Committee for State Security) could engineer all sorts of awkward situations. Foreigners were still a race apart, and even a diplomatic pass did not guarantee a quiet life.

I was to meet Aleksandr Nazarov, head of the Ministry's Foreign Department. For reasons known only in the Soviet bureaucracy (and probably the KGB) he had been extremely helpful in setting things up. On receiving a formal request for an interview from the Embassy he had not merely named an institute where I could discuss the placement of graduates, but also arranged for me to go to his office first, and meet a junior colleague who would accompany me there.

I went to the Ministry by metro, which was less convenient, but vastly more interesting than the inside of an embassy car. The Foreign Department of the Ministry was located in the Institute of Architecture, on Zhdanov Street, in the centre. It was in an nineteenth-century building with an ornate and pleasing facade. But the Ministry of Higher Education was not a particularly prestigious organisation, and on entering I found the interior to be quite shabby, be-lying the formerly elegant high ceilings and marble staircase. No decorating had been done for decades, and the ubiquitous brown and cream paint looked as though it had been applied by drunken peasants. The dour woman who checked passes just inside the entrance (most Soviet institutions, important or otherwise, had a doorkeeper) told me to go up to the first floor. On reaching it I found a doorplate with A.A. Nazarov on it. I knocked on the double-leafed door.

"Come in," said a female voice. I found myself in an outer office, confronted by a fat, ill-dressed secretary. It was all very Soviet. "Mr. Matthews? Yes, Aleksandr Aleksandrovich is ready to receive you." She got up and waddled to an inner door which was slightly ajar. She opened it a little further, and looked inside.

"Aleksandr Aleksandrovich, Mr. Matthews is here!"

"Show him in, please."

Nazarov's room was larger and lighter than the anteroom, but no less shabby. The occupant, a small thick-set man with a square face and crinkly black hair, had the reserved and slightly wary manner adopted by all Soviet officials who dealt with foreigners. A copy of the UNESCO guide to scholarships lay on his desk, its brightly coloured jacket contrasting strangely with the drab surroundings. Since Russian students could not normally dream of going abroad, the volume was no doubt used mainly as a token of international status.

"Good morning, Mr. Matthews," Comrade Nazarov began in a friendly enough tone. "I gather you are interested in the way we organise employment for our graduates."

"Material for my dissertation," I explained. "I've been working on it for some years already."

"These things take time," said Nazarov sympathetically. "I hope you will enjoy the visit we have arranged for you this morning, and find it useful. This particular institute trains engineers for our light industry. I have asked one of my younger colleagues, Comrade Vadim Popov, to take you there."

Nazarov pressed what looked like a genuine nineteenth-century electric knob on his desk and the secretary reappeared. "Would you ask Comrade Popov to come along, please?"

I do not know where Comrade Popov had been secreted (he was not in the outer office when I arrived) but he came in almost immediately. Fair, curly-haired and blue-eyed, like many Russians, he was short and extremely well built, his movements betokening great physical strength. The deep lines on his forehead and the confidence in his eyes gave him an air of considerable maturity, though I guessed he was in fact only three or four years my senior. My first impression was that although he was on the Soviet side of the fence, in personal matters he could probably be relied upon.

"Please introduce yourselves," said Aleksandr Aleksandrovich, Russian fashion.

Vadim Popov seemed pleased to see me, and after we had shaken hands, and thanked Aleksandr Aleksandrovich, he led me down to the street. To emphasise the importance of the occasion the Ministry had actually laid on an official car to take us to the institute. And indeed, when we got there, I found that the director had organised a much grander affair than I anticipated. Half a dozen teachers and administrators awaited me, seated around a great table and eager to answer questions about how their graduates were employed. The matter was regarded as an example of superior socialist planning which could be safely demonstrated to the outside world.

I had always been rather shy at academic gatherings, perhaps because my modest family background did not predispose me to that sort of contact. So although there was no language difficulty, I got through my questions in a few minutes, and had little more to say. Indeed, at that point it looked as though I would inflict on my hosts the terrible indignity of not taking up enough of their time. Fortunately, Popov stepped in and kept things going for the extra hour or so expected: so I was very grateful for his help. After we had finished, and were driving back to the centre of Moscow, it seemed only polite to ask him to have lunch with me, though (I thought) he could hardly accept. Mere mention of the word "embassy" was normally enough to send Soviet citizens scurrying off for safety. Much to my surprise, he agreed to come.

"Let's go to the Cafe Ararat," I suggested. "It's near." It also happened to be one of the more interesting corners of Moscow. Here, in a rather bogus Armenian decor, to a background of 'decadent' American jazz or a Western version of 'Black Eyes' you could observe the Moscow *jeunesse dorée* consuming Caucasian fried pasties and Armenian cognac, that is, after the usual long wait. Nobody went to a Soviet restaurant those days unless they had two or three hours to spare.

Over lunch we got to know one another a little, and switched to first names. Vadim had graduated in Korean at the Institute for Eastern Languages, and was teaching Korean history at the prestigious Institute for Oriental Studies. He also had a part-time job at the Ministry headquarters, which was why, he said, he had been called in to accompany me. He was just finishing an MA dissertation himself and was obviously secure in the Soviet academic hierarchy. But he was very secretive about his background: apart from mentioning an 'uncle' who was a man of influence, and had promised him thirty thousand roubles to buy a car for his birthday, he would say nothing. 'Popov' is a common Russian name, and even if it was genuine, nothing of his background could be deduced from it.

It soon became apparent to me that although Vadim was in an academic job, anyone less scholarly it would be difficult to imagine. He assessed his work mainly in terms of salary. He had a good sense of humour and a liking for vodka (though he was evidently no drunkard). His main interests lay in sport – he had once won a trophy for swimming – and in the opposite sex. He could produce the sort of irresistible, lascivious look which other men envied. He collected postage stamps, not so much for their intellectual interest as for their investment value; each set was stored for sale in the future. He evinced a keen interest in cars – particularly their prices and running costs – in the West. Why did we have such high accident rates, he asked, as he had read in the papers? I explained the system of obligatory insurance, as far as I understood it.

"Ah," he said, "It's clear, isn't it? If you don't have to pay for damage, it doesn't matter whether you crash or not!"

When he asked me whether Catholicism was a branch of Christianity, I decided that his grasp of Western culture was not all that good, either. He had a robust Russian disdain for anything lying to the east of Soviet frontiers, including Korea. He had never been there and evidently had no wish to go. Like most of his compatriots he was a victim of the Soviet censorship.

On the whole, despite such minor discrepancies of outlook, the lunch went exceedingly well, and I thought that if by some miracle we could continue meeting, he would make a very interesting friend. When I got back to the Embassy that afternoon I went to Chancery and gave a brief account of my official visit. The Embassy, in its isolation, welcomed staff activities which might reveal a little of what was going on behind the Russian screen, as long as such activities were registered and did not present a threat to security. I submitted Vadim's name in the accepted fashion, and went back to the little room at the end of the corridor where I did my translations. "Have a nice lunch?" asked Fay, my secretary. Anybody less Russian than she it would be difficult to imagine.

*

In fact, the lunch had been a welcome relief from the embassy round, which I was finding increasingly claustrophobic. Most of the staff lived in specially designated diplomatic flats around Moscow, and were taken to and from work in embassy cars and minibuses, so as to spare them the rigours of the local bus and metro services. It was very convenient, but I used public transport whenever I could. I shared a flat with Bob Longmire, a small, bespectacled and congenial colleague, just off the Sadovo-Samotechnaya square. Like all diplomatic accommodation it was well furnished with imported items, and apart from a few things – the heavy double windows, drab wallpaper, antediluvian sink and stove – it resembled a middle-class flat almost anywhere on the continent. The diplomatic block in which it was located, however, was insulated from the outside world (as was the Embassy itself) by a special branch of the Soviet militia – huge, threatening men who kept a twenty-four hour guard at the entrance. Anything less like the crowded slums of Moscow, where occupancy was commonly said to be up to three people a room, could hardly be imagined. Not that foreigners were ever invited into them!

The only Russians who could get into our little haven were the maidservants from the "UPDK", the Soviet organisation which controlled all domestic help for foreigners. The maids had KGB clearance and were commonly thought to report on the hapless souls who employed them. Bob and I had a woman called Lidia who was hopeless at nearly everything, and unbelievably lazy. She was also physically attractive and clearly available for compromising adventure between the sheets, the kind of person, in fact, that the UPDK usually provided for diplomatic bachelors. Neither Bob nor I were tempted, but the dust got so bad that I asked Bob whether it would not be better to get someone else. The UPDK maids were outrageously overpaid by Moscow standards, anyway, and we should be getting our money's worth. "No point in trying," said he. "They might send us someone even worse. Lidia serves the food nicely when people come to lunch, and at least she has a soft spot for Shura." Shura was our Siberian tabby then showing signs of pregnancy.

Apart from the stringent security arrangements, and the Russian fear of foreigners, the diplomatic community was also isolated by the language barrier. Apart from translators like myself, very few people knew Russian. The embassies were socially inbred to an extraordinary degree. I found myself constantly attending lunches and dinners in flats very like our own, and meeting only people from other missions. The food and drink were usually excellent, but obtained through the same mail-order firms, or bought by servants like Lidia at collective farm markets which most Russians were too poor to use. There were airmail editions of foreign papers, fashionable magazines, the latest novels for discussion by embassy wives who had little else to do.... A kind of numbing sameness was encountered everywhere.

The guests at these gatherings tended to be sorted by seniority and branch, so that a Head of Chancery (for example) would not normally be invited to dine with his own radio operator. The elite of the Foreign Office comprised 'Branch A', who alone were entrusted with diplomatic work, and could advance to the exalted status of ambassador. Bob and myself, though specialists in our own right, and on the diplomatic list (I was actually bottom), were merely 'Branch B'. A lot of these social practices may have been inevitable, and were taken for granted: but the embassy round in general was a far cry from Russia outside the double windows. I kept thinking I was in the wrong place.

There were, however, amusing episodes, like Prime Minister Harold Macmillan's visit in February, 1959. Before he arrived an admonitory circular went around saying, in effect, that this was a big thing, and everyone was expected to go into overdrive. Bob Longmire proudly told me that he had been chosen to take a diplomatic bag down to Kiev, which Macmillan was also to visit. Why our Prime Minister should need a diplomatic bag on a day's visit to the Ukrainian capital, I could not understand, but such was the arrangement. "It's not our business to ask," said Bob, who was an obedient sort of chap. "It's just required." While Macmillan was in Moscow everyone scurried around looking serious, and doing extra jobs. It probably did no good whatever.

When the time came for Khrushchev to see Macmillan off at the airport I was involved myself. The powers that be decided to supplement the clutch of Branch A diplomats in the departure party with a couple of people from the research section. On arrival at the airport I and another colleague, Ray Hutchings, joined the official line to shake hands with the two leaders. Our presence provoked an objection from an arrogant Chancery man but we stood our ground and were rewarded by the brief grasp of two prime ministerial paws.

That was not quite the end of the story, however. After Macmillan had boarded his splendid aeroplane the whole departure party, including Khrushchev and an air marshal or two, had to wait on the tarmac as the engines were started and the craft turned for take-off. We all, to a man, found ourselves directly in the jet stream, and sprayed with a fine rain of aviation fuel. After what seemed an age, the aircraft moved off, and the rain stopped. Only when the plane was airborne could we retreat to our cars, wondering how on earth we were going to get the awful smell out of our winter furs.

★

Even when one was away from the Embassy, contact with Russians was greatly inhibited. The man in the street knew only too well that most foreigners were followed by KGB operatives, and any association could easily lead to 'unpleasantness' – a threat of dismissal from work, an interview in the Lubianka, or (alternatively) pressure to maintain a relationship and inform on a regular basis. The KGB-imposed restrictions were ridiculous, as the great majority of embassy staff had no nefarious intent, and lacked the qualities needed for spying anyway. But very few Russians were prepared to take the risk, interesting though it may have been to have a 'capitalist' friend. On the other hand, the embassies, apprehensive about KGB penetration, discouraged staff from friendship with Russians. Hence the system of listing outside meetings.

More adventurous spirits tried to break out of the circle by learning a little Russian, going to the theatre, travelling in the provinces. The Russian speakers like myself could associate more easily, but we were watched more closely, and suffered more from the pervasive fear of foreigners. One of my great pleasures, in fact, was to go off walking in the streets of an evening and observe the antics of the operatives (known as 'goons' in embassy circles) as they tried to keep up with me. Getting away from them was virtually impossible, because they worked in squads, with radio cars, and passed their quarry on, one to the other. However, making them break cover was an unending source of fun. One of the best ways, I found, was simply to start running. If they were not to lose you, they had to run as well, revealing all. It was particularly hard on the middle-aged and fat. Of course, such pranks were most undiplomatic, and I said nothing about them at the Embassy.

Superficially I fitted into the diplomatic round fairly well: I was quite presentable, had some training in Russian affairs, and I was listed as a third secretary. But after a few weeks' employment it became clear to me that I was very much a square peg in a round hole. I decided that I had no interest, like Bob, in making a Foreign Office career below the true diplomatic level. I desperately wanted to be in Russia, rather than in Her Majesty's Embassy. Apart from that, an upbringing in a rather poor working-class family in the Hafod, Swansea was not the best prelude to the social demands of embassy life.

My childhood world (shared by millions of other people) featured houses without running (let alone hot) water, no bathrooms, telephones, cars or even books; poor, war-damaged schools; and no foreign travel (a bit of hitch-hiking came only when I was a student). Most of the men were labourers, while the wives stayed at home attending to endless domestic chores. Apart from that I had a couple of extra disadvantages – separated parents and a crippled grand-mother. So although my father had taught me 'table manners', and we were always warm and well-fed, I lacked the upbringing, graces (and monied appearance!) required in diplomatic circles. My indelible South Wales accent, without any proper command of Welsh, gave it all away.

Of course, I would not for a moment have laid claim to sympathy, because I had obviously been so much more fortunate than most of the boys around me. I had received an extended education, landed a good, if temporary, job in Moscow, and had decent career prospects. But there is no doubt that my upbringing made me a most unusual choice for Foreign Office employment, and I would not have obtained it without the backing of an Oxford college. The Foreign Office certainly took a long time – several months – to give me security clearance. I mention my background in some detail because it explains, in some measure, my bemused disdain for the social games I observed in the diplomatic community, and contributed to the drama which followed. The Russians were always on the lookout for gullible foreigners of proletarian stock, people who may have borne the brunt of 'capitalist exploitation'.

★

A friendship with Vadim offered welcome contact with the real Russia. I soon found that he was willing to go on meeting me, and during the months that followed we did so regularly. It was clear that he enjoyed some official protection, because he would telephone me at the embassy flat. Only one other Russian had ever done that – a student – he had been rapidly summoned to the Dean's office and warned of expulsion if he did it again. All foreigners' lines were, of course, tapped.

Vadim always had plenty of money and loved to frequent Moscow's best restaurants. So we went back to the Ararat, then the Metropole, the Sofia, the Peking, the Baku, and ended up more than once in the two gypsy restaurant barges on Moscow River. I loved the raucous singers, their colourful dress, tambourines and heavy-footed stamping, and I was quite happy to tolerate the indifferent food to hear them. The atmosphere was very Russian, and few foreigners were to be seen. Occasionally, too, Vadim would get tickets for some popular theatre performance, although I was no great theatre-goer myself. My parents had no interest in the stage, and had not nurtured one in me. War-time Swansea was not the best seeding ground for thespian endeavour.

Having entered his name on the embassy list once, I did not bother to provide updates on our meetings – I was afraid some fool in the hierarchy would order me to stop. My silence may have been 'irregular', but I was not particularly concerned because Vadim never showed the least interest in the Embassy, or in my work there. I had no access to highly sensitive information, though he was not to know that. Mostly we talked about the West, Vadim's amorous conquests, and the best ways to enjoy yourself in Moscow. Our meetings were apparently quite innocuous, but the mere fact that I went to them widened the psychological gap between myself and my embassy colleagues. But why, I thought, go to diplomatic parties if you could spend the time with a real Russian of more or less your own age? Although Fay, I think, had her eye on me, I had formed no emotional attachments in that sphere.

Then, one evening, my relations with Vadim took an entirely unexpected turn. He had telephoned me to suggest that we met not at a restaurant, as usual, but near the Manezh building in the centre of town. We would go on somewhere from there. I was intrigued, and agreed; the meeting was fixed for seven o'clock the following Saturday evening. When the time came I took the crowded trolley bus and alighted near Manezh Square. The Manezh is typical bit of early nineteenth-century Moscow, an enormous, yellow structure, formerly the home of a tsarist riding school. It had long since been turned into an exhibition hall by the Soviet authorities.

At that hour it was dark and deserted, and there was hardly anyone to be seen on the broad Mokhovaya Street outside. A little further along, at the junction of Kalinin Prospect, I was just able to make out Vadim's squat figure. He was standing by a large black ZIL – an official car with curtains drawn across the back window. I felt distinctly uneasy. This was, after all, Moscow, and as a diplomat I was vulnerable. Had my friend Vadim organised a trap, the sort of 'provocation' I read about in the security circulars? Would a couple of plainclothes heavies jump out of the vehicle and snatch me? There was no one there to observe it, anyway. Vadim took a few steps towards me, a smile of welcome on his face.

"Hullo. How are things?"

"Fine," I answered. "You've come with a car, I see."

"Well, I thought to hell with it, instead of going to a restaurant, let's go out and have dinner at my uncle's dacha. So I got him to let me have a car to get there. With a driver." He paused expectantly.

What should I do? Accept Vadim's invitation at its face value, and enjoy some genuine Russian hospitality at a dacha? Or follow strict embassy instructions and refuse? The meeting had not been approved, of course, and the car was chauffeur-driven, with all that that implied. I could have no idea where I would end up. Had I known it, this was to be one of the great turning points in my life. But I have always been inclined to take risks, and the decision took only a second or two.

"Excellent, Vadim," I said. "Let's go."

The door closed, and we drove away. Instantly the feeling of unease gripped me again: I could just perceive, in the gloom, a third person on the back seat. Vadim put the light on for a moment, and I found that the man beside me was small, plump and benign, with gold-framed spectacles and a pleasant face, in a word, hardly of KGB ilk. I relaxed a little. "Meet my friend," said Vadim, leaving us, in the Russian way, to introduce ourselves.

"Igor Orlovski," said the man.

"Mervyn Matthews," I said, "from Great Britain."

Igor, I learned, was a gynaecologist researching the womb at a Moscow Institute. As we got talking I found he was not without a sense of humour.

"My supervisor," he said, "gave me the idea. He thought it would be interesting to find out what effect womb enlargement has on the mother's brain. How do I do it? I fit electrodes to female rabbits' scalp and blow air into their wombs. My professor told me to blow, so I've been blowing for months. We haven't found anything yet, though."

Then he told me about the things that really interested him – Russian classical writers and music. Vadim sat silently with the air of a satisfied host.

The car sped through the Moscow night. We must now be approaching – or have passed – the forty-kilometre limit which diplomatic personnel were not allowed to cross without permission. Another cause for apprehension! Also, I was sure we had left the main highway to Leningrad, and were out into Moscow Province, God knows where. Vadim must have sensed my concern. "We'll be arriving soon," he said.

And indeed a few minutes later the car slowed almost to a halt outside a compound surrounded by a blank wooden fence. I glimpsed a shadowy figure waiting by the roadside, and a gate slid open noiselessly. The car passed through and we coasted down what appeared to be a long, tree-lined drive. We made a sharp turn and stopped in front of one of the largest wooden dachas I had ever seen. The impressive front door was open, and a light burned in the porch. A frail little woman, evidently a housekeeper, was standing there, ready to welcome us. We got out of the car, acknowledged her smile and went in. I found myself in a large, if bare, entrance hall with a number of doors leading off it. Vadim seemed thoroughly at home.

"Let me show you around," he said. "Take your coats off."

First he led us into a large dining room lit by a heavily shaded lamp – all the electric lighting in the dacha seemed to be underpowered. An enormous table stood in the middle and I noted with pleasure that it was laid for a substantial meal. From the dining room Vadim took us into what was doubtlessly intended to be the glory of the establishment – a hall with a full-size billiard table. A set of snooker balls nestled in a frame on the green baize, and well-made cues stood in a rack against the wall.

"After supper," said Vadim, "we'll have a game. Let me show you upstairs."

We trooped up a broad wooden staircase which led to a spacious landing, again with many doors. Two or three of the rooms were bedrooms: but the largest, matching the billiard room downstairs, was for reception. It was furnished with ponderous, Soviet-style arm chairs and a few enormous oil paintings, including one of a Russian forest scene. There was a real stone fireplace with a blazing log fire, a rarity in Russia. My exclamations of surprise pleased Vadim, who clearly wanted to impress. At the end of the room a set of french windows opened onto a balcony, but the evening was moonless and chilly, so we did not venture out.

"You are well set up here, Vadim!" I said, thinking of the overcrowded Moscow tenements. He grinned confidently.

"Yes," he said, "I come here quite often with my friends."

I did a quick reappraisal of his social status and raised it significantly.

The three of us went downstairs and took our places at the dining table. The servant, who had been keeping an eye on us, went off to the kitchen to get the first dishes: and Vadim busied himself with one of his favourite tasks – opening bottles of vodka. Two kinds had been provided, the ordinary, Stolichnaya, and a more aromatic kind, with pepper, called Pertsovka. While my host was thus engaged I looked at the table again. Generous plates of caviare, black and red, smoked salmon, the mouth-watering white flesh of Volga sturgeon had appeared. The cutlery was of a heavy, Victorian type, in silver and gold: there were quaint little stands for the knives and forks such as I had never seen before. Like the rest of the dacha, the table produced an impression of pre-revolutionary opulence. I had never seen anything comparable at embassy parties, generous though they could be.

We gorged ourselves shamelessly. Vadim began with the inevitable toast to further visits, and urged us to gulp more vodka. Igor obviously had no difficulty in keeping up with him, while I tried not to drink too much, as I was not particularly used to it, and vodka went to my head quickly. Nevertheless, I soon felt a strong inner glow, and reality faded slightly. Igor lapsed into a permanent broad grin.

I have little recollection of what was discussed on that highly convivial evening, but politics and Korea were certainly absent. I think we concerned ourselves with the more immediate problems of life: Vadim's prowess at swimming and basketball, how everyone, capitalist and socialist, needed money, and, of course, women. Igor told us about his frequent visits to the Moscow Conservatory, which was not very far from where he worked. He did not have to buy tickets, he said, because the girls at the door knew him, and after a day of inflating rabbits he could get in for nothing. The alcoholic haze thickened. The servant came and went, bringing wine and clearing away empty dishes. At one point she appeared with a platter of steaming boiled potatoes and butter: in all their simplicity they tasted marvellous.

The meal finished about midnight, and Vadim proposed that we have a game of billiards. It was enjoyable but did not last long; although no one was impossibly drunk, Vadim seemed to be the only person who could aim straight. Then we went upstairs where coffee and brandy were served. We lounged before the flaming logs which provided the only light. At times the flames would brighten and illuminate the faces of my companions, already sleepy. Sometimes the glare was strong enough to light up the oil paintings in their massive frames. At about one o'clock the servant came upstairs and told us that the car was at the porch. It was time to go.

Little was said on the way back to Moscow, we were all too tired. But for me it was a memorable evening, and I was glad I had got into the ZIL. It had enabled me to catch yet another glimpse of a Russia which was utterly beyond the reach of most foreigners. However, a small problem still awaited solution. It would be entirely inappropriate for me to be seen getting out of an official Soviet car in front of the diplomatic block at two o'clock in the morning. Although my colleagues were a clean-living lot, and probably long abed, one of them might well be up for a cup of cocoa, and look out of the window. The car would arouse all sorts of suspicions. So I asked the driver to stop a couple of hundred yards away, in the Sadovo-Samotechnaya Square, where I could alight unseen. Fortunately, Bob Longmire did not hear me coming in at that unearthly hour. If he did, he never mentioned it.

A New Friend

★

One evening a few weeks later, when I was looking through the airmail edition of *The Times*, my attention was attracted by a small notice which stated that a group of officials from the British Council in London would shortly be leaving for Moscow. They were coming to negotiate an Anglo-Russian 'cultural exchange' agreement, which would contain, for the first time ever, a provision for exchanging post-graduate students.

This, I thought, might be just what I was looking for, a chance to leave the Embassy, yet stay in Moscow and get some Russian friends. I had made one or two when I first came to the Moscow Youth Festival for a few days in 1957, but I had thought it better, as an embassy employee, not to contact them. I knew that the American students who had managed to install themselves in Moscow and Leningrad universities lived a life far less constrained than my own. They had Russian friends and were unfettered by diplomatic 'privilege'. They lived in student hostels, coming and going as they pleased, without militiamen at the gate. If an exchange agreement were concluded, and I could get myself into it, not only would my life change for the better, but I could also press on faster with my magnum opus on Soviet employment problems. A move to Moscow University would mean living on a student grant, which was far less than I was getting at the Embassy, but it would evidently be sufficient for my needs. Next morning, as soon as I got into the office, I was foraging for memorandum paper in my untidy desk drawers. Everything in the Embassy started with a memorandum.

The first step was to approach Ted Orchard, our bearded and occasionally fearsome head of section. He agreed to support my application, so my next step was to rid myself of any security rating which might make the Foreign Office reluctant to see me transfer to a Soviet institution. In fact I had only low-level clearance which allowed me sight of confidential office circulars warning of 'provocations' and changes in security rules. Given the degree of Soviet penetration of the Embassy (we employed Soviet staff for lesser duties, and had discovered microphones installed behind the wainscotting in 1948) the security element was almost laughable. But my name came off the list, anyway.

Events moved quickly. I applied to the British Council for one of their places: word came back that my name was acceptable, and would be included in the list about to be submitted to the Russians. That, however, was the easy bit. As everyone in the Embassy knew, the idea of anyone on the diplomatic list transferring to student status at Moscow State University – given the unbounded suspicion of the Soviet authorities – was hardly credible. In fact I was told that the Ambassador, Sir Patrick Reilly, actually said so. The Embassy applied to the Soviet Foreign Ministry on my behalf, and sure enough a refusal came back. This meant that I was much worse off: not only had I demonstrated to the Embassy that I was happy to leave the hallowed portals, but I had no niche to shelter in instead.

★

Apart from that, things had taken a bit of a downturn in the office, for I had just collected my first reprimand. One day, a few weeks earlier, the diplomatic bag brought a letter to me from Max Hayward, who was a Fellow of St. Antony's at Oxford and one of Britain's finest specialists in Russian literature. He told me that a friend of his (no name was mentioned) was compiling a complete edition of Boris Pasternak's poetry for publication in America, but could not find some of the poet's earlier work in western libraries. Pasternak was still alive, and living in Peredelkino, a village near Moscow, but as a result of the *Doctor Zhivago* scandal he was in disgrace and virtually incommunicado. His novel had evoked the ire of the authorities because it was not 'socialist realist' and had been illicitly published abroad. A visit from Westerners seeking other work from him could cause him extra difficulties. Max asked if I could find the poems and some small articles in the Lenin Library, copy them out (there were several dozen), and find a safe way of getting them to Oxford.

He said specifically that I should get official permission before doing it. That was the problem: Ted Orchard was a decent sort, but I feared he might hesitate to approve the work, and my using the diplomatic bag to send it out of Russia. The Russians, if they ever found out, would claim that the bag had been used for 'anti-Soviet activity', and would protest. The fact that they never would, and that the aim was to save great Russian poetry for posterity, would not, I thought, fit the F.O. mindset. So rather than court an official prohibition I decided, for the time being, not to ask, but get on with the copying. The problem of getting the poems out of Russia could be addressed later.

A substantial list duly arrived from London. I was told that some poems had been published in several variants and needed to be checked line by line. It was clearly a hefty task, but I set to work with a will. Every evening, for three or four weeks, after supper at the flat, I would take the trolley bus down to the Lenin Library, too preoccupied with the task in hand to tease the goons following me. My ticket admitted me to the 'Professors' ' reading room, a tall, gloomy hall with oaken desks, where decrepit academics read in silence for hours on end. A few tired aspidistras added to the atmosphere of terminal calm. Generally I would have preferred to work in the crowded public reading rooms, with lots of young Russians whispering to one another, but as a foreigner I was not allowed to do so.

Rather to my surprise I had no problem in ordering the works, despite Pasternak's disgrace, and the slim volumes arrived from the stacks, one by one. Evidently the KGB staff who almost certainly monitored foreigners' reading lists had missed it, or were not interested. At first I wrote each line out in longhand, and had the sheets photographed by a friendly military attaché, so as to have a second copy. There was a regular library photographic service, but I was afraid to use it. Soon, however, I discovered that the library rules did not prohibit the use of personal cameras, so I bought one that was suitable for close work, and took it with me.

That speeded the work up enormously, though I always felt uncomfortable because it made a noisy click which reverberated around the hall. I also feared the KGB might find out through a member of staff and use the noise as a pretext for cancelling my ticket. Indeed, one evening the girl at the desk told me that I was transforming the Professors' room into a photographic laboratory – but she did not stop me. Apart from the occasional annoyed glance, none of the readers seemed to take much notice. I learned how to do my own developing and back at the flat, late at night, I would lock myself in the bathroom and process the evening's spools. Usually Bob was out, or had gone to bed, so I did not have to tell him. Despite my inexperience and total lack of interest in photography, all the shots came out. A little brown, perhaps, but no matter.

As the manuscript and photographs accumulated, the problem of getting them to England resurfaced. The only possibility apart from using the bag was to ask someone with diplomatic immunity to take them through the customs. But no one seemed to be going just then. So after a few days' deliberation I drew a deep breath and put them all into a couple of thick envelopes, and dispatched them by the bag, on two consecutive weeks. They were addressed to Max at Oxford, and no one, I thought, would be any the wiser. They looked like thick letters, and the contents were perfectly innocuous, anyway.

Happy to have the task off my hands I settled back into my various routines, buying books in the Moscow bookshops, translating Soviet news items, and hearing about Fay's visits to the American Embassy Club. I awaited a word of thanks from Oxford with pleasurable anticipation. About a week after the second envelope had gone off, however, I got an internal telephone call from Hilary King, the Head of Chancery, asking me to come over and see him at the end of the working day. I was puzzled, for he had no direct involvement in our section, and would not normally contact me.

"Mervyn," he said when I went into his office, (all first names at the Embassy, except for the Ambassador, who was 'H.E.') "it has been brought to my notice that you have sent two unauthorised envelopes to London by the diplomatic bag."

"Yes," I said, "I didn't think there would be any problem."

"You know that the bag should not be used for this sort of thing. The Embassy is very vulnerable to complaints from the Soviet side, and if the Russians found out there would be real trouble."

I was silent.

"And as a member of the embassy staff you should not have collected that material at a public library. I presume you did it in Embassy time, too."

"I certainly did not," I replied, deeply hurt by the suggestion. How dare this man, who hardly knew me, presume that I was misusing Foreign Office time?

"Well, Mervyn, there it is. Please refrain from that sort of thing in the future!"

"I'm sorry."

I made my way sadly to the embassy car waiting to take us back to the flat. To be reprimanded in this way over Pasternak's poetry was unbelievable: it seemed to me that the Foreign Office had displayed a shameful subservience to Soviet administrative demands. Beyond that, there was some kind of check on private letters in the Moscow bag (a practice which could be beneficial only to our Russian adversaries). An authoritative figure in London had refused to support what most people would regard as an entirely admirable act. Beyond that, I was personally offended by King's imputation. The only positive element in the situation was that the envelopes had been allowed through. A year or so later, when I was back in Oxford, Max Hayward came to my room and gave me (without comment) a fine, five-volume set of Pasternak's poetry. It was my reward.

*

My social image at the Embassy, such as it was, also suffered a blow. Silly though it may seem, the blame lay mostly with our cat Shura. She was normally kept in the apartment, but one day, somehow or other, she came into contact with a sensuous tom, and there ensued an alarming pregnancy yielding no less than eight Siberian kittens, of which seven survived. Lidia was delighted, and took them off to Russian homes, one by one. She would wrap each in a scarf before departing, and hold it to her cheek, smiling at us and fluttering her long eyelashes to invite compliments.

"We can't have any more of this," said Bob firmly, after the last one had gone. "She'll escape again, and the whole house will be overrun with cats. There's a place where they spay them somewhere. Can you find out about it and take her over?"

As the junior partner in the household I agreed, in fact I thought it would be amusing to see a Moscow vet. But when the day came, instead of ordering a taxi, like a normal embassy employee, I decided to wrap the animal up in a scarf, Lidia fashion, and take her over by tram, as part of my policy of exploring Russian life. I found the stop and boarded the ageing vehicle. It was crowded, with a fair selection of the Moscow public, one or two of whom glanced at me curiously. They could not tell I was a foreigner, but were intrigued by the cat.

At first everything was perfectly all right, and the tram rolled down the tree-lined boulevard. Then we started going around a curve, with juddering and loud squealing of wheels. Shura panicked and leapt from my grasp. I jumped up to catch her, and an old peasant woman screamed – Russian peasant women had a known propensity for screaming. In a moment there was a minor pandemonium, with people shouting "Catch it! There it is!" When I called "Shura!, Shura, come back! Shura! Sorry, comrades!" the passengers caught a hint of a foreign accent, which greatly heightened their interest. An old man with a fur collar started to complain about foreigners with cats on trams, and for a moment I thought they might stop the vehicle and call the militia. Greatly to my relief we managed, by collective effort, to catch the animal, and I got off at the next stop. That was the end of the incident, but I was unwise enough to tell someone in the Embassy, and I was sure (from a few arch enquiries about the cat's health) that the unflattering story had got around.

There was also a subtle down-grading in my accommodation arrangements (embassy life, I had found, was full of subtleties). Bob Longmire, with whom I had so much in common, moved out to a place of his own, and two people who were not on the diplomatic list replaced him, one after the other. They were both very pleasant, but had no interest in Russia, Moscow was just another posting for them. Bob took Lydia with him, and I sacked her replacement when it became evident that she was eating the best food in the fridge. Then, as my future became more uncertain, I could not easily get a replacement. So the embassy accountant duly informed me that I had lost my servant allowance as well.

By the end of June it was evident that my one-year contract with the Embassy would not be renewed. I did not want to stay in the Foreign Office, long term, at Branch B level, but I enquired as a matter of course whether anything else was going. Only a Branch B job in Warsaw, I was told, and at a lower rating. I turned it down forthwith. Clearly, the end was nigh. I braced myself for a return to Oxford in the autumn, and long hours of research in the libraries there.

I was still, of course, meeting Vadim, and one evening a few weeks later I told him, I think over an Azerbaidzhani shashlik, that I would not be staying in Moscow for a second year.

"The Embassy will not be renewing my contract as a third secretary, as I hoped," I said. "In any case, now that the student exchange is starting, the translator scheme I came under may be cancelled. Your Ministry of Foreign Affairs won't let me transfer to Moscow University. So there's nothing to be done, it looks as though I'll be off!"

Vadim had a very deliberate way of pouring vodka, and I remember him doing so on that occasion. He smiled.

"Don't jump to conclusions," he said. "let's see whether anything can be shifted. I'll find out whether my uncle can help."

Given the minor miracle his uncle had produced already, in terms of an official car and a dacha, I thought there might well be something in what he said.... And sure enough in due course I was called into Chancery to hear the amazing news: the Embassy had received a note saying that the Ministry of Foreign Affairs had reviewed the matter and had no objection to my accepting a place as a research student at MGU (to use the common Russian acronym). No one could understand it.

I was absolutely delighted. In terms of dates, too, things worked out well. The exchange scheme had started, and I could go straight to Moscow University without returning to England. On my last working day in the office (it was already late November) H.E. called me in for a farewell handshake – I was, after all, on the diplomatic list. Obviously, Sir Patrick knew about the glitches in my performance, and that in Foreign Office terms I was heading precisely nowhere. But he did not show it.

"So you're going to Moscow University," he said. "Most unusual.... I wonder why the Ministry allowed you to do it?"

I had no clear idea myself, but I could hardly tell him it had been organised by my Russian friend's uncle. There was a long, long silence as he waited for an explanation. I said nothing. Eventually he

gave up and we amicably shook hands. "Good luck," he said. Had
he but known it, that was one of the happiest moments of my life.

I loved having presents, so as a sort of leaving present to myself I
set up, with the help of the embassy travel office, a ten-day trip to
Central Asia, visiting the ancient towns of Tashkent, Samarkand,
Kokand and Bukhara. When I told Vadim about it he said he would
get the Ministry to send him out for an inspection job, and meet me
somewhere en route, but that seemed distinctly far-fetched, even for
him, and I rather dismissed the idea. Meanwhile, I looked forward to
the journey immensely.

★

The sands of the Kara Kum desert moved almost imperceptibly
under the wings of the old, vibrating propeller plane. I had already
visited Tashkent, Samarkand, and the sleepy town of Kokand. I
found them to be a strange mixture of the oriental and colonial: the
Central Asian khanates, of course, had been under Russian tutelage
for a century or more. I was thrilled by the ancient mosques, blue-
tiled, domed and partially destroyed by earthquake; picturesque
minarets from which the emirs' victims had occasionally been
thrown; bazaars where shashlik braziers gave off an acrid smoke, and
a blind beggar might recount a long epic from memory. The local
people (Uzbeks and Tadzhiks) tended, however, to dress like
Russians, and the shops and offices were heavily Sovietised. As far
as I could tell, there was no KGB surveillance in the streets, which
was a welcome relief after Moscow.

I was now on the last leg of my journey, flying to the ancient
walled city of Bukhara. It was my first sight of a desert ever and,
frankly, I was disappointed. Although the day was fine the sands
below looked grey and uninviting, quite unlike the bright Moroccan
wastes Bob Hope, Bing Crosby and Dorothy Lamour had crossed in
the films I had seen in Swansea. But a lady in the visa section of the
Embassy (the one who burnt sensitive documents in an iron pot) had
been to Bukhara, and said it was well worth a visit. She had been
horrified by the former emir's dungeon where unfortunate souls
endured the agonies of being bitten by sheep lice. She had also seen
camels in the bazaar. That was the sort of stuff I was after. Back in
Moscow, at Sadovaya-Samotechnaya, my worldly chattels were
packed ready for transportation to the University. A final two days in
exotic Bukhara befitted the rapid improvement in my fortunes.

A small dusty town soon became visible, and as the aircraft lost
height I accepted one of Aeroflot's nasty little sweets which were

supposed to relieve ear pain. I had been shamefully lax about reading up on the area before I travelled, and when I got off the plane I was surprised to find it so cold. We were in November and the sunshine, though brilliant, did not warm. Outside the little airport I found a battered taxi and clambered in. My suitcase was damned heavy because it contained a portable radio. As a minor embassy chore I had agreed to monitor the reception of the BBC Russian service over local jamming, even though it could cause trouble if the local KGB searched my luggage and mistook it for a transmitter.

The taxi driver, a tall sallow man with an oversize blue nose, was fairly talkative. He was, he told me, a Bukharan Jew, a well recognised variety in those parts, but my first ever. As we drove into town he told me something about the new building which was going on, along with the destruction of the useless old walls. "We are very proud of our new hotel," he declared. "That's where you're staying. It's only just finished."

Bukhara was obviously less developed than the larger towns I had visited, though it was the same mixture of colonial and Soviet building. One also saw blank clay walls which sheltered traditional Uzbek households, and wooden Russian izbas. We drove down some side streets, along an unmade road. In these modest surroundings the new Bukhara Hotel was quite impressive – a neat block with a restaurant sign on the front. The driver deposited me at the entrance, and after a little altercation about the weight of the suitcase on his part, and the clearly exorbitant fare on mine, he drove off. Shivering slightly I picked up the suitcase and pushed my way through the swing doors in anticipation of a welcoming gust of warm air. But the vestibule was, if anything, colder than the street outside. Indeed, the receptionist had moved her table as near the entrance as possible, and sat muffled in a winter coat and scarves.

As I approached she took her gloves off and reached for the registration forms.

"I believe you have a room for me," I said. "I hope it's a bit warmer than this!" She looked at me reproachfully.

"It's a *new* hotel," she said. She was a Soviet Russian and as far as she was concerned no further explanation was needed: the idea that everything should work from the word go was almost an insult to honest Soviet builders.

"They haven't delivered the fuel yet. Your room is on the third floor. Can you carry your case upstairs? The lift hasn't been switched on."

There was nothing for it but to manage as best I could. As I struggled up, cursing the radio and looking down at the steps so as not to trip, a pair of neatly-trousered legs came into sight, descending: above them, as I looked up, I saw a woollen sweater, and the young, but lined face and curly hair of... Vadim Popov. I was genuinely astonished, as I had more or less discounted his promise to meet me in Central Asia – it had seemed too far-fetched. We shook hands warmly.

"Vadim! So you made it, after all."

"What do you mean, 'after all'? I told you I would be coming *navernyaka*, that's 'certainly'."

"But what are you doing here?"

"What do you think?" he winked. "The ministry sent me, to discuss administrative matters with a colleague. Let me help you with your case. God almighty, what have you got in this?"

"I bought a few books in Tashkent," I said, which was also true. He lugged it up the remaining stairs and we quickly found my room. It was only a little way along the corridor from his own.

"What are your plans for today?" he asked.

"Obviously I want to have look around Bukhara."

"Excellent. We'll do it together. Best in the afternoon, when I'm free. I'll get an official car and pick you up here at three o'clock."

The fact that he appeared at ten past four, while I was patiently drinking tea in the hotel restaurant, didn't seem to matter.

"I'm sorry, I was held up," he said. "But let's be off."

An old Moskvich was waiting outside and we piled in. The tour was considerably faster than I would have wished, or normally expected from a Russian historian. In the course of a brief hour we saw the market place, the minaret from which the emirs threw their enemies, some mosques and the famous dungeon. Apparently two Britishers, the good Captain Arthur Connolly and a diplomat called Charles Stoddart, had been imprisoned and died there in 1842. They had been caught up in the so-called 'Great Game' between Russia and Great Britain, as each strove for influence over the Central Asian khanates. We also visited the municipal museum with its paintings of people having their throats cut, and went on to see what remained of the great town walls. Then we had some greasy shashlik and plov back at the market place.

Vadim's haste was unwelcome, but it did not surprise me. My friend regarded historical monuments as being of interest only if they had girls in them. "There's only one thing left," he said as we finished eating. "That's the Emir's summer palace outside the town."

We drove off along yet another dusty road. Despite the brilliant sunshine the weather was no warmer than on the previous day. The yellowing leaves of the vines which stretched along the roadside and the occasional olive tree gave the Uzbek countryside an autumnal appearance. The former emir's palace, we found, had been transformed into a rest centre for tired Uzbeks, but the season was now over and it was closed. The palace itself was a smallish building in extensive gardens, now deserted. We walked around it and came upon a large tiled pool with a little water on the bottom. We sat down on the terrace at one end.

"You can just imagine the emir," said Vadim, giving free reign to his fancy, "sitting here and looking over his wives and concubines bathing. He'd say, 'Well, I'll have that one today!' Vadim paused to enjoy the thought, as a light breeze rustled the leaves, and the shallow water lapped against the edge of the pool.

"I've got some good news for this evening," he continued. "An old friend of mine from the ministry, Volodya, is organising a welcome at his house. There should be some girls there."

"Wonderful," I replied, "and tomorrow is only my first day as an undiplomat."

"I think we're going to have a good time in Bukhara, too."

★

Volodya lived some distance from the hotel, and since we did not have the car outside working hours it took us a long time to find it. The outskirts of the town were very rustic and unlit, but fortunately we had the moonlight to help us. Volodya inhabited one of the Russian-style, wooden houses with a fair-sized garden, and a front gate. When we at last pushed it open he hastened down the path to meet us. He was middle-aged, jovial, and already quite drunk. He led us in and introduced us to the family, that is, his elderly parents and two younger sisters.

Another splendid meal awaited us, with the largest turkey I ever saw in the Soviet Union. We ate, drank, and danced to old American hits played on a mechanical gramophone. I wondered how on earth they had got there. Everybody got rather drunk except Volodya's mother, who sat silent and mildly disapproving behind the turkey. Another girl, small, plump and a little older than I, had been invited to keep me company. She was called Nina and I was told she had a job in Tashkent: actually, I found her quite likable. By the time the party came to an end the moon was high in the sky, and we all went out to admire it from a veranda at the back of the house. Nina, it turned out, was also staying at the Bukhara Hotel so the three of us left together. Vadim suggested that the sisters follow us later, when the parents were abed. Volodya ambled down to the gate with us, and

30

at the very last moment revealed the true object of his hospitality.

"Vadim, my dear fellow," he said forlornly, "any chance of a job in Moscow?" Vadim smiled, but said nothing.

The foyer of the hotel was silent and most of the lights turned out. I waited until Vadim had started to climb the stairs and turned to Nina. "You'll come to my room in a little while?"

She nodded and squeezed my hand.

I mounted the stairway rather unsteadily, and made my way along the corridor. When I reached the outer door of my room I was surprised to see a faint shaft of light under it. Strange! Surely I had not left the light on? What was up now? My head seemed to clear of the vodka fumes in a moment. I applied the key to the lock, and stepped into the small vestibule. The light was coming through a fanlight, as the inner door was still closed. Inside I heard the tinkling of glasses.

Whoever was inside had heard me coming in. Suddenly the door opened and a man emerged: he was standing against the light and I could hardly make out his features. I felt the familiar sick feeling in the bottom of my stomach that I experienced when I was being followed by the more malevolent goons in Moscow. Clearly, I had disturbed a couple of KGB men searching my luggage, or taking the radio to bits.

"Who are you?" I whispered angrily. so as not to wake anyone along the corridor, "Let me go in!"

The goon, quite unperturbed, edged his way forward, pushing me to back into the corridor.

"I'm sorry," he whispered back, "we've been repairing the electrics."

"At two o'clock in the morning? And there's nothing wrong with them," I hissed. "You're no electrician..."

He did not want to get into an argument about his calling.

"My mate has finished, now," he said, and a small man in a black cap (perhaps another Bukharan Jew) emerged, though without any tools of the trade. Unlike his companion he looked a little sheepish.

"Good night!" they said, and were gone. I went into the room, but could not see anything that had been disturbed, and the radio was evidently OK. But the glasses on the table suggested that the visitors had decided to have a quiet drink while they were on the job. Somehow they must have known that I would be away for an hour or two.

The incident was ludicrous, but I sank down on the edge of the bed with a heavy heart. So even in far-off Central Asia, after leaving the Embassy, I was still being watched! Would Vadim get into trouble? Of course not, if he had befriended me already he had little to fear. But what about the others, Volodya and his family? A few minutes' thought convinced me that in all likelihood they were not at risk, either – they hardly knew me.

I began to shiver, my God, it was cold. Better get into bed quick. I found my pyjamas and started to undress. I was down to my underpants when there was a soft tap on the outer door. My first thought was that it was Vadim wanting to continue the party. I went to the door and opened it a few inches. A diminutive figure stood in the corridor.

"Nina! What do you want?"

In a second she had pushed her way inside, undeterred (or perhaps encouraged) by the fact that I was undressed.

"Mervyn!" (my name sounded wonderful, pronounced by a female Russian voice). "I thought I'd come and help you get to bed."

Her grey eyes ran over the coverlet, she sounded more like a school mistress rather than a bedmate. But a bedmate was something I did not want just at that moment. The KGB had just been around, and might still have me under observation. Joyous copulation could be re-categorised as rape, and if things went in that direction I would be in deep trouble. I could imagine Nina clasping me in a steely embrace and screaming for help, which would be immediately forthcoming, because it was waiting outside in the corridor.

"Ninochka," I cried, "I think I can manage by myself, thank you!"

"Well, I'm not going until you've been nicely tucked up. Don't stand there in the cold!"

I wondered whether I should tell her about my recent visitors, but decided not to. Either she knew already, or would be too frightened. But in the twinkling of an eye she had pushed me back onto the bed and was on top of me.

It would be nice to relate that events took their natural course, but I must admit that with the KGB lurking around, I doubted greatly that I would be able to rise to the occasion. I freed myself from her clinging embrace, and managed to usher her out, protesting, into the corridor. Then I closed the door, dashed back to the bed and settled under the blankets. A fine opportunity had been missed, but at least I was safe. I lay there for a while, listening. All way silent, and there was no sign of Vadim or Volodya's sisters. Perhaps, I thought, they were too tired (or tipsy) to continue the party. And gradually I drifted off to sleep myself.

When I saw Vadim next morning I decided not to say anything about my nocturnal visitors – it could do no good, and perhaps make him less willing to associate with me in future. The radio was apparently intact, and there seemed to be no complications – no call from the hotel manager, no militiamen. As for continuing the party, it seemed that the girls had just not turned up. Vadim was a little sheepish, and I suspect he had just fallen asleep himself: in any case, he did not raise the matter either. We took the plane back to Moscow, as planned.

★

On looking back, the past assumes a new significance. It is clear that by the autumn of 1959 my life in Russia had taken a strange turn indeed, but one I did not fully comprehend. The changes had come about mainly with Vadim's help, though he himself seemed to wield no power. He had consistently befriended me, with no apparent benefit to himself. Obviously, it was interesting and prestigious for a young Russian to have contact with a Westerner. But why was he so keen to keep things going, especially as we were personally not very compatible? He had none of my passion for foreign languages, classical music, or interest in social and political affairs. His manner could occasionally be a little aggressive. And who was this influential 'uncle'? If anyone had asked me, in that summer long past, how all this hung together, I would have said (perhaps with a trace of youthful self-flattery) that in the Moscow of the day I was a rare acquaintance whom Vadim did not want to lose.

For my part, our friendship did not seem sinister or dangerous. The Foreign Department of the Ministry of Higher Education, where he worked part-time, was certainly under some sort of KGB control, but so was most of the Soviet bureaucracy. In any case, for me there were scarcely any security implications: although I had signed the Secrets Act, my job at the Embassy had not involved perusal of secret material, and I had removed myself from the 'restricted circular' list. Beyond that, I always regarded myself as intensely patriotic, and would never dream of acting to the detriment of Great Britain. If things were going reasonably well, I thought, (and they were), then I could stay in Russia and enjoy the Moscow life, without seeking too many tedious explanations. Vadim had helped me, but he had done so voluntarily, and I was not bound by any promises. If any problems arose, they could be dealt with according to circumstance. Meanwhile, it was all rather exciting.

Two. The KGB Reveals Its Hand

Back in Moscow – it was now mid December – I loaded my suitcases into a car graciously provided by my former employers, and the chauffeur drove me out of the diplomatic world. We made our way quickly around the great ring road (there was not much traffic in those days), and passing the fine, miraculously preserved Church of Nikola v Kamovnikakh, proceeded along Komsomol Prospekt. The Prospekt crosses Moscow River over a long, sloping bridge and leads, a little further on, to the Lenin Hills, which overlook Moscow from the south. We stopped in front of the main entrance to Moscow State University. It was the grandest academic institution in the country, housed mostly in one of Stalin's so-called 'tall buildings'. I had attended a public lecture there during my brief 1957 visit, and of course seen it many times from a distance. But I never guessed that one day I would actually be living there.

One could not fail to be impressed by the complex of buildings some thirty storeys high, with huge wings, incongruously pinnacled towers, and a gigantic portico. Massive metal statues depicted young men and women bending studiously over books, absorbing knowledge for the benefit of their homeland. The whole structure, ponderous and oppressive in the extreme, reflected Stalin's appalling tastes in architecture. Endless driveways and scruffy lawns (the Russian climate is not kind to grasses) created an impression of emptiness around.

I had always thought MGU looked like a forbidding castle in a boy's adventure story, but when we arrived that evening the facade was studded with hundreds of small, brightly-lit windows which beckoned cheerfully. As I got out of the car I thought of the little room which would be my own, a light-to-be, no doubt, in one of the wings. "There's no place like home," I said to the chauffeur, pulling my cases out of the boot, and I laughed at my own joke. I would be living among Russians, and everything would be so different from life in the embassy compound: a mere room instead of a flat, canteens instead of elegant dining tables, a library instead of the small room with Fay. A new, and as I hoped, much less constrained existence lay before me.

Having got past the security desk, just inside the vast hallway, I made my way through a throng of students and found my floor and room. There was always (I was told) an acute accommodation problem, and I had arrived well after term began. So I was put into the so-called 'hotel' – a floor reserved for occasional, usually senior, visitors. My room, however, was more or less identical with those in other parts of the building – small, with an oversized and draughty window, yet sufficient to live in. The furniture comprised a sort of sofa bed, a writing table, and a cupboard: the fact that it was so much less commodious than in the diplomatic block did not concern me in the least. At the end of the corridor was a kitchen with a stove for boiling water and cooking.

I soon discovered that self-catering skills could save an hour's queuing in the students' cafeterias, or a long wait at the lifts to get to the professors' restaurant, which was not quick, either. The student meals were hardly worth waiting for, mainly watery borshch and cabbage soup, wet potato purée, tough meat or fat salami. The only thing I really enjoyed was a strange kind of minced liver soup which I had never tasted before. The prices were nominal, so little could be expected by way of culinary endeavour. I had of course made a point of eating in a few public dining rooms while I was at the Embassy, so I had a good idea what to expect. It was part of the real Russia.

Students living on the main floors were supposed to do their own cleaning – a consequence of Khrushchev's half-baked attempts at egalitarianism. But in the hotel we had a daily cleaner, one Anna Pavlovna, a thin, pallid woman who always appeared in a headscarf and black overall. Anyone less like the socially aspiring Lidia it would be difficult to imagine. She was of peasant stock, and seemed to embody the very spirit of the land. Although she was only in her early fifties, her main aim in life was to reach her middle fifties, in order to claim a modest retirement pension, and work no more. For much of the day she rummaged around with buckets and brushes which she kept in a mysterious dark cupboard behind the soil pipes.

Anna Pavlovna always had a detailed knowledge of what was available in the student shop, and once came back carrying a string bag with about a hundred loose eggs in it, no doubt many days' sustenance for herself and her young son. Her husband, she told me, had been killed in the war. She would do bits of shopping for the hotel residents and could be quite helpful. She also tried to better her lot by doing laundry, though this was strictly against the rules. She asked for presents such as English biscuits and washing powder, and (it was said) informed on any foreigners in sight. Indeed, I soon found that she was quite likely to barge into my room without knocking, presumably in the hope of catching me doing something nefarious which could be usefully reported to the hotel management (in other words, the KGB). She hoped in this way to improve her standing in the trade union and get better holiday vouchers.

Anna Pavlovna was evidently the thin edge of the KGB wedge, and as I quickly realised, my dreams of freedom from surveillance were not to be realised. The hotel doorway, though inside the main building, was guarded around the clock by several middle-aged females, each more ogreish and inquisitive than the last. They almost certainly spied on us, for the same reasons as Anna Pavlovna: and as they were all terrible gossips, I imagine they enjoyed doing it. It was rumoured they got a special reward for calling in the Komsomol Morality Patrol whenever they suspected intimacy between the sexes.

Of course, had I thought about surveillance matters more soberly, I could have foreseen that even in that wondrous castle things could not be otherwise, given the large number of foreign students. The 'organs' were said to occupy the whole of the ninth floor in one of the towers, which is why the lifts did not stop there. As for day-to-day surveillance, it turned out not to be as intrusive as at the Embassy, but I discovered at least one goon post in the building, and goon cars were constantly parked in front of the portico. This meant that the KGB could get an operative on to any of the inhabitants quite quickly.

*

Various formalities had to be dealt with. The morning after my arrival I went to the Department for Foreign Students and got my pass, an essential document, given the stringent checks at all entrances. Apart from the Russian passion for verification, there was indeed a need to stop outsiders slipping through: some people, it was rumoured, lived illegally in the students' quarters for years on end. The University was like a little town, with its own food shop, sport and health centres. In Soviet terms, it had nearly everything.

I found I had been attached to the highly conservative Department of Economics, which was under the stultifying control of a dreadful man called Yagodkin. Dean of the Faculty and Secretary of the all-important Party Committee, he automatically suppressed any thinking which, in his narrow view, might subvert Marxism-Leninism. He nominated a thirty-year old, mildly hostile party stalwart by the name of Feliks Mikhailovich Volkov to be my supervisor. Feliks Mikhailovich was a sports cyclist and a disciplinarian. He made it clear that he expected me to hand in research findings at least once a week, which by the relaxed standards of Oxford was unbelievable.

He set the tone of our relations by describing my initial work-plan as "confused, incomplete, and murky", a harsh judgement indeed, because in my view it was just sloppy.

In his analysis of Soviet labour problems, Feliks Mikhailovich rigorously adhered to the usual outmoded Marxist categories. I soon realised that I could gain little of value from him, and I tried to meet him as rarely as possible. After a time we settled down to a meaningless game of exhortations, half-promises and excuses. I attended a few lectures, but found very little of use in them. Soon I turned to digging things up for myself in the Professors' reading room of the Lenin Library, and there indeed I spent most of my time. As the months went by I managed to extract a body of material which was to stand me in good stead later.

The Faculty of Economics, did, however, have one unexpected advantage. It was located in the old university building on Mokhovaya Street in the centre of town, and there was no room for a goon post inside. The KGB therefore had to operate from cars parked in a yard directly under the lecture room windows, and if you looked out you could see who would be following you after lectures. That on occasions could be very convenient.

★

Most, if not all, of the exciting things in life happened outside the lecture rooms and libraries. Naturally, I got to know some of the foreign students. Among the Britishers were Martin Dewhirst and Gerald Brooke, and there was also the Frenchman Georges Nivat, who specialised in Russian literature and had been with me at St. Antony's College, Oxford. All were to play a part, sooner or later, in my Moscow activities. Now that I was no longer in the diplomatic service I was able to contact friends from my first visit to Russia: they included Igor Vail', the poor student who lived on Kropotkin Street, Valerii Shein, who worked for the Moscow Theatre organisation, Volodya and Laurissa Yakubovich, a student couple who lived in a cramped flat behind the Lenin Library.

Of course I also maintained a close relationship with Vadim. He had an official pass and could get into the MGU hostel without being met or invited. He came to my room once or twice and borrowed a gramophone for me, old but serviceable. I had just begun to collect Bach records, as Soviet long-players were very cheap, and I was very grateful. Vadim also – no doubt with his uncle's permission – organised another evening out at the dacha. He invited a male friend of his, a skiing instructor, and some girls, one of whom was for my pleasure. True, she was a little fat, and ten years too old, but at least she was there. We all went skiing in the moonlight, on the edge of the woods. Occasionally I would let the others go on ahead, and stand alone among the pine trees, enjoying the snowy silence. Despite the efforts of the instructor I kept falling over (my coordination was never particularly good), but mercifully I avoided injury, and it was all extremely enjoyable. We went back to the dacha for supper, billiards, and various other activities in the enormous beds upstairs.

★

A month or two after I had moved to the University, Vadim rang me on the corridor telephone, a call which (had I but known it) was to change the direction of my life again. That very day, he said, he had successfully 'defended' his Candidate thesis (which was a sort of M.A.) and thought the occasion should be marked by a banquet. In fact he was shortly going to give one for a number of friends in a private room at the (extremely expensive) Praga Restaurant on the Arbat. Would I like to attend? I would be the only foreigner there.... An academic dinner would not normally have attracted me – I was always somewhat shy in company – but Vadim seemed anxious for me to go, and I felt that with him present the occasion could be quite lively. So I agreed.

When I arrived at the Praga I found a company of about a dozen academics, mostly old, weary, and not too far from death. Vadim, as a matter of fact, seemed quite out of place among them. Nobody had very much to say, and to begin with there were several awkward silences: Vadim's assured smile, however, melted the ice, and as the vodka began to flow everybody loosened up. Inevitably, the meal began with a series of toasts in honour of our host. One of the people who rose to speak was clearly of a different background. Still in his thirties, he had a broad, handsome face, high cheekbones, and swept-back hair. There was a strange grey streak above his temple, which would have distinguished him throughout life. He was beautifully dressed, and obviously much at ease. Vadim told me in a whisper that his name was Aleksei.

Aleksei offered a short, but elegant toast, with all the required phrases. "A great pleasure to propose this toast, comrades... Vadim has worked hard in his chosen field of endeavour... well-deserved success... a fine contribution to Soviet oriental studies... an agreeable colleague... a keen interest in Soviet sport... a promising future in which we wish him well..." And so on.

Aleksei was on the other side of the wide table, and though he glanced at me once or twice we did not speak. That was probably a good thing, because as the meal progressed I got rather the worse for drink. Regardless of Vadim's invitations, I was no habitual drinker, and the evening eventually disintegrated into a blur. God knows how I got back to MGU. A few days later, however, Vadim telephoned again, and told me that Aleksei would like to invite us both to the theatre. They lived in the same block (which I gather was on Novoslobodskaya street, not far from the centre of Moscow) and Aleksei was a 'referent' – a sort of research assistant – to Vadim's mysterious uncle. He 'handled information'. I was a bit surprised that someone who had not even spoken to me should extend such an invitation, but I presumed that like Vadim, Aleksei might enjoy associating with foreigners, and had some sort of authorisation to do so.

We all met, and the theatre visit – it was opera at the Bolshoi – went quite well. Aleksei, as I anticipated, showed himself to be a man of some refinement. He was married and had a daughter whom he wanted to get into the national ballet, which was one of his passions. He did not admit to speaking English, but when he used the occasional word it was properly pronounced. In fact, he told me later that he had spent several months with the Soviet delegation to the United Nations. He was not without humour, either, and once declared that my English accent was fine once you took the trouble to get used to it. But he seemed very well disposed towards me, and anxious to continue our acquaintanceship. I decided I would accept any other invitations he offered, and see what ensued. In Russia something usually did – I had come looking for adventure, anyway.

Soon there was an invitation to dinner at a leading Moscow restaurant. It was not to be turned down, especially if it replaced supper in the Lenin Library cafeteria. We met in the main hall, and Aleksei brought his wife Ina Vadimovna. She was a tall, elegant creature, beautifully dressed in blue. Her gold ornamentation included a solid bracelet with a watch inset. I had never seen one before.

"My wife," said Aleksei modestly, "is a typical Soviet woman." An image of Anna Pavlovna and her string bag of eggs flashed through my mind: typicality, I thought, is not easily defined. But I was surprised at Aleksei's apparent willingness to be seen dining with me in public – diplomats ate in these restaurants quite often, and someone from the British Embassy could easily have walked in and taken an interest in my companions. But Aleksei always seemed incredibly self-assured.

As the weeks went by I found that he to some extent replaced Vadim as a social companion, though he was older and sometimes adopted a tutorial, almost authoritative, air. He invited me two or three times for dinners *à deux* in the private rooms of expensive restaurants, not least the Georgian 'Aragvi' and the Russian 'Moskva'. The tables invariably gleamed with expensive glass and cutlery. Aleksei knew something about wine, and usually ordered Tsinandali or Mukuzani – the best Georgia had to offer. He was always very talkative, the conversation usually centring on my social background, political views and career. ("Do tell me something about yourself, Mervyn, and how you find our country. We are very proud of it," etc., etc.)

The gulf between life as I had known it in working-class Hafod, and as Aleksei experienced it in the Moscow élite, was so wide as to be almost unbridgeable. I was sure he understood little of what I told him, partly because he tried to fit everything into inappropriate Marxist patterns. Hardly anyone in the Hafod knew about Marx, except perhaps to confuse him with the Marx brothers of Hollywood fame. Lenin was more distinctive, and may have fared a little better. When the talk turned to Russia I did my best to sound reasonable, and expressed some cautious approval of Soviet education. But it was not easy for me to talk about Soviet successes – I was too conscious of the darker side of the picture.

Little by little, Aleksei steered the talk closer to intelligence matters, though without asking anything specific about embassy personnel. He was curious about the rules for reporting on Soviet acquaintances, particularly some recent changes which I had never heard of. There was nothing I could have told him, or would have wished to: he was trying to imply that any difficulties in contact were due to unfounded British suspicions of his countrymen. ("At the same time the Soviet Union has to be very careful about foreign spies, Mervyn".) He had a great contempt for MI5 and MI6, ("The work of British intelligence is quite dreadful"). There was nothing I could say to that, what with Burgess and Maclean safely in Moscow, and God knows who else still working for the Russians.

As I sat at the table, listening to his urbane Russian, the only Welsh spy joke I knew ran through my mind. A Russian spy is sent on a secret mission to Treorchy (or somewhere like that) to make contact with an undercover agent, a certain Mr. Llew Jones, whose address he has lost. On arriving, the Russian goes to the local fish and chip shop, obviously a centre of social activity, and asks in innocent tones if anyone knows where Llew Jones lives. "Llew Jones?" someone answers. "There's three of them 'ere, mun. But are you foreign, like?" "Yes," said the Russian, with a strong accent, "I'm from Madagascar". "Then you must want Llew Jones the spy," came the answer. "It's the second house on the right down Chapel Street."

I didn't dare recount this to Aleksei, because he could not possibly understand anything about Llew Jones's or fish and chip shops. But I did once tell him that the KGB operatives caused a great deal of merriment in the foreign community. Suddenly, he was listening with great attention, though I knew I had little but nonsense to relate. I told him, for example, that some of the goons could be seen playing dominoes in a room under the Kamenny Bridge, a few yards from the British Embassy, while awaiting call-out. After the meal (it was a lunch), Aleksei said he could take me back to the Lenin Library in the car, but he would ask to driver to take a swing past the bridge, so that he could see the premises himself. And indeed, on walking past it some time later I noticed that the den had evidently been shut down. Had I been a little too flippant? I thought ruefully. It was not my aim to improve the efficiency of KGB surveillance practices.

★

One evening, in the spring of 1960, when we were well into the Tsinandali, Aleksei looked at me across the table and said that he had decided to take "a more active interest" in my career. There was a pause and I looked suitably pleased. Then he went on.

"I would like to know, Mervyn, whether you have any travel plans while you are at MGU."

He must have realised that he would strike a responsive chord. Foreign students like myself might not have been doing much serious work, if the truth be told, but they were not normally allowed to make journeys outside Moscow. They were supposed to keep their heads down and concentrate on their studies – quite apart from the problems of getting tickets and finding hotels.

"I don't have any plans, but I would love to go somewhere. You know the problems. I am also tied down at the Faculty."

"No doubt leave could be arranged. Where would you like to go?"

I thought of a few exotic spots.

"I have always wanted to go to Mongolia."

"I'm afraid that's not very practicable, it's a foreign country, you know," said Aleksei, assuming a serious air. "Passports, visas, frontiers... I mean somewhere within the confines of our great socialist land."

"I would love to see Siberia," I said. "Novosibirsk, Lake Baikal, the great rivers."

"And the new Bratsk Hydroelectric dam," Aleksei added encouragingly. "I think we could get there without too much of a problem.

It will still be cold there, but... we will winter in Siberia."

And so it was decided. Aleksei would, of course, attend to all the permissions and hotel reservations. At the end of the evening we parted on better terms than ever. Was there no end to the exciting surprises in the wonderland that was Russia?

As I travelled back to the university on the metro, however, and looked at the (invariably morose) Russian faces around me, I had to admit to myself that Aleksei's proposal had its downside. Having dinner with him was one thing, letting him organise a trip into the distant provinces was another. This was no ordinary gesture, there was obviously something behind it. It took our acquaintanceship into a more questionable dimension. Why should he be befriending a hapless foreigner like myself? His intelligence connections were becoming ever more obvious, though he had never mentioned anything specific. Perhaps he hoped to persuade me to help the USSR.

Possibly, at that point, I should have broken off our relationship. But when one is young one is naturally egotistical, over-confident. I thought that if the KGB considered me valuable, and wanted to give me a smashing time in Russia, so much the better. I had never given Aleksei any indication that I would work for the KGB – I was possessed of a strong sense of patriotism, anyway. I had told him very little about the Embassy. Beyond that, there was no effective way in which I could be forced to cooperate; I had never had, nor was I likely to have, any intelligence information for anyone, least of all the Soviet Union.

All in all, I reckoned that I had held my own quite well. I had gained enormously from associating with Vadim, and if anything went wrong I could simply leave Russia. As a member of the cultural exchange group I did not fear arrest – I had broken no laws and the political implications for the Soviet side would have been too negative. So I comforted myself with the thought that I would not be travelling with Aleksei on false pretences: he had made no specific requests, and I had given no undertakings. Better play along and see what would come of it.

Had I but realised it there were profound misapprehensions on both sides. Only years later, after I had spoken to defectors in the West, did I appreciate the intensity of the pressure on KGB officers to recruit foreign nationals, the seriousness of the game then being played around me. For his part, Aleksei was dealing with quantities which he could scarcely understand either – my earlier life in Swansea, attitudes inculcated into me at British universities, unseen but real Foreign Office prejudices. It is not surprising if he grossly overestimated his powers of persuasion. The crude Marxist theories which influenced KGB recruitment policy predicated that a Westerner of poor background could only respond positively to the great Soviet experiment.

★

On the morning of the 18th April Aleksei picked me up at MGU in his splendid ZIL. I had never actually seen him in outdoor clothes, and I found he was dressed in a fine brown overcoat and light black shoes, not the clumsy attire one might have expected for a traveller to Siberia. I knew that Aleksei had been to New York, and although good tailoring was available in Moscow (if you could pay for it) the garment seemed very un-Russian to me. I had donned my thick, inelegant Co-op overcoat and boots. Aleksei was in a good, holiday mood, and we chatted through most of the journey. It was then, as I recall, that he made me his only compliment ever: "You have a clear head, Mervyn," he said. "A very clear head." (It was some time before I came to reflect, ruefully, that it was not clear enough.)

Everything went according to plan and we flew off to Novosibirsk in the same type of heavily vibrating aircraft that had taken me to Central Asia. Novosibirsk was a sprawling town, with familiar Russian-style eighteenth- and nineteenth-century buildings in the centre and monotonous, Soviet-style suburbs. There was a great area of slummy wooden izbas close to the river, and traces of snow everywhere. Aleksei and I stayed at a hotel on one of the main streets, and I was immediately struck by the deference the manageress showed us. Clearly, she regarded my companion as a very important visitor, and as a consequence provided us with the best steak and chips I ever had in Russia. I was delighted to find a local telephone directory in my room, as these items, though heavily censored, were highly prized in the West. I had never stolen anything in my life, but fully intended to filch it: unfortunately the hotel security must have divined my dishonest intent, for the directory disappeared shortly before we were due to leave.

Despite my lack of enthusiasm for the theatre I had to concur when Aleksei suggested going to see the Novosibirsk ballet. "Very mediocre, really," he declared as we walked back after the performance. "But all you can expect here, I suppose." Again and again during the trip he exhibited a strange mixture of pride in Soviet achievements and condescension towards Russian provincialism. Clearly, he regarded himself as a fastidious Muscovite who travelled abroad, frequented the capital's best restaurants, and enjoyed a lofty official status. He had little in common with the "unwashed Russia" around him, to quote Lermontov's famous expression. As the days passed the contradiction became ever more apparent to me, but of course I said nothing.

Next day a local official was on hand to show us around, and he told us about a local scheme to grow vegetables under glass. Aleksei questioned him at length for my benefit. We spent time viewing the new township for academics (Akademgorodok) and I found the building, by Russian standards, very neat and attractive. We took a wonderful day trip along the vast, meandering river Ob' on a little white cutter which stopped at straggling villages for passengers to board and disembark. Aleksei and I went ashore a number of times over the rickety gangplank, and he photographed me in my Co-op overcoat.

I did not, however, dare suggest photographing him. Perhaps I should have proposed that a third person take us together, though he would probably have refused that as well. We were accosted by a local man who smoked papirosy – the cheap but strong Russian cigarettes favoured by the proletariat. He claimed an unlikely friendship with Anastas Mikoyan, who had been a close associate of Stalin and leading figure in the CPSU. One met the strangest people, I thought, even on the River Ob'. Aleksei disregarded him completely, as though he were of a different race.

The little town of Bratsk, on the river Angara was our next port of call. The Russians had built a massive hydro-electric station there, and though critics expressed doubt about the economics of it, officially it was always held to be a great success story. That is how Aleksei wanted me to see it. Transport was not easy: we flew there in the smallest passenger plane I had ever seen, seating only a dozen or so, face to face. The flight was very bumpy and uncomfortable. The aircraft flew low, crawling slowly over the endless snowy forest. When we arrived a land-rover type vehicle was waiting to take us over roads and tracks covered by up to two feet of liquid mud.

Bratsk itself was a very rudimentary sort of place, with scattered wooden houses, unmade roads, no particular centre. Aleksei arranged for us to be shown around the great dam, which took up most of a day: I was left with a sad impression of conifers, melting snow, construction sites and emptiness. We stayed in one of the wooden huts, and had boiled pilmeni, a Siberian version of ravioli, served with vinegar and butter, for supper. Towards the end of the day our tempers became a little frayed, for Aleksei was having trouble with his sinuses (something he often complained about), and I was impatient about the endless wait at table. "Don't embarrass me,

Mervyn," he chided. We were supposed to leave the next afternoon in the same small aircraft, but again there was a problem, because the weather was poor and the plane not ready. It finally took off in the evening and we followed another vibratory flightpath, this time to Irkutsk.

Our visit to Lake Baikal, which came next, was the most interesting part of the trip. Said to be the deepest lake in the world, at fifteen hundred metres, Baikal was still ice-covered and extremely beautiful. The weather had cleared and there was a lovely blue sky. The chairman of a local collective farm, an active, grey-haired man was our guide for this leg of the trip. After telling us about the farm he led us out a hundred yards or so over the frozen lake to see local men fishing through holes in the ice. It was judged to be a good method because the fish came to the holes for better-aerated water. As we walked back, and were still a few yards from the gently sloping shore, I was horrified to feel the ice yielding a little under my feet. I never knew that ice bent – it was evidently thinner near the lake's edge. There had been no movement underfoot as we walked out, and we were evidently returning to a slightly different spot. I looked at Aleksei in alarm, but he was quite unconcerned and trod quietly on.

"It's easy to be calm when you are on top," he said. "It's the thought of being underneath that is frightening."

I reflected that my life in Russia was a bit like that, coloured by feelings of apprehension and possible collapse. But so far I had been lucky.

"The chairman is a very nice chap," I said, changing the subject as we set foot on dry land. "And he seems very able. But what kind of promotion can he hope for, living out here, in such an isolated spot?"

"Promotion?" said Aleksei, adjusting his shirt cuffs, as he sometimes did. "He doesn't need any. He's perfectly happy to work for his socialist homeland here, on Baikal."

We stayed overnight in a picturesque Russian izba in the nearby village of Kul'tuk. It had a high wooden fence and a great stack of logs outside – evidently the remains of the winter fuel. I imagine it was the best dwelling in the village, which is why occasional visitors were housed there. It comprised one great room with a tiled stove for heating and divan beds along the walls.

There was no privacy, and Aleksei and I slept in our underwear. I had never, of course, given Aleksei's nether garments a thought, but I was interested to note that they comprised a white singlet and briefs. This was highly unusual, for (as I well knew) European-style underwear was absolutely unobtainable in Moscow. The Russian male wore loose black shorts which did not show the dirt and required less scarce washing powder. I did not sleep very well, probably on account of the unfamiliar surroundings, and suddenly, in the middle of the night, I heard Aleksei talking in his sleep. I pricked up my ears in the hope of hearing some interesting secrets, but alas, it was just one long, unintelligible mumble. Nothing to be gleaned there.

I was greatly disappointed by the food. I had anticipated tasty traditional cooking, either Russian or Buryat-Mongolian (which was the local nationality), but our kerchiefed hostess produced from her ornate rustic cupboard only tin after tin of standard Soviet preserves. Perhaps in a place like Kul'tuk tinned food was highly regarded. There was no plumbing, of course, and a patch of levelled earth down the garden served as a latrine. I noted that Aleksei did not use it (presumably because it was beneath his dignity).

We had a car at our disposal and next day Aleksei ordered the driver to take us towards the Mongolian border, which was only a few kilometres away. The terrain was mostly flat and uninteresting, with scattered birch trees. Any bit of Gower, I thought, was more attractive. There were hardly any people around, and most of them seemed to be drably attired Russians. I saw no colourful local costume.

Before we left Moscow I had thought it quite possible that Aleksei might take advantage of the trip to propose some sort of cooperation, though in my slightly naive way I did not think it at all certain. How different things look with hindsight: it was the main object of the trip! The crunch came shortly before we were due to depart, during a late lunch in the VIP lounge at Irkutsk airport. After a lengthy discourse on the need for peace between nations Aleksei put his cards – or a few of them – on the table.

"Mervyn," he said, "I should tell you that I work for the *Komitet po mezhvedomstvennoi informatsii* [Committee for Interdepartmental Information], and we would like to enlist your aid. Peace is the main problem of our time. Would you be prepared to work for Soviet intelligence, and help us achieve it? You could begin by mixing with the staff of the British Embassy, and giving us some information about them."

The moment had at last come for me to make a firm refusal. I tried, however, not to be too abrupt.

"I can well envisage situations in which I could help the Soviet organs, Aleksei," I said. "But that would be on two conditions. Firstly, the help should be entirely of my own choosing."

"And the second?"

"That the help I gave would not be in any way detrimental to the interests of my country. I am a very patriotic person. Unofficial contacts such as ours can be very useful without infringing anyone's national security."

Aleksei had done most of the talking, as usual, and had been extremely persuasive. Now he was silent. Slowly and deliberately he lit another fine cigarette (he smoked only the best Soviet brands). There was no doubting his disappointment.

"Well," he said slowly, "I had the impression that you wanted to help us...."

"I have given no promises."

"Well, I thought your mind was made up. But perhaps you want to consider the matter further."

The meal was at an end, and with it the conversation. We left the table. I had given him what I considered to be my final answer, but now that the situation had been fully clarified, I wondered what he would say to his superiors. Obviously, he must be responsible to someone.

He tried to put a brave face on it, but could not altogether conceal his feelings. As we flew back to Moscow I found that a subtle change had taken place in his attitude towards me. He allowed himself, for the first time ever, to make critical comments. I had not been sufficiently impressed by the Bratsk dam, he said, I was a 'carper' and 'playing politics'. He grumbled about the breakdowns we had experienced in the transport, implying the difficulties had not been justified. At the same time he was careful to avoid anything like a rupture in our relationship. It could, in fact, have come to an untimely end when the plane touched down at Omsk. As we were crossing the tarmac to go to the airport building I noticed that one of the tyres had burst (in fact they all seemed to be badly worn). Aleksei would not comment.

When we arrived in Moscow we were, as I expected, met by his official car. I made a point of offering to pay my share of the travel expenses, but he would not hear of it. He said we would meet later.

★

Back at MGU life continued as usual – the hostel, canteen, metro journeys to the centre, tedious encounters with Feliks Volkov, and (more pleasurably) meetings with Russian friends. There was a short and totally unexpected visit by Nina from Bukhara. She telephoned me and we met for a meal. Apparently she had come to Moscow on some sort of official business, but proudly showed me a blouse she had bought in the GUM multiple store on Red Square, something quite unobtainable in Tashkent. There was no particular intimacy between us (the logistics of getting her into MGU were daunting), and I wondered whether she had other motives for contacting me. And how did she find my number? I could not have given it to her in Bukhara. Perhaps Vadim helped her. If she had any ulterior motives, they did not surface. On the very same weekend I had a telephone call from Tolya, a young historian I had met during a short visit to Yalta when I was still working at the Embassy. He was quite charming, with his lovely southern accent. Yet his unexpected appearance in Moscow, and readiness to see me prompted the same questions: had he really come, just for a few days, to do some research? Moscow was a strange place.

As far as I could see, I had lost nothing by the showdown in Irkutsk, for both Aleksei and Vadim seemed anxious to stay on good terms. Indeed, they kept on doing me small favours. I told Aleksei that I would welcome a bibliography of Soviet books on my research topic, and sure enough, a few weeks later, Vadim brought one along. It was very good and had clearly been done by a competent hand. Vadim found me some quite lucrative historical translation work through *Progress*, the main Soviet foreign-language publishing house. Aleksei continued to express an interest in my career, and even said he could help me get back into the Foreign Office, thereby revealing how little he understood the social subtleties involved.

Then, early in June, Vadim suddenly came up with another fun-laden idea. What about making a trip of ten days or so down to the Black Sea coast, just the two of us, each paying his share? The sea might still be cold, he said, but there wouldn't be many tourists and it would relatively quiet. I thought this would be a splendid thing to do, and without KGB complications, except that (like the trip to Siberia) it would require special leave from the University. Vadim said his uncle could fix that as well. So the jaunt was arranged. The spot for repose and merriment was to be Gagry, a small coastal resort in Georgia (more precisely in the province of Abkhazia), which Vadim had visited before.

We flew down to the nearest airport, (I believe it was Sochi) and took a taxi onwards. Gagry turned out to be a delightful township nestling at the foot of luscious hills, with a clean pebble beach. Vadim got us rooms in a little wooden hotel with a splendid veranda looking out on to the sea, one not normally used by foreigners. I was pleased to note that there was no KGB surveillance – nothing obvious, at least. The food was good, Georgian style, and we started a very relaxed holiday.

Everything was just right, except perhaps for the cold sea, though Vadim boasted that he could go in half a dozen times a day. I could manage only once or twice. We did a delightful day trip along the coast on a cutter (just like the one on the Ob'); the little galley on board sold no drinks except vodka. We stopped in a tiny Abkhazian harbour which seemed to be inhabited entirely by grey-skinned men in black cloth caps. The women were kept out of sight.

The absence of surveillance must have been apparent to the few holiday-makers around, and I found no difficulty in meeting them – mostly young people in tourist groups. We did a wonderful bus trip up to Lake Ritsa, one of the most beautiful spots in Georgia, and saw Stalin's personal dacha on the far bank. I took masses of photographs, and no one seemed to mind. Rowing boats were available not far from the hotel, and I spent a few unforgettable hours floating alone on the quiet water, watching the forest-clad hills of Abkhazia in the sunlight. I also met rather a nice girl who was staying in the hotel and did not have any hesitation about coming back to my room. How different from Moscow!

I suppose strange things had to happen even here, and they did. One day Vadim suggested that we spent a few hours at a well-known beauty-spot in the hills. We could get there without difficulty by train, he said, as the line ran close to Gagry, though there were only a few trains a day. For some reason we arranged to meet on the little platform, but having got there I found I had left my money at the hotel. I returned to get it, and misjudged the time needed. Anyway, when I got back to the railway line I found that the train had just left, and Vadim was stamping up and down in a towering, spluttering rage.

"Where the hell have you been? We've missed the train now. We can't go."

I was surprised at his reaction.

"Well, it doesn't matter all that much, does it? We can spend the time on the beach, as usual. Perhaps tomorrow?"

"But I had set my mind on going there today!"

Nothing more was said, but I could not understand why he should have reacted so badly. We were not pressed for time, and could easily have gone on another day. In the event the idea was abandoned: but it took him until the evening to get over it.

A few days later, on the 8th June, there was a much more serious development. In the afternoon I returned to the hotel alone, leaving Vadim on the beach. As soon as she saw me the manageress called me over to the reception desk and told me that someone had just telephoned. I was astonished, as I didn't know a soul in Georgia, let alone Gagry. So who on earth could it have been? The person, she said, would ring again at six o'clock.

I spent an uneasy hour or so lounging on the balcony, with Vadim nowhere in sight. What could this mean? The telephone rang at the appointed time, and when I put it to my ear I was greeted by a familiar voice – Aleksei's. I told him I thought he was in Moscow. No, he said, he was here, on the coast, staying at another hotel. Could I meet him at the round pond in the park at eight o'clock that evening? Did I know it? There was a kiosk alongside, where they sold champagne, but at that hour the spot would be deserted. As far as I was concerned, there was no problem about the location, I knew it well: what did worry me, and worried me greatly, was Aleksei's presence in Gagry.

What was he up to this time? Had the KGB cooked up something nasty? There was nothing I could do but agree to meet him. Incredibly naive though it may seem with hindsight, the thought that Vadim might have been directly involved in setting this up never entered my head. If asked at that moment, I would probably have replied that he organised the trip in good faith, purely for pleasure: and that Aleksei, on finding out about it, had decided to latch on, using my isolation and vulnerability for his own (as yet unclear) purposes.

I got to the pond in good time and waited, alone in the darkness. There were no holidaymakers in sight. I listened to the chorus of frogs on the warm night air, and peered along the paths. Then, just about eight, I heard the crunch of a footstep on the gravel, and discerned a tall figure approaching. Aleksei was, as usual, calm and collected.

"Hello, Mervyn, having a nice holiday?" he asked, nonchalantly.

"Yes, of course. Everything's fine. But what brings you here?"

Aleksei did not answer directly.

"There are some matters which we have to discuss urgently," he said.

I looked at him expectantly.

"I would like you to come to room [he mentioned a number] in your hotel a little later this evening. At nine o'clock. OK? There's no need to say anything to Vadim."

"Can't we discuss it here?"

"Better at the hotel."

"OK!" In circumstances like this there was no question of my refusing.

"See you shortly, then." And with that he turned on his heel and walked off.

I stood looking at the dark water of the pool for a few minutes, feeling more apprehensive than ever. The ice was bending underfoot again! Why hadn't he told me what he wanted straight away? If he was going to start anything serious, I would have to get back to Moscow, and even out of the Soviet Union, pretty quickly. This game could not go on for ever.

At the agreed hour I found the room where we were supposed to meet and tapped lightly at the door.

"Come in!"

It was large, dimly lit, and contained yet another surprise. Aleksei was not alone: next to him, at a table, sat a heavily-built man in his late forties, with a broad Slav face and fair, but thinning hair. He had the cruelest eyes I had ever seen. Like Aleksei he was wearing a suit, but it seemed ill-fitting, and I was struck by his crude, Soviet-style sandals. Aleksei was always fashionably shod and would not have been seen dead in them. Curiously enough, the footwear typified the social difference between them. And when the older man spoke, it was with an uneducated, peasant intonation, far from Aleksei's cultured utterance. There was no food in sight, but it didn't matter, I couldn't have eaten it anyway. The evening was clearly not going to be congenial.

"This is Aleksandr Fedorovich, my boss," said Aleksei, rather coldly.

"How do you do," I said.

Aleksandr Fedorovich just glared.

"We've come down to discuss your position and your intentions. As you know, we have taken a favourable interest in you, and you have indicated that you can help us. We can help you, too, in the future. But so far you have done nothing."

For my part silence again seemed to be the best response.

"A person of your working-class background should be only too ready to support the cause of socialism," said Aleksandr Fedorovich. "Your father was a docker, wasn't he, and your family was poor."

I nodded.

"You told Aleksei your father didn't drink wine. And why didn't he? Because he couldn't afford it. Because he was being exploited. Now you can do something about it."

I was astonished that someone so utterly divorced from the realities of my childhood should bring up this particular detail. Aleksei must have entered it in the KGB files. All the barrels of beer and bottles of whiskey that had gone through my father's digestive system in the Working Mens' Club in Wind Street had evidently not been noted.

"The time has now come for you to prove your loyalty to our cause," Aleksandr Fedorovich continued gravely. "We want you to obtain information for us about certain foreigners in Moscow."

"I'm afraid I can't help you," I said. "I've talked about this with Aleksei already. If there were ways in which I could help, I would be happy to go along, provided they were not damaging to British interests."

The conversation soon started going around in circles, and got rather ridiculous. Aleksei claimed that that I had promised to help, while Aleksandr Fedorovich kept repeating, under the impression that it would help: "Why didn't your father drink wine, Mervyn?"

Things were at their most tedious when the door suddenly burst open (it had not been locked) and a middle-aged woman ran in, screaming, "Help, save me, stop him –"

Aleksei jumped to his feet.

"What's the matter?"

"There's a Georgian drunk after me, he's trying to rape me!"

The mere rape of an unknown female was of no interest to KGB officers with an important interview on their hands, and Aleksei firmly pushed her back out into the corridor and closed the door. Her pursuer had evidently disappeared, or was perhaps waiting for her in another part of the hotel, for we heard no more of her. Frankly, I was too concerned with my own fate to worry about hers. Aleksandr Fedorovich and Aleksei were now turning to threats.

"We know," said Aleksei gravely, "that you have been guilty of immoral acts."

"All too few," I thought. In the preceding months I had sown a few wild oats, some as a result of Vadim. Aleksei probably knew about my innocent brush with Nina in Central Asia, the girl at the Vadim's uncle's dacha, and possibly a girl who lived in a circular room near the Ministry of Foreign Trade building, and had made herself suspiciously available. There was also the girl I had just met in Gagri. But I had only been in one Moscow brothel ever, and the total of conquests was extremely modest compared to what Vadim (or for that matter my theatrical friend Valerii Shein) had achieved. I thought rather than argue about numbers it would be better to put on a show of contrition.

"I can't think of anything serious," I said. "No immorality or offence was intended."

"If the Komsomol finds out about it," said Aleksandr Fedorovich, "there will be a big scandal in the newspapers, and you will be shamefully expelled from the university and from the country. Everyone will know."

There was another meaningful pause.

"The time has now come to say finally, yes or no," said Aleksei.

They both looked at me expectantly.

"Then the answer must be No," I said. "Nothing would ever persuade me to work against my country."

Aleksandr Fedorovich wanted to continue his interminable urgings, like a catholic priest desperate to convert a sinner before death. But Aleksei stopped him.

"He won't change his mind now," he told him. "I think we should finish for the time being."

"We will have to meet again," said Aleksandr Fedorovich. "Where shall it be?"

"Let's hire a rowing boat," I said, in all seriousness. "It will be pleasant on the water."

"Not proper working conditions," he barked. "I think we had better meet again here. We will let you know the time."

The meeting had gone on for about two hours. When I got back to my room I sat down on the bed and considered the situation. There was no doubt that this latest crisis was much more serious than the last, and it seemed unlikely that I could hold the KGB off any longer. They had given me an ultimatum. They would hardly, I thought, imprison me, or cause a morality scandal (which wouldn't have worried me), but they could easily get at my Russian friends, arrange some sort of harassment or an 'accident' – it had happened to others. I decided next morning I should make arrangements to fly back to Moscow on the first available plane, pack my stuff at the university, and leave the Soviet Union. The danger flag was flying, but escape still seemed to be fairly easy. I didn't sleep very much that night.

Next morning I found Vadim and told him I was going back to Moscow. He seemed very surprised: but once more I was to be surprised myself. Half an hour before I was due to leave the hotel there was another telephone call. It was Aleksei again. I told him I was just on the point of leaving, in fact by a helicopter service to the airport, but he asked me to stay where I was, because he and Aleksandr Fedorovich wanted to see me once more.

"You can't go, there isn't any transport, anyway," he said.

"What about the helicopter service?"

"It's a spoilt telephone," said Aleksei, using Moscow slang for misinformation. "Go to the same room at twelve o'clock."

I knew that if they wanted to stop me leaving they could easily do so, and I had little alternative but to go to the meeting. At least Aleksei did not seem particularly threatening or angry. When I entered the room at the appointed hour I found, to my immense relief, only him, with no sign of Sokolov. In fact he was quite friendly again.

"Mervyn," he said, "Aleksandr Fedorovich has got into touch with Moscow on your behalf, and fixed things. A decision has been taken at the highest level not to put pressure on you."

"I'm delighted to hear it, Aleksei."

"Better to wait until you come to understand the correctness of our proposals yourself. Aleksandr Fedorovich has acted decisively, and I think you should be grateful to him."

"Please pass on my thanks," I said, rather dryly.

Yet another crisis was over. Aleksei and his dreadful companion would be going back to Moscow, and leaving me in peace.

★

The remaining days at the resort were quite enjoyable, despite all that had happened, and I returned to the capital with Vadim as planned. It had all been very dramatic, but the outcome still allowed me to regard my relationship with the KGB as an exciting game which could cost me little or nothing. I remained puzzled by the contrast between the two men who dealt with me: Aleksei, so sophisticated, and Aleksandr Fedorovich, so crude. Was it just a matter of generational turn-over in the organisation? Or was Aleksei in fact the senior of the two men? Though from my point of view it made little practical difference.

Looking back, I think there were two elements in the situation which I did not appreciate, even after the Gagry events. The first was the sheer administrative effort which the KGB had put into recruiting me. Although I was paying for the Gagry visit myself, their intervention there required a new, significant input of time and resources. They simply could not grasp the fact that they were wasting their time: apart from misjudging my political attitudes, and over-estimating my attachment to Russia, they grossly exaggerated my potential as a spy. I did not disabuse them on any count; perhaps, to be quite honest, I should have.

The other element which I did not fully appreciate was the role played by Vadim. Although he had introduced me to Aleksei, and worked miracles with KGB backing, I still took him at his word, and regarded him as completely trustworthy. Only later did I suspect that he knew a great deal – perhaps everything – that was going on behind the KGB screen, and may have advised Aleksei on the best way to handle me. He must have been aware of the planned confrontation at Gagri, which is why he was nowhere to be seen on certain occasions. Probably I was being handled not just by two KGB officers, but by two KGB officers and an active, part-time volunteer.

How astonishing that I did not realise it at the time.

★

Back in Moscow and I continued my desultory work at MGU and my more serious activities at the Lenin Library. In the evenings I saw Russian friends – those who were too inconspicuous to fear the KGB, or were willing to take some risk. Apart from street surveillance everything went quiet on the KGB front. Aleksei invited me out to dinner a few times, but tried no new initiatives. I was supposed to return to England with the post-graduate group in July, but since life seemed relatively peaceful, even with the goons, I decided to try and stay on for a few weeks and enjoy the Moscow summer. In the autumn I would be returning to Oxford to complete my dissertation: time did not press.

I asked Aleksei about it, as he still professed an interest in my well-being, and he said it could be done. However, as my staying on alone might look a little peculiar, and raise questions in people's minds, I asked him if he could arrange for my fellow student, Martin Dewhirst, to stay as well. The pretext would be that Martin, like me, had joined the group late (the Soviet authorities had been reluctant to give him a visa). Aleksei thought this was a good idea, and I put in my formal application. Martin got his extension as well. To make me feel grateful, I suppose, Aleksei told me that if it had not been for my intervention Dewhirst would have been off to London with the rest.

During our last dinners, a few of Aleksei's remarks stuck in my mind. My intransigence at Gagry, he said, had got him into trouble: he had called his boss, Aleksandr Fedorovich, out on a wild goose chase. One evening Aleksei accused me of collecting information for the Embassy (though I was doing nothing of the sort), presumably to test my reaction. Then, in the middle of August he told me that an acquaintance of mine, Olga Vsevolodovna Ivinskaya, had just been arrested on a charge of 'speculation'. I was very upset to hear it, for I admired her greatly.

★

I had met Olga Vsevolodovna through Georges Nivat. Georges was small, very likable, and devoted to literature. He was also clearly destined for a distinguished career. In Moscow he would complain volubly about the acrid smell of Vietnamese cooking in his corridor, which was, he said, 'ruining his life'. One of Georges' main interests at the time was Boris Pasternak's poetry, and he had made contact with the poet and his family, or more precisely, Pasternak's close friend Olga Vsevolodovna and their daughter Irina. The women lived with another son, Dmitrii, in a flat on Potapov pereulok, near the centre of Moscow. Irina was outstandingly beautiful, with fair hair and blue eyes. Her mother was a quiet and dignified figure.

Times were hard for the poet and those around him. He was an essentially apolitical man, and the scandal over his unorthodox novel *Doctor Zhivago*, which was published abroad in 1958, had disturbed him greatly. The Khrushchev leadership launched a press campaign against him, and he was expelled from the Union of Writers. One day soon after I arrived at MGU Georges offered to take me out to meet him at his dacha in the writers' village of Peredelkino, but I was much too shy. Although I had helped to get his early poetry abroad, I knew little of his work, and had not read *Zhivago*. What could I, an unknown post-graduate, say to so great a writer? I declined the invitation.

I did, however, spend one lovely afternoon at another dacha in Peredelkino which Olga Vsevolodovna was renting so as to be near him. Irina had invited some of her friends along, and the atmosphere was very cordial. One of them, a very attractive girl, invited me to go out for a walk among the dacha gardens, which were green with summer foliage. She was a very pleasant companion, and we both felt it was a good moment for dalliance.

"What do Russian women really want in life?" I asked. "It's a mystery to me."

"They only want one thing," was the serious reply. "They want to be loved."

The remark somehow stuck in my mind. Back at the dacha I amused the company by catching a little frog. Memory is a strange thing – I can still feel it wriggling in my hand.

Alas, that is the only happy interlude I can recall in the Ivinskaya affair. The family had every reason to believe, as close associates of Pasternak, that the flat in Potapov pereulok was closely watched – their old cleaner Polina was certainly being questioned about them. But Olga Vsevolodovna was a brave woman, and welcomed contact with foreigners, believing it gave them some protection against official persecution. When I went there on one occasion she graciously offered me some fine chocolates which could only have come from abroad. "Do not forget us," she said, as I left. "Come again."

Georges sometimes stayed at the flat, though it was possibly illegal, as foreigners were supposed to live only at their registered address. He fell deeply in love with Irina, and his feelings were reciprocated.

Soon he made a proposal of marriage, which was accepted, and they planned what Georges hoped would be a beautiful Orthodox marriage in a Moscow church. Since he was a Catholic, the ceremony would have to take place behind the altar, but this would only add colour to the occasion. Georges told me he was drawing up a list of guests.

Then everything went terribly wrong. In January, 1960 there was a small-pox scare in Moscow, and Georges and I were vaccinated together at the MGU clinic. Georges was in the queue immediately in front of me, and I noticed nothing untoward about the procedure. However, he had a reaction which put him into hospital for several weeks. The Westerners at MGU helped one another in time of need, so naturally I went up to Sokolniki, where the hospital was located, to visit him. I found him very cheerful and alert, but suffering from what was said to be a blood infection. How he had got it no one knew.

After that he had several bouts of a serious skin condition lasting months. One day he telephoned me urgently from Potapov pereulok and told me to bring the British embassy doctor straight away, because he was very ill. I contacted the doctor and found he was most unwilling to leave his office in the embassy building, perhaps because he did not fully believe me. But I insisted that the matter was serious: I knew the gentleman was not overburdened with medical duties, as I had once heard him say, all but seriously, that doctoring on Sofiiskaya naberezhnaya was money for old rope.

We met in the centre of town, and went over to Potapov. At first I could not find the flat, because on all previous occasions Georges had led me there. The doctor declared that he was not going to waste any more of his time, and was returning to the Embassy forthwith. Fortunately, just then I found the flat, and we went in. Thank God I had managed to persuade him to hang on, for we found Georges in bed with a terrible, suppurating rash which defied diagnosis and clearly needed immediate treatment. The doctor tore up some sheets, bound the affected areas, and told me to get Georges to hospital as soon as possible. The rash took some time to clear, and in the spring Georges went back to France to recuperate.

Boris Pasternak died on the 31st May, and there was a well-attended, though unofficial funeral. The poet's demise meant that the family was more vulnerable than ever. Georges returned to Russia, although a little earlier than he desired, because the Soviet Embassy in Paris would not extend his re-entry visa. He and Irina now applied for a date to get married at the so-called 'Palace of Weddings' on Griboedov street, the only place where foreign partners could be registered. There could be no question of Irina being allowed to go abroad to get married in Paris. The couple were given the 20th June as a date for registration, but by this time Georges had had a relapse and was in hospital again. Irina's attempt to smuggle him out to meet a second date (16th July) was frustrated by the appearance of a guardian nurse at his bedside. Now Irina fell ill with the same mysterious disease. The third date she got fell just after the 10th August, when Georges's visa was due to expire.

The situation was an absolute nightmare. The infection was highly suspicious, but I could not bring myself to believe that it had actually been implanted by the KGB, the idea being just too evil. So without mentioning that aspect, I asked Aleksei to help. He was, as I expected, entirely noncommittal. Georges knew I was trying to do something, but he thought it was through a minor official of the Ministry of Higher Education – I could not tell him I was in contact with the 'organs'. Soon after, the French Embassy found that it could not get his visa extended either, and his bright hopes for marrying the lovely Irina were dashed. On the 10th August it was my sad task to accompany him to the airport with Olga Vsevolodovna and a friend of his from the French Embassy. It was the saddest of journeys for all three of us: Irina was too ill to get out of bed.

A few days later, after Georges had left the country in tears, Aleksei raised the topic unexpectedly at dinner, but only with another distressing revelation. "That woman you asked about [he meant Olga Vsevolodovna] has just been arrested on contraband charges," he told me. I was stunned, and lost all appetite. I may have been the last foreigner to see her before it happened. "She was involved in smuggling foreign currency," Aleksei continued, referring no doubt to the *Zhivago* royalties, "and other matters. She was morally corrupt." Aleksei would not cede an inch from the official line. "It's a bad family, Mervyn," he said, protectively, as it were. "I would advise you to keep fifteen kilometres away from them." I learnt a little later that the Ivinskaya flat had been searched and some material confiscated. On the 6th September poor Irina was herself arrested, though still ill, and taken to the Lubyanka. She describes events as she experienced them, with great clarity, in her memoirs *Legendy potapovskogo pereulka*. And what about the mysterious illness? Later, on reading Solzhenitsyn's autobiography *The Oak and the Calf*, Irina found a description of similar symptoms. An attempt had apparently made to poison the writer when he was living in Rostov, and the preparation used was called 'ricin'. Irina discussed strong evidence for poisoning in an article she wrote for the Russian émigré newspaper *Russkaya mysl'* in June 1992.

★

On the night before I was due to leave Russia, Aleksandr Fedorovich invited me to dinner, in other words he called me in for another working-over. On this occasion he was more affable, but told me he was anxious to gain my allegiance, and wanted me to write a statement to that effect. At first I refused, but I gave in when he agreed to let me word it myself. I wrote a short paragraph saying (and here I quote the key words) "that I would always be loyal to the cause of peace and better understanding between nations". The statement itself was completely innocuous, but afterwards I regretted having written anything at all. There was no knowing whether the KGB would try and use it against me. "Whether it will ever surface again" I noted later, "remains to be seen". I left Moscow on the 26th September, 1960, after two very eventful years.

★

Some of my experiences in Russia may have been scary, but for me the country glowed with excitement, and I was anxious to return. My next opportunity came in May 1961, in connection with the British Exhibition in Moscow. I got work as an interpreter on the British Council stand. The exhibition was held in the great park of People's Economic Achievements, in one of Moscow's northern suburbs, and I was lodged in a shabby hotel nearby. But travel to the centre was not too difficult, and I could meet old friends after work.

I thought it would be a good idea to maintain my friendship with Vadim, which meant of course bringing Aleksei into the picture. I was well aware that this could lead to more trouble, but I was rather reluctant to lose Vadim, whom I liked, anyway. Aleksei would know through the KGB network that I was in Moscow, and if I did not telephone him, he would almost certainly telephone me. It was perhaps better for me to take the initiative and retain a psychological advantage. I bought presents for both of them – a lighter with 'Vadim' engraved on it, and chocolates for Aleksei and his wife, Ina.

After I arrived Vadim and I kicked off with dinner in, of all places, a tripe restaurant that he had discovered, followed by an evening in the old Sundukovski Steam baths in the heart of Moscow. That, too, was an interesting experience – steaming halls, air almost too hot to breathe, and bunches of birch twigs to beat yourself with. A skinny old man with a long beard and a loin cloth went around mopping up and keeping the place clean. We finished, like everyone else, sitting around in white sheets and drinking enormous glasses of beer.

My dinner with Aleksei, on the other hand, was the usual refined affair, with gleaming table cloth, beautiful glasses, irresistible food. But he told me, to my dismay, that Aleksandr Fedorovich wanted to meet me as well. Could I please give him a ring, I had his number, hadn't I? I decided to do so, because I was, as usual, under street surveillance, and could be picked up at any time. However I let things hang for a few days before telephoning the dreadful man from a kiosk in the street. Better not use the British Council phone at the Exhibition, I thought.

"Aleksandr Fedorovich! How are you? It's Mervyn."

When I heard his voice I froze: he was more unpleasant than ever.

"Why didn't you ring me before?" he grunted. "I've been waiting. I want to see you."

"I'm very busy at the Exhibition just now. Let's make it the day after tomorrow."

"That doesn't suit me," replied Aleksandr Fedorovich imperiously. "We must meet tomorrow, about midday. When can you get time off? A car will pick you up, better in the centre somewhere. Let's fix a spot and the exact hour."

Next day I was, of course, waiting at the kerbside, and the car appeared promptly. It was a chauffeur-driven Volga (Aleksei always used the bigger and more prestigious ZIL) and alas, Aleksandr Fedorovich was in it. My stomach turned over as I got in. I would only be in Moscow a few days more, but what would happen this time? We went to have lunch in a private room at the Sovetskaya Hotel on Leningrad Prospect, but as I anticipated, the conversation did not facilitate digestion. My host demanded, at least ten times, that I should get to know a French interpreter who was working at the Exhibition, and find out what he was really up to. I refused outright, so I never knew exactly what was behind the demand. In the end Aleksandr Fedorovich gave up trying, but only after arranging to meet me again a day or two later.

Just as we were finishing the meal a small incident revealed Sokolov's complete unconcern for the workers whose fate he was supposed to champion. The waitress, fat and harassed as most of them were, came and asked if he could settle the bill, as she was just going off work. I imagine she wanted to get the tip that would normally go with a large meal, and perhaps settle up with the kitchen, where she may have been charged for food herself. That was sometimes the practice in Soviet restaurants. "We haven't finished yet," said Aleksandr Fedorovich, although we had. She went off hesitantly, no doubt worried about settling. In any case she had lost the hoped-for tip, and I felt quite sorry for her.

After she had gone Aleksandr Fedorovich had suggested prolonging my visa, so that I could make a trip down to the Black Sea Coast with Aleksei. I had already had enough of that, and confronted by my obvious lack of enthusiasm he dropped the idea. He did, however, pull some roubles notes from his pocket – not a great amount – and insist on my taking them, no signature, no strings. Rather weakly, I pocketed them. There were no consequences, but I later regretted having done so. Aleksei had once given me a small, elegant Georgian drinking horn, but it seemed natural to accept a gift like that from him. Sokolov was different: I felt I had sullied myself in taking cash from so odious a person. But the incident was over in a moment, and there was nothing to be done afterwards.

I arrived at the next assignation to find Aleksei waiting for me – alone. Was I relieved!

"Aleksandr Fedorovich has left Moscow for the time being," he said. "He asked you about a French interpreter, didn't he? That was only a trial balloon. What he really wanted to know, in concrete terms, was how you could help us."

"Well, we've discussed that already, Aleksei," I replied.

He nodded understandingly, and the conversation moved on to inconsequential matters. The door was again left open for further cooperation – but on my terms. I left the USSR with the rest of the party, as planned, on the 5th June.

*

On my return to Oxford, I found that a number of strange things were going on there, too. The hand of the KGB was not entirely absent from the city of dreaming spires. I usually took an interest in Soviet visitors, and one day I met a certain Igor Rozanov, whom the Soviet government had sent over on the cultural exchange. Somewhat older than the average student, and a specialist in Chinese, Rozanov had been selected to spend a year at Exeter College. Obviously, he was no ordinary Russian student, such as I had known in Moscow. When I got talking to him he did not hesitate to boast about his fine career prospects in the Ministry of Foreign Affairs. And it was surely no coincidence that (by his own admission) he knew Vadim Popov! My God, I thought, it *is* a small world. When I spoke to Vadim later, in Moscow, he confirmed that "their dachas were indeed close together."

It did not take me long to develop an active dislike of Rozanov: he seemed impervious to the benefits he was enjoying at Oxford ("Who needs two rooms, anyway?"), and was invariably negative in his comments on Britain. Given the overcrowding and hardship I had seen in Russia, I found his condescension most distasteful, and I was soon taking good care not to see much of him. He partially blew his cover by joining the Soviet Embassy soon afterwards. If one of his tasks was to keep a line open to me on behalf of the KGB, he did not fulfil it very well: but he had at least registered his presence. I wrote letters, incidentally, to both Vadim and Aleksei, using box numbers which they gave me. Aleksei replied as though he were a student at Moscow University, offering to help me locate research materials. He added meaningfully that he would be happy to see me again in Moscow.

The KGB, it seemed, was not the only organisation anxious to enlist my modest services. Something else was stirring, but from a different quarter. One of my closest friends at St. Antony's was the émigré Sergei Utechin, an able historian from the Volga. He had left Russia during the war, and was an active member of an organisation called the NTS (the Russian acronym for People's Labour Union). The NTS was dedicated to overthrowing the Soviet regime and establishing democracy in Russia, but few people (except its own members) took it seriously. It functioned mainly on the basis of the enthusiasm of its leadership and its dreams for the future. The Soviet authorities were, however, delighted to use it for scare tactics, representing it as a real threat to Soviet power. In Russia, membership of the NTS was a treasonable offence.

Sergei invited up to Oxford a Russian friend called Georgii Khan, a strange name to the Russian ear, who, said Sergei, was interested in meeting students with Russian interests. He would like to talk to me. Georgii turned out to be a fat, sociable man in his mid-forties, with (it would seem) hardly any knowledge of English. We had a few talks about the situation in the USSR, and he revealed that he was also a member of the NTS. He was looking for people who could take anti-Soviet material to Russia, and even liaise with NTS members there. He hinted that I might be able to help them in this regard: indeed, he showed me some of their literature, closely printed on tiny sheets so that it could be easily concealed about one's person.

Of course I was sympathetic to democratic NTS aims. But given my contacts with the KGB, my sojourns in Russia were complicated enough already. I could not be involved with the KGB *and* the NTS at the same time. So I told him that I could not help him. Nevertheless, Mr. Khan – who subsequently changed his surname to Miller – was to play a significant part in my life.

★

Things moved forward one evening in the summer of 1963, after dinner at St. Antony's College. By then my D.Phil. thesis on Soviet employment had gone through, I had spent a year at Harvard, and had been elected to a junior Research Fellowship at the College. This gave me short-term membership of the Senior Common Room, whither the Fellows normally retired after dinner to enjoy a mixture of arch conversation, newspaper reading and booze. The SCR was graced on that occasion by the presence of none other than Prince Dmitri Obolenski, who taught Russian and Byzantine history. Charming and slightly erudite, and a genuine Russian nobleman to boot, he was involved in organising the cultural exchanges with the USSR. Our conversation was brief, but – for me – very exciting.

"I gather," he said, suggestively, "that the British Council has not been able to find enough students to fill the Moscow quota again."

"Really?"

"Would you be interested in going?"

"I've been on an exchange before, and I'm probably too long in the tooth."

"I shouldn't think so," said the Prince. "Could you get the time off from the College? Would you have a suitable topic of study?"

The upshot was a formal application, interviews and a grant to spend another academic year in my favourite city. I had learnt a little about Russian surprises by now, so before leaving Oxford I thought it wise to deposit with a friend an outline of all my contacts with the KGB, to be passed on to our security services if anything untoward happened.

I am going back to the USSR, leaving England on the *Kalinin* next Sunday 1st Sept. [1963]. I am wondering whether Aleksei will get into touch with me again. It is possible that he will, and that some new forms of pressure will be thought up.... Last year I wrote an article on the Soviet censorship based on a confidential list of banned books which I saw in Yalta. The article appeared anonymously, but the authorship may have been traced. That would amount to a breach of the [Soviet] laws on state secrecy. The book I have written on Soviet youth problems, again, might give grounds to the Soviet authorities for legal action against me. It may be out while I am still in Moscow. On the whole, however, I think that my position as an exchange student will provide some protection: more [important] is the fact that I have no access whatever to sensitive information, so I can be of little immediate use [to the KGB].

I do not intend to contact either Aleksei or Aleksandr Fedorovich. If there is any trouble, it will mean that they have contacted me.

signed: W.M. Matthews

Three. A Red Sweater

Ifound that very little had changed at Moscow University when I returned in the first days of September, 1963. This time I was lodged in the main hostel. My first room was too noisy to sleep in, so after a week or so of repeated requests the Department for Foreign Students gave me another on the 6th floor of zone G. There I found I was sharing a two-roomed 'block' with a Chinese student called Wang. He was a pleasant neighbour, but terrified of being too friendly with a 'capitalist' – the Chinese kept a sharp eye on one another. In the absence of a cultural agreement between Peking and Rome, Wang had been sent to Moscow University to study Italian, which unfortunately meant learning Russian first. Despite this slight inconvenience he seemed very contented with his lot.

The watchful eye of the *dezhurnaya* at the Hotel desk back in 1960 was replaced by that of the *starosta* on floor six. *Starostas* (the word means 'elder') were chosen from older students who were enthusiastic members of the Komsomol and didn't mind doing a bit of informing on the side. We had a lad from Grozny, the capital of Chechnya, who was politically enthusiastic and studied economics. He seemed to take an interest in me just because I was a Westerner, but we got on quite well, and as time went by he even asked me one or two small favours, like translating letters into English. His name was Ruslan Khasbulatov: neither of us dreamed that he would eventually be elected Chairman of the Russian Supreme Soviet, and contend for the leadership of all Russia.

As for the other people in the corridor, I made one or two slight friends, but at thirty-two I was by now really a bit too old to mix easily with the undergraduates. Apart from that they were no less wary than before of getting close to a foreigner, especially with someone like Ruslan around. The goon posts were still there, and more often than not I was followed when I left the building.

With a dreadful inevitability I was again placed in the Faculty of Economics with Volkov as my supervisor. Yagodkin was still there, and worse than ever: everyone in the department seemed to be caught in an ideological time warp. Yagodkin did not like the sociological character of the topic I proposed, and imperiously thrust upon me a standard undergraduate research theme. As a consequence, my efforts for Feliks Mikhailovich were even less enthusiastic than the first time around. After a few weeks, in a spasm of despair, I applied for transfer to the Faculty of Journalism so that I could work on the Russian *feuilleton*, which had always amused me. When this move was firmly blocked, I lost interest in MGU altogether. I was, however, expected to provide F.M. with lists of the books I had read, so I made a point of going to the Lenin Library from time to time and writing notes which I could flash before him.

A matter that concerned me more was the possible re-emergence of Aleksei and his dreadful colleague Aleksandr Fedorovich – in fact, I thought about it almost daily. I telephoned Vadim, as a friend, knowing that contacting him would make little difference to KGB intentions: they would again be aware that I was in Moscow. Sure enough, on the evening of the 22nd November, I was called to the telephone. Somewhat apprehensive, I walked along the dimly-lit corridor to the desk where the instrument was located. And once more I heard Aleksei's measured tones.

"Hello, Mervyn, back in Moscow!"

"Yes, indeed...."

"Why haven't you telephoned me?"

I made some unconvincing excuse about being busy.

"I think," said Aleksei, "that we should meet!"

But I already made my decision on that score. Although I wouldn't have minded seeing him for a friendly chat, I knew that was impossible – his motives could only be sinister. And Aleksandr Fedorovich was about the last person I wanted to clap eyes on.

"I'm sorry, Aleksei, I won't have time."

There was an awkward silence, and for a few moments I wondered how the conversation would end. In fact, he had little more to say, and we both put down the receivers. He did not ring again.

★

Nearly everything that was interesting to me took place outside the walls of the university, as before. One day, as I was walking past the famous statue of Yurii Dolgoruki, the prince who had founded Moscow, I had a most pleasant surprise. Whom should I bump into but Irina Ivinskaya. She was with a young male friend, and the three of us sat down on a bench for a few minutes to catch up on the news, or more accurately, the course of disaster. I did not want to talk to them for long – if I was under KGB surveillance it might do them no good.

Irina was as beautiful and composed as ever, and not visibly affected by her two years' imprisonment for 'contraband'. The sentence had been three years, but was reduced for good behaviour. She had managed to get a place at the Pushkin Literary Institute – mainly, she admitted, on account of her closeness to Pasternak, whose works were widely admired, despite official disapproval. Irina was very able, but even bright young Muscovites could not normally dream of being admitted to so prestigious an establishment. Olga Vsevolodovna was still in a camp, and not very well, but she had survived half of her eight-year sentence, and hoped for early release also. According to prison rules, Irina was allowed to visit her at long intervals. Georges had not been permitted to return to Russia. The conversation was animated, but we parted sadly, realising that it was better not to continue an overt friendship.

I spent time at the homes of old friends, like Valerii Shein and the Yakuboviches. Igor Vail' as a student at MGU, had a pass and could visit me in the hostel. A new friend, Vitalii Listsov, who studied electronics, invited me to his family house on the outskirts of Moscow, and we spent an afternoon skiing together. In October I had a lavish shashlik dinner with Vadim at the Baku, an Azerbaidzhan restaurant on Gorki Street. I found that his *modus vivendi* had not changed in the slightest. There were no obvious KGB overtones, and we paid half-and-half for the meal, as of old. Subsequently I saw less of him, mainly because my circle of acquaintances widened in a most unexpected manner.

One evening Valerii Shein said he would like to introduce me to his cousin, also called Valerii. Valerii Golovitser and his sister Galya had lived with the Sheins when they were children, after the untimely deaths of their mother and father through illness and accident. The family was Jewish, and very cohesive. Galya, a beautiful and spirited girl, married an Italian communist and had been whisked off to live in Teramo, a small town in Abruzzi: it was relatively easy for members of foreign Communist Parties to get their Russian wives out of the country. Her brother dreamed of joining her, but he was politically suspect and had never managed to obtain an exit visa. The problem was that he liked associating with foreigners, particularly people in the artistic sphere, and had been called in to the KGB for 'talks' more than once.

The three of us first got together in Shein's flat on Stankevich Street, just off Gorkii Street. Valerii Golovitser was about five years younger than I, short but gracefully built, and very carefully dressed. He had thick black hair, a pale complexion and dark sensitive eyes. One sensed his use of a foreign aftershave, probably from a shop in Teramo. His main passion in life was ballet, which he saw as often as he possibly could. He was a great admirer of the ballerina Maya Plisetskaya, and even knew her personally. He had a menial job and little money, but had perfected various means of getting into the theatre without paying, to settle into what would now be called 'no show' seats. He had dreamed of being a dancer himself, but as he was a little too short, and could not afford full-time study, he was taking a part-time course in theatre studies. He also collected classical records (the hobby I had started myself when last at MGU), and he said that if I went to his room he would show me some. I thought it would be interesting to get to know him better.

We met again one evening at the Kropotkinskoe metro station, which stands at the end of one of Moscow's delightful tree-lined boulevards. I will always remember him running up, eager-faced, as I waited in the leafy half darkness.

"I live on Ryleeva Street, on the Arbat," he said. "Not very far from here. Come on."

We reached the house in a few minutes and entered the dirty hallway. Like most of Moscow's older buildings, it contained several large flats on each floor. Formerly they were no doubt quite elegant, but in Soviet times were usually occupied by several families, one to a room, and Valerii's flat was no exception. He showed me the communal kitchen and the bathroom: the peeling walls and rusting pipes exemplified a proletarian underside of Soviet Russia which was not pictured anywhere. Valerii had his own room with a large and attractive window, though it was also in sad need of redecoration. He had filled it with pieces of valuable antique furniture, elegant but quite out of keeping with the general dilapidation. His interests extended beyond ballet to most forms of art.

We had nothing particular planned for that evening, so we just lounged on his divan and talked about life. Valerii took out some of his Bach cantata records and presented them to me, and since I knew how difficult it was to find them in Moscow, I much appreciated his gift. My relative indifference to matters of the theatre did not mean that we had nothing to talk about: as far as I remember we touched on the trials of living in post-Stalin Russia, life abroad, the various activities of Moscow dancers and actors. There was his friend Venya, for example.

"Venya was here yesterday," he said, "my actor friend."

"What play is he in?"

"He hasn't got a job at the moment. But he is quite talented. He was telling me whom he had slept with."

"A long string of beautiful girls."

"No," said Valerii, "a long string of beautiful boys," and laughed meaningfully.

"In some ways the world is the same all over," I exclaimed.

Inevitably the topic of the KGB came up.

"Valerii Shein says you've had some trouble with them," I said.

"Yes," he replied. "But they haven't called me in recently. The last time was on account of thieving at the *Izvestia* packing depot where I work. They were convinced I was involved, though I wasn't."

"Why did they think you were?"

Valerii laughed.

" 'Well, Comrade Golovitser,' the officer said to me, 'you can't possibly live on the wage you get from *Izvestia*. You must be doing something on the side. Otherwise you'd starve.'"

Valerii was a likeable person, and we quickly became good friends. From time to time he mentioned another close friend of his, a girl called Mila (short for Ludmilla) Bibikova, who was also dear to his sister Galya. Mila, said Valerii, had had an even tougher childhood than they – her parents had been arrested when she was little, she and her elder sister had been brought up in orphanages, where she had contracted tuberculosis. Family misfortune and a passion for the theatre had brought them together. I was intrigued by this sad story, and ever anxious to enlarge my circle of Russian friends, asked if I could meet Ludmilla.

"Of course," said Valerii, "no problem at all. If I ask her, she'll come running. Especially if I tell her you are Estonian. She lives nearby, she's got a room in a communal flat on Starokonyushenny pereulok."

Perhaps Valerii wanted to do her a favour by getting her a foreign friend. She was evidently as courageous as he, and did not fear the consequences, though my being 'Estonian' would make things a bit less threatening to begin with. There was, however, another small problem: my shyness about meeting people. I thought it would be a bit strange if he invited her around as a blind date, since we might not like one another, and it seemed a bit crass, anyway. Perhaps, to avoid mutual embarrassment, it would be better if I could see her first, perhaps at a distance? I asked Valerii whether this would be possible.

"It can be arranged," said Valerii. "We're going to the Bolshoi Theatre tomorrow evening. If you wait outside when it finishes, you'll see us leaving. Keep a sharp eye open, or you'll miss us in the crowd."

At ten o'clock I was waiting in the square in front of the great Bolshoi portico. Moscow is cold in October, and gusts of wind carried snowflakes over the broad pavements. Everyone was heavily dressed. After a while Valerii emerged, easily distinguishable by his fine, upright posture and expensive *ushanka,* or fur hat. He was accompanied by a girl probably in her late twenties, in a Russian headscarf. She was short and limped noticeably. I watched them as they went off in the direction of the Arbat, engrossed in conversation. That brief glimpse got me over my shyness, so when I saw Valerii next I asked him to invite her to his room so we could meet.

Mila turned up a couple of evenings later, having been warned, I am sure, that an eligible foreigner was in sight. The first thing I noticed about her were her eyes – grey, sharp, but very kind, with a wonderful smile. Otherwise you would not have described her as a beauty, like Irina, for example. Her features were very Russian, even Tartar, with the characteristic high cheekbones and slightly olive skin. Occasionally at that time I made notes on what was happening, though they were infrequent, and partly in my own bad Welsh, because I feared that they might fall into the hands of the KGB. On the 28th October I wrote that Mila was "of very strong character, but utterly charming, intelligent". She Russianised my name into *Mervusya* as soon as we met: it was the first time I ever heard it. Valerii had mentioned that she was not very graceful in manner, grace not being a quality easily acquired in Soviet orphanages. As far as I could see, it didn't matter.

★

We started meeting regularly. I learned that her life story was even more tragic than Valerii had suggested. Her father had been a communist party official in the west Ukrainian town of Chernigov, and headed the department of ideology. He had also worked as party organiser in the famous Kharkov Tractor Works and had been awarded the highly regarded Order of Lenin for his efforts. But in October, 1937, together with thousands of others, he had been arrested on trumped-up charges of treason and (as the family found out later) tortured and shot. A few weeks later Mila's mother, Marfa Platonovna, was arrested merely because she had been married to him. Soldiers came to take her in the middle of the night, and Mila's first memory, as a child of less than four years, was being awakened by a soldier with a gun. Her elder sister Lena screamed as their mother was dragged away down the street. Marfa Platonovna was sent off to a prison camp in Siberia, where she endured appalling conditions until her release in 1949.

Mila and her sister were at first lodged in a children's prison (the only accommodation immediately available), then separated and sent to different children's homes. In February 1938, Mila contracted measles and tuberculosis of the hip, spending three years in hospital. The treatment must have been primitive, because a fistular infection developed, the joint was immobilised and the leg badly deformed. When war started she was evacuated to a home in a little town called Solikamsk on the edge of the Urals, where she survived starvation, sometimes through eating grass. Some years later the surgeons managed partially to correct the deformity, but she never regained movement in the hip, and the illness somewhat inhibited her growth. Even so, she considered herself lucky, as most of the children who had been ill with her died. The tale was a harrowing one and she was reluctant to dwell on it.

The sisters were reunited only in 1944 when Lena set out to look for her, and got her transferred to another orphanage in Saltykovka, near Moscow. The tragedy ended, in political terms, only after 1953 when Stalin died and their mother was able to live freely in Moscow, without fear of persecution. Her father was, in the hallowed Soviet phrase, rehabilitated in 1955. Like many 'repressed' children Mila evoked sympathy from the people who came into contact with her. She concealed her suspect political parentage (an accepted practice) and got a place in the Faculty of History at Moscow University. After graduating she was taken on to help with historical research in the well-known Institute of Marxism-Leninism. Like many of her colleagues she retained her staunchly anti-Soviet views – but kept quiet about them.

Mila seemed to be a very sincere person, and listened to my accounts of my own childhood in Swansea with great interest. The various bombings of the town, the relative poverty of my family and break-up of my parents' marriage, which had been my own miserable lot, were small beer compared to her dreadful experiences. Nobody in our family had ever been imprisoned and nobody had ever been shot. I had never had any hunger pains to ease, my main worry during the war being to make my four-ounce sweet ration last the week.

As the weeks went by our friendship deepened. Mila lived in Starokonyushenny pereulok, (Old Stable Lane) an old street right in the centre of Moscow. It still retained a few traditional wooden houses and small, nineteenth-century villas among the newer blocks. Soon Mila started inviting me back to her tiny room in a communal flat not unlike Valerii's. It had deep double windows looking out into a small yard, yellow wallpaper, and a door thickly padded for warmth and quiet. There was space only for a wardrobe, a divan bed, a small table and stools which could be tucked away underneath it. The room could be noisy, too, for it adjoined the communal kitchen, and the family in the next room liked to have late-night parties – with an accordion. However, she kept it very clean, and it took on a homely aspect for me.

I found myself spending most of my evenings there, preceded by a strange routine. On my way from the university hostel, followed at a discrete distance by the goons, I passed close to Valerii's flat on Ryleev Street. I would usually call in for a chat, and perhaps pick up some more records. Then I would try and shake the goons off before going on to Mila's: usually they were unlosable, it was just that I preferred them not to know my every move. When I gave the requisite number of rings on the doorbell she would open the door, greet me with a smile and usher me in to her little cell, if possible without attracting the attention of the neighbours. Then we would have tea with blackcurrant jam on antique plates (she liked old china), and an embroidered Ukrainian tablecloth. After a while the food got more elaborate, with milk for the tea and a full evening meal, my favourite being fried sturgeon. In those days it was still a relatively cheap fish – for foreigners, that is. The saucepan with the boiled potatoes that went with it was carried in from the kitchen and wrapped in a blanket to keep it warm.

The communal kitchen, with its blackened gas stove, one small table per family, and all-pervasive smell of salted cucumbers, was best avoided. It was almost impossible not to bump into the neighbours there, and they were all terribly inquisitive about 'Mila's foreigner'. Maria Ivanovna, one of the fattest women I have ever seen, was the worst. She was intensely curious about my foreign accent, and keen to know where I came from – I never told her (or anyone else) in the hope that they might think I was from somewhere politically safe, one of the Baltic republics, perhaps. The neighbours were not only uneasy – everybody knew foreigners attracted the attention of the KGB – but envious as well, as the smell of sturgeon betokened an unaccustomed opulence.

Still, the evenings at Mila's were congenial and intimate, marred only by her Russian habit of leaving the little top window open for blasts of frosty air to come in. It was a wrench to go out into the bitterly cold winter street. When leaving the flat, usually late at night, I would cast an eye along the snowy pavements to note, as a matter of interest, who would be following me back to the university.

I went on seeing old friends, including Vadim. When I told him about my growing friendship with Mila he seemed mildly embarrassed, as though that was not the sort of thing a foreigner should do. But of course, his reaction was quite irrelevant: my life became ever more centred on Starokonyushenny pereulok. And with Mila waiting for me there I had no incentive to travel outside Moscow. I joined the student group for a weekend in the ancient town of Vladimir, which was only a few hours away by train, but I refused to do a tour of the Ukraine. Nobody took much notice. Instead Mila introduced me to some of her friends (she was very sociable) and took me back to meet her family. With that my Moscow days acquired a dimension usually denied to foreigners, something I had dreamed about while working at the Embassy. Even Vadim never invited me home, in fact he was always silent about his background.

Mila's sister Lena was a big, impressive woman, who had married a charming man called Aleksandr (Sasha) Vasin. He was of relatively opulent peasant stock, but the family had been dispossessed during the collectivisation of the Russian village in the thirties. Sasha had fought well in the War, lost a leg, joined the Communist party and risen to high rank in the Ministry of Justice. He was always very secretive about his job (even the family had no clear idea of what it was), but I discovered from his telephone number that he was head of the powerful department of finance. This of course gave him useful contacts throughout the Soviet Union, and enabled him to place his wife in a legal job, though she had no qualifications except reliability. Lena (short for Elena) had, incidentally, changed her name: her parents originally called her Lenina to demonstrate their patriotism. They intended to call her younger sister Stalina, but happily baulked at the last moment and settled for Ludmilla.

The family was thus very much part of the new Soviet bourgeoisie. Lena and Sasha lived in a comfortable two-roomed flat on the prestigious Frunzenski Embankment of the Moscow River, had a small car and a little dacha outside Moscow (though it was a far cry from that of Vadim's uncle). None of the the family had ever been abroad except Sasha, who had once had a holiday in Bulgaria, Russia's most servile satellite. There were two rather beautiful teenage daughters who were supposed to be studying, but spent much of their time philandering.

Of course, as far as the family was concerned, any association with me required courage, for Sasha could have been questioned, and possibly disciplined, on account of it. It was highly unusual for Soviet families to invite foreigners to visit them at home. His authoritative position, Mila said, gave no guarantee of invulnerability to KGB. By now Marfa Platonovna was living in a nice room in another part of Moscow, she invited Mila and me over for a meal, too.

★

Little by little the frosts began to ease, and the Moscow spring made its bare, watery appearance. In the emotional sphere, my relationship with Mila was getting serious. Looking back, I can pin-point the moment my fate was sealed. It was one grey, February evening on Starokonyushenny pereulok, soon after the snow had cleared. I had spent an afternoon at the flat, and when we left, at dusk, Mila for some reason had to go off in another direction. I said good-bye to her, and after a moment turned to watch her going off down the street. Suddenly, for no discernable reason, I realised I was profoundly in love with that lopsided figure, and I could see no future for myself without her. Call it what you will, glandular chemistry or love.

And with that realisation a sea-change came over my Moscow existence. I knew that even if the path of 'true love' were smooth and led towards marriage, the next few months would bring a lot of administrative problems. I could not simply take Mila off to England, for Soviet citizens did not have the right to go abroad, as Georges Nivat and Valerii knew only too well. She could only leave as my wife, which meant getting the marriage registered by the Soviet authorities in Moscow. Under Stalin, marriages with foreigners had been banned altogether, but though they were now formally permitted, they were still regarded as undesirable and often impeded. The KGB would doubtlessly be involved, if only to ensure that no one with access to state secrets went abroad. Since state secrecy went down to such menial matters as postal deliveries, I wondered how an employee of the Institute of Marxism Leninism would fare. Regardless of these difficulties, my mind was made up: but I decided to wait a while before making the actual proposal. Little did I know that yet another surprise was in store for me.

*

On the morning of the 6th March I went for another of my pointless meetings with Feliks Volkov at the old Faculty building, and on leaving I noticed that KGB surveillance had been greatly intensified. Usually I had a couple of goons watching me, but on that morning there seemed to be many more. I felt uneasy, as I had done so often before in Moscow, but on the other hand I had not done anything really amiss, and had no reason to expect trouble.

I had earlier arranged to ring Igor Vail' at home, and possibly call in to see him later in the day, to discuss a small personal matter. He tried to dress reasonably, and a few weeks before I had sold him a few small articles of clothing, the most important being a red sweater.

I also asked him to take a dark brown suit I had no need of and sell it in a state Commission Shop, since under Soviet law foreigners could not do so. I knew, however, that Igor had not taken the suit to the shop, as he thought he could get a better price by selling it to some African student. When I had last seen it, it was hanging on the wall in the small room which he shared with his mother. I wanted to know how far he had got with this business, and pick up the money for the sweater.

But, given the intensified surveillance, I thought it might be better not to go there at all. I found a telephone booth and rang him up.

"Igor, how are you?"

"Fine, where are you now?"

"In town. Things aren't all that good. You know we arranged to meet this evening?"

"Yes, you're coming here at seven."

"Well, perhaps it's better if we put it off, you can guess what I mean."

"Put it off? Why?" Igor sounded startled, and a little hoarse.

"Well, I don't like coming in certain circumstances."

To any Russian that remark, coming from a foreigner, would have been crystal clear.

"It doesn't matter at all," said Igor, nervously. "Come along. I look forward to seeing you."

"OK."

I put down the telephone rather perplexed. He certainly knew what I was hinting at, but he seemed very anxious for me to come, nevertheless. I wondered why.

And so at seven o'clock, in the gathering darkness, I made my way to his flat on Kropotkin Street. It was in an old nineteenth-century town house near the metro where I met Valerii. Igor's was the only communal flat I had ever been in where the lavatory was actually in the kitchen (though behind a modest screen). As I approached the house in the gloom I saw someone who was obviously watching it from across the street, so I went for a little walkabout through some gloomy alleyways and yards. There was not much hope of shaking off the surveillance, but I thought I would (as usual) give them a run for their money. If they did not actually see me going in, so much the better.

Eventually I slipped in through the front entrance and climbed the dirty stairway to the top floor, where Igor's communal flat was situated. I gave the required three rings on the doorbell and Igor opened the front door, apparently in the best of spirits.

"OK?" he said, with a welcoming grin. "Come in!"

I followed him quickly into his room, as usual, to avoid the attention of neighbours. There another surprise awaited me.

Igor had always ensured that his mother was out (in fact I only saw her once ever) and we invariably had the room to ourselves. But on this occasion two strangers – middle aged men in dark suits – were sitting on the bed, also smiling.

"These are friends of mine," said Igor, unctuously. "They are interested in buying your suit, or anything else you have for sale."

"Yes, we'll buy anything you have," said one.

I was alarmed: Igor had not said anything about 'friends' coming: something was clearly wrong. Foreigners were not allowed to buy or sell anything to Soviet citizens, and discretion was essential, even for tiny items. What was Igor up to?

"I think I'll be off," I said, and backed towards the door.

"No, no," said Igor, jumping up to restrain me, "don't go. They'll give you a good price."

"I'm not interested."

On seeing that I was on the point of leaving anyway, one of them stood up and drew an official pass from his pocket. It showed that I was being dealt with by a certain Captain Kazakov.

"We are from the Criminal Investigation Department of the Ministry for the Preservation of Public Order," said Kazakov, "and we are arresting you as a 'speculator'."

The idea was to pin a speculation charge on me! So that's why the surveillance had been increased. Charging me was not difficult, as 'speculation' was defined as any kind of buying and selling for profit, including the few small items I had sold Igor, at his insistence. If convicted I could be fined or sentenced to a term of up to two years' imprisonment.

Escape was impossible, and probably pointless: they could get me at the University, anyway. Kazakov ordered Igor and myself to go down to the street, where a militia car was waiting. We were both taken along to the 60th Militia Division Headquarters on Maly Mogiltsevski pereulok, just behind Smolensk Square. After a short wait I was led into a large, dark office to be interviewed by the officer in charge, a man who introduced himself as Mizurev.

Igor stayed outside, and I saw no more of him that evening. Presumably he was released by prior arrangement, perhaps with a word of gratitude for his histrionic performance, or a dire threat to his enrolment at the university. The officer, after taking my name and some personal details, laboriously wrote out a *protokol*, Russian-style, saying that I had been involved in speculation, and describing the circumstances of the arrest. He then handed it to me to sign.

I refused outright, without even looking at it. I knew such formalities were meaningless: *protokol* or no, I was the victim of an operation which would inevitably put me back into the hands of the KGB. Indeed it was almost certain that the KGB had organised it all from the beginning. In any case, they would find out what had happened very quickly and use it for their own purposes.

So what could I do? And with Mila now very much in the picture? Only two paths were open to me. I could either let matters take their course (which could lead to some sort of prosecution, possibly confinement, at the very least expulsion from the country) or I could try, once again, to find a common language with the 'organs', and stay on at liberty in Moscow. If I wanted to marry Mila and get her out of the country, this second course was the only way forward. I was trapped.

I looked at the militia officer.

"Can I make a telephone call?" I asked with a certain condescension. "I have to speak with the KGB." The militia was a very down-market organisation, and everybody knew it. I doubt whether the officer was expecting that particular request, though he must have known that the case was unusual. Whatever the explanation, he readily agreed.

Sokolov's number was in my notebook – I always carried my telephone numbers around with me. Although when I phoned he was not there, I was told he could be found, and I should await his call. I sat there in silence at the officer's desk: neither of us had anything to say. About half an hour later the telephone rang. It was indeed Sokolov, despite the late hour. If he knew what was going on, he must have been pleased to have such quick results. For my part, for the first time ever, I was glad to hear him, as I was desperate to get out of my immediate predicament. The militia could easily have kept me in a cell for several days.

Aleksandr Fedorovich did not sound in the least surprised, but said he would help me, and told me to go on waiting. Another half-hour passed. Then there was a stir outside the office, and who should come in but Aleksei, self-assured as ever, but with a worried frown on his face. It was our first meeting for two years. I was taken into the corridor while he arranged my release: and a few minutes later I found myself sitting with him on the comfortable seat of his chauffeur-driven ZIL, on my way to the university hostel. Was I relieved.

As one who had fully mastered western conventionality, Aleksei enquired after my Mother's health in Swansea. It was, I told him, all right, but would have been considerably worse, had she known my circumstances at that moment. Aleksei expressed sympathetic agreement.

"Yes, Mervyn, you are in trouble!"

'Trouble' was not an adequate description of my plight: the impact on my proposed marriage could be catastrophic. Sokolov's confident manner over the phone, the ease with which Aleksei had secured my release, and indeed all the events of the day, tended to confirm my suspicion that this was a carefully-planned KGB job. But why were they still so desperate to get me, more than three years after their attempt in Gagry had failed? They must have realised that I had no access to sensitive information abroad, and was unlikely to have any. In Russia my potential as an informer was limited, and it would disappear altogether when I left.

Looking back, I can discern several reasons for their ardour. My KGB case officer (perhaps Aleksei himself) was no doubt more reluctant than ever to see all effort put into recruiting me wasted. I was on the books, as it were. I had refused to renew contact, time was passing, and half of my planned stay in the country was over. Something had to be done. The KGB may also have suspected that I was developing an emotional attachment which as good Soviet citizens they did not favour. There was a more general consideration which was pointed out to me three decades later by Oleg Gordievsky, who (before defecting) occupied a responsible position in the KGB himself. Any officer who recruited a foreign agent had a very easy time in the service afterwards, and Aleksei could hope vastly to improve his career prospects by suborning me.

We drove back to the magical towers of MGU in virtual silence, though Aleksei indicated that I, he and Aleksandr Fedorovich would have to meet soon. I did not sleep that night. As I lay there, listening to Wang snoring next door, I wondered what would have happened had I not telephoned Sokolov: did I play into his hands? Hardly. The outcome would surely have been much the same, give or take a day or two.

I was only to see Igor Vail' once more. A week or so later we encountered one another outside the old Arts Faculty building on Mokhovaya Street. He gave me a wan, embarrassed smile, and would, I think, have spoken: but I was so upset that I walked past him. Later he told Valerii Shein that he had warned me of the trap by wink and nod, as he opened the front door, but there was no truth in that. I understood at the time that he was hardly to be blamed, in so far as he was a poor, vulnerable student who would succumb to any threat of expulsion for the university. He may also have been threatened with a speculation charge himself unless he helped the militia.

★

Next day, at Starokonyushenny, I told Mila there had been a more or less successful attempt at provocation at Igor Vail's, but I did not go into much detail. There was no immediate danger of my disappearing, I said, my 'guardian angel' Aleksei had reappeared, so arrest was unlikely. She was aware, of course, that I had been under KGB pressure in the past, there had been no point in my hiding it from her. She took the news very calmly, without tears or hysterics. Indeed in one sense it must have seemed perfectly natural to her: she had spent her entire life under the shadow of the 'organs' and I was, after all, a vulnerable foreigner. She looked at me with her grey green eyes.

"Well, that's life in Moscow," she said. "Would you like some more tea? By the way, Lena and Sasha have invited us out to the dacha this weekend. Would you like to come?"

"Of course, it would be wonderful."

Indeed, over the weeks that followed, as the sun got warmer, we went there a number of times, enjoying the quiet atmosphere, drinking smoky tea from a samovar, and eating spoonfuls of the wonderful blackcurrant jam. Mila and I would go for walks in the young birch wood nearby. I was also called upon to put in some hard labour digging the vegetable garden, and helping poor Sasha carry buckets of water from the well. In Russia everyone was expected to lend a hand. It was all very congenial – a welcome break from the awful strains of Moscow – though Lena did tell me not to speak to the neighbours: the presence of a foreigner might make people feel uneasy.

★

There now began a difficult – perhaps the most difficult ever – period in my life. My first meeting with Aleksei and Aleksandr Fedorovich was arranged quickly, in fact for the evening of the 9th March. I was told by telephone to go a room in the Moskva Hotel, right in the centre of town. Of course, I knew there was no point in ignoring the summons, as the KGB would simply have me picked up and delivered me – or had me taken directly to the airport for prompt dispatch abroad. The goons at MGU could get me easily enough, the locks being laughably inadequate. In any case, I knew that another spate of threats and pressures was about to begin.

I walked down the broad, carpeted corridor of what was one of Moscow's most prestigious hotels, reached the number I had been given, and knocked.

"Come in."

On entering the suite, large and luxurious, as expected, I found two hard-faced men sitting and waiting for me at a polished table much as they had in Gagry some three years before. A familiar game had to be played, with the same opponents: Sokolov – crude and aggressive, with his lower-class Russian: Aleksei – sophisticated and elegantly spoken. But the dice were now heavily loaded against me. I had been formally charged with speculation by the militia, and I had marriage to Mila to consider.

Sokolov began the proceedings by putting a heavy briefcase on the table close to me. He did not open it, but as we talked he kept on asking me to repeat words which he said he had not heard. The case obviously contained a tape-recorder, but why he should have needed one in a place like the Moskva, which everyone believed to be heavily microphoned, was beyond my comprehension.

"So, you've committed the serious crime of economic speculation, Mervyn," he said, "selling clothes. Apart from the matter of anti-Soviet propaganda. And now you are asking us to get you out of your difficulties. The law of our country is very strict about these things, and you are in real danger of arrest."

I was silent.

"The only thing you can do now is to cooperate fully and honestly with the Committee."

"Yes, Aleksandr Fedorovich is right," said Aleksei. "We've been very patient with you, and you have not helped us at all."

There was very little I could say in reply, and subsequently they did most of the talking. All three of us were – up to a point – bluffing. On the one hand, we all knew that to imprison me for a trivial offence would draw unfavourable attention in the West, and raise questions about unsavoury Soviet attempts to suborn foreign students. Moreover, it might have damaged exchanges which the KGB was using for espionage purposes. On the other hand, I had to pretend that I was scared stiff: I was, of course, extremely apprehensive, not so much of prosecution, as of being driven out of Moscow.

The meeting dragged on for the better part of four hours. Despite their insistence, I said as little as possible – I preferred them to think they had me on the run. Finally, Aleksei came to the point.

"What we want," he said, "is a written declaration of your loyalty to our cause."

"All right," I said reluctantly, "I will give you one."

"I'll dictate it to you," said Sokolov, no doubt mindful of what I had written before. The luxuries of the suite included an old-fashioned pen, a decorative inkwell and paper, so I set to, composing some bits myself and taking Sokolov's dictation on others. "I persuaded the Soviet people to turn against their government," I wrote, "but I regret it, and will not do it in future. I am ready to collect information on individuals and institutions abroad and on foreigners in the USSR." Since I had no security contacts whatever, and would take jolly good care not to get anyone into trouble, I regarded this undertaking as ridiculous, rather than treasonable. But like the earlier script it was certainly better not written.

Having got his statement, Aleksandr Fedorovich rose and put it carefully into his pocket. Other meetings, he said, would now be required. I should phome him a few days later (he gave me a date and a time) and I would be given further details. Then he took his briefcase and left the room, leaving Aleksei and me alone. But another interesting development was to follow.

There was a long and thoughtful silence. Aleksei was obviously sad, and did not conceal it. Perhaps he was comparing his original hopes for cooperation with the realities of the moment. When at last he spoke he addressed me by the familiar Russian 'thou', (*ty*) which he had never once used before, though we had always been on good terms. We had always used the politer 'you' (*Vy*). Either the room was indeed not microphoned, or he did not care.

"Yes, Mervyn," he repeated, "things are in a bad way. I was looking at your dossier in the office. It was bulging.... The situation is very serious."

"But I have given you the statement you asked for."

"Can't you see," he said earnestly, "the whole situation has changed. Even if you cooperate with us, it's not the same now. We know you are not doing it of your own free will. We were looking for someone who believed in our cause and volunteered information willingly. Now it's an enforced relationship. Not much good for us."

There was nothing I could say to that.

"What can I do, then?" I asked.

"I think," Aleksei continued with astonishing candour, "that the best thing is for you to leave Russia.... Just find some pretext to make a visit home, immediately. Some family problem, your Mother's health.... And when you've gone, we'll refuse re-entry. Surely you can think of something?"

"I'll give it some thought, Aleksei," I replied. "I can't say just at this moment."

Suddenly I, too, felt sad. Aleksei was an adversary who had tried to get me to do something – betray my country – that he would never himself have even considered. Yet there was an element of friendship in our relationship, and he being really frank and helpful, perhaps to the detriment of his service. For an instant I wondered whether I should confide in him regarding my marriage plans: but no, I thought, with this sweater business, things had gone too far. He would only react negatively, and KGB officers were the last people to confide in.

We parted. The situation was indeed dreadful. Aleksei had indicated the simple way out, but I could not take it. I was trapped. Still, I reflected as I made another metro journey back to MGU, I had some reason to be satisfied with the meeting. The threat of immediate expulsion from Moscow had been lifted, and the path to the Moscow Palace of Weddings was still open, provided Mila would tread it with me. The next practical step was to propose marriage: not perhaps in the present tense circumstances, but without waiting too long, either. Evidently, I had some time in hand.

★

I made the proposal at Starkonyushenny on the evening of the 27th March. We had finished drinking tea and I thought it was probably best to do this when we met next evening. I helped Mila carry the dishes into the communal kitchen. The flat was quiet and the kitchen was empty. We embraced by the gas stove, oblivious to the smell of gherkins and a tiny gas leak.

"Let's get registered," I said suddenly, using the Soviet jargon of the day.

"Oh, Mervusya!"

She may well have been expecting something of the sort, yet she seemed a little uncertain.

"Let's think about it a bit," she said. "Perhaps you'll change your mind. No hasty decisions."

Mila, I had found, was never one to leap to positive conclusions, but in fact she said 'Yes' the next day. She must have realised that apart from the immediate political dangers (the loss of her job, her room, or even her Moscow residence permit) marrying a foreigner would mean a big break with her past. She had never been abroad, England was far away, and re-entry to Russia not guaranteed. Of course, the chance to emigrate like Galya was wonderful: but living in the West was not without its fears, either. I imagined she was somewhat overwhelmed by the prospect, though she did not show it.

★

Now I had to turn to the real problems of organising the registration

– with the fate of Georges Nivat very much in mind. I did not know much about it, but tedious procedures would certainly have to be gone through, on the British as well as the Russian side. I would have to inform the Embassy, because I would eventually require a British entry visa for Mila: but beyond that, I found, the Soviet side required some sort of notice of consent. It would all take time, and I had to keep a dialogue going with the KGB at least until the marital bond had been established. As my wife, Mila would automatically acquire the right to a Soviet exit visa. The Soviet authorities might well chose to ignore it, and keep her in Russia, but there would be a proper basis for intervention at a diplomatic level. Just about that time, coincidentally, we met a handsome Canadian student who was planning to marry a ravishingly beautiful Russian girl: somehow, we knew that their union would go through without difficulty. Ours might not.

There was no alternative to contacting the Embassy again, this time as an outsider. Like most students in our group I had kept as far away from the compound as possible. The KGB probably registered all visits, and association with diplomats could easily jeopardize the safety of Russian friends. All the more so as the official who dealt with the students was a rather officious man called Thomas Brimelow. He was second-in-command and invariably seemed wrapped up in procedural niceties. I suppose he did a reasonable job in Chancery, but it would be difficult to imagine anyone further from the problems of living in the real world of Moscow.

My relations with him had already been soured by an incident which appeared trivial at the time, but indicated how inflexible embassy staff could be. Before I left England the editor of a well-known publication called *The Annual Register of World Events* had asked me to provide him with a write-up of developments in Russia, and since I had not managed to finish it in Oxford I had had to bring it with me to MGU. This, however, raised the problem of getting it back to London, as the Soviet post was heavily censored. The best alternative was... the diplomatic bag. But the bag remained, as in 1959, a hallowed institution, and diplomats still feared any Soviet complaint about it being used for non-diplomatic purposes.

Soon after I arrived in Moscow I thought it reasonable to explain the situation to Brimelow and request him to despatch the article to London by bag: he could scarcely have known about the Pasternak poetry fiasco several years earlier. So I reluctantly telephoned and asked to see him. When we met in his office he naturally quibbled about non-diplomatic usage, but took my envelope and said he would send it off with a covering letter. My presumption was that the problem was thereby solved. How wrong I was.

About five weeks later he telephoned me at MGU and asked me to come to the Embassy and see him again. His call was most unwelcome, not only because it betokened further, undesirable contact with diplomats, but also because it implied there was some kind of problem. When I got to his office he handed me my envelope, in his usual matter-of-fact way, together with a covering letter, taking up a whole sheet of foolscap, from another official called Edward Youde in London. Youde explained that the Bag Could Not Be Used For This Sort Of Thing, so the item was Being Returned. Clearly, there was nothing more to be done through Brimelow. Faced with this ridiculous situation, I had to cast around and ask a student who was travelling to London to take the article through the customs at his own risk.

When, towards the middle of March, I went to see Brimelow and told him of my intention to get married he was, as I expected, rather indifferent. Students' emotional entanglements were beyond his day-to-day remit, and took his attention away from the serious diplomatic round. However, he did seem to know all about the procedures. He told me that the Consul, Kenneth Kirby, would have to issue a Certificate of No Impediment for presentation to the Soviet authorities. Unfortunately, an application had to be displayed on the embassy notice board for three weeks before the document could be issued. I was profoundly disappointed to hear it: the ground was burning under my feet. How could I possibly hold the KGB off for three weeks, in addition to any further period required by the Palace of Weddings? I asked him if he could not get it through sooner.

"Oh, no, no," said Brimelow, in his terse, slightly Northern tones. "And you need to be sure that any document you present to the Soviet authorities is valid, don't you?"

Surely, I thought, the Russians could have no idea about waiting periods, and would not have refused to accept any Certificate of No Impediment if it came from an official source? I had no means of knowing whether Brimelow had discretion in the matter or not: if he did, he chose not to exercise it. I arranged to see the Consul and left the embassy compound in a thoroughly despondent mood. Brimelow had again revealed a difficulty, instead of solving one. I could only press on, regardless.

In the university hostel, strange to relate, my predicament was regarded with some merriment. One day I happened to tell a friendly student that I was trying to get married, and was having trouble with the KGB. He told everyone straight away, so boys would come up to me in the corridor, laugh, and say, "How are things going, Mervyn? Organs after you again, are they? Ha, ha, ha!" Khasbulatov hovered in the background, but said nothing.

★

The certificate, a fine document, beautifully typed, was issued on the 22nd April. At last Mila and I could do something positive. The next day we went along to the Palace of Weddings in Griboyedova Street to apply for registration. Soviet law permitted marriage to foreigners 'on a common basis', yet foreigners were not allowed to use the more modest local registry offices, where procedures were quicker.

The Palace, we found, was a fine, low-built town house, at least a century old, with (it seemed) the original panelling and lovely parquet floors intact. We were received by the deputy head, a man called Pokhomov. He accepted our application to register, but said that the first slot available was on the 9th June, nearly seven weeks hence. Many Soviet couples were waiting to use their admirable facilities, he declared, and there was no way he could fit us in earlier. Mila and I had no particular interest in being married in elegant surroundings, but we had no alternative. Pokhomov handed me the standard invitation card with the date and time on it: 11.00 am. I tucked it away for safe keeping.

★

Weddings are almost always family affairs, even when they take place in strange circumstances. So there was the question of informing my widowed mother in distant Swansea. Usually we exchanged letters every week, and although none of the ones I sent to her survived, I always kept hers. Like many mothers she was somewhat intrusive, and as a rule I told her little about my affairs. Most of her missives at that time were filled with accounts of the local rainfall, commentaries on her asthma, and (for several weeks running) enquiries about a parcel which had not arrived in Moscow because she had put a tin of ham in it. Hermetically-sealed goods were not allowed through.

I did not at first tell her about Mila, partly because I did not want her to worry – and send interfering letters – and partly because I did not know how things would develop. On the 1st of April, however, I wrote to tell her I was thinking of getting engaged, and the following week I wrote to say I intended getting married. Unfortunately she received the letters on consecutive days, leaving her no time to adapt to the staggering news. The response was as immediate as the postal service allowed.

"DON'T get married in Russia, Mervyn, [she wrote on the 15th April]. It will create too many difficulties. Use your common sense. The Soviet authorities might not allow the girl to come to this country. I have read of it happening – even if you are married. I hope it won't be a case of marrying in haste and repenting in leisure. How long have you known her?

The shock you have given me this week has upset me and made me feel really ill. My chest is terrible. I am going to ask the doctor tomorrow if he can put me into hospital until I feel better. You could have told me something about it a while ago, surely.... The worry is murdering me. Come home and think it over.... I never thought you could be bowled over so easily... the reaction now is that every time my thoughts turn to you I have an ache in my stomach.... I am afraid that you might go to live in Russia and be lost to me forever. You had better try and put my mind at rest or I will be in a mental home.

A few days later, however, she calmed down: "Please understand, Mervyn, I was never opposed to the idea of you getting married.... But I am not happy to think of what the outcome of a Russian wedding would be.... If I was feeling well enough I would make arrangements to fly out to Moscow to see what is going on..."

There was no question whatever of her "flying out to Moscow" – she had never been abroad in her life. But had she known the true situation she might indeed have ended up under sedation.

★

Sokolov was now calling me to meetings at central hotels once a week or so. Perhaps he changed the location for exaggerated security reasons. No one else was ever present, and although he sometimes tried to adopt an avuncular attitude, I found him as obnoxious as ever. "Don't blame me, Mervyn," he would say, with a slightly shame-faced smile. "You got yourself into this mess. The KGB could easily have you imprisoned for your anti-Soviet activities. Now think how you can help us." He told me at one point that he had been a boxer, and had travelled briefly in West Europe, taking in London and Oxford. Since he apparently knew no English, I suspected he had worked as a low-grade security guard.

He was obsessed with gathering what he deemed to be 'useful information'. He wanted to know how certain scholars in England and America (mostly quite prominent people) regarded the Soviet Union. He asked about security at the British Embassy, entry procedures for the Foreign Office, and F.O. personnel. He was also interested in the so-called "security briefings" for British Council students, the good old NTS, and foreigners in Moscow.

Security matters were utterly beyond me, and most of my knowledge of the NTS came from newspapers. Since nearly all of my free time was taken up with Mila, I rarely saw the British students, let alone people from the Embassy, and now I had another good reason to avoid them. But I imagined that Sokolov, having found a likely 'source', was obliged to pump me anyway. I was careful to give him only facts which could be obtained from people's published works (if you knew where to look), or were relatively innocuous. I never revealed any foibles which could be used to compromise personal acquaintances, even those who were persona non grata, and would never come to Russia. On getting back to my room at the University I would note the gist of the conversation, so that at least I had my own record of it.

The interplay with Sokolov was stressful because I was trying to give so little away; but apart from that, simply dealing with him caused me considerable anguish. "The last week has been agony," I wrote soon after the meetings started. "I really don't know how I have lived through it." At the later meetings we would sit for long periods in complete silence; once he turned on the television and watched it for an hour or more, ignoring me until he thought it was time to go home. I do not know whether the KGB paid overtime rates, but he always kept me quite late. At one point, perhaps to increase the pressure on me, he accused me of having anti-Soviet conversations with (unnamed) students.

At first I said nothing to him about my love for Mila. I presumed that the KGB already knew about it from their surveillance of my movements, and I did not want to provoke any intervention before we had obtained a date for registration. But as soon as the day was fixed I decided to tell him of my intentions – it might mollify his masters a little. In the event he seemed to be as disconcerted as Vadim, and brushed it off.

"Mervyn," he said with a sour smile, "isn't that rather hasty? If she is an honest, hard-working girl she shouldn't be drawn into any dishonest operations."

"What do you mean?" I retorted angrily. "There could never be any question of 'dishonest operations'."

On the 6th of May, in order to avoid one of the horrible assignations, I actually cut my foot. Next day I went to the university clinic to register a temporary disability, and the doctor obligingly issued certificate No. 386 of the 7.V.64, "Left sole cut, released from study until 9.V.64". I was well aware that if I failed to turn up without good reason Sokolov might take it as a sign of protest and get me expelled from Russia forthwith. I kept the certificate.

I did not know how long I could keep him quiet with loads of nonsense, and I expected trouble at each of the meetings. It came, sure enough, on the 18th May, some three weeks before I was due to get married. When I arrived at the Moskva that evening I found Sokolov in a very nasty mood indeed. Possibly, there had been a realistic appraisal of the stuff he was getting from me.

"You have not been helping us properly," he barked. "All we get from you are useless bits of information about the green lawns of Oxford! You know perfectly well what you are doing. Now we want you to tell us about your Soviet friends."

"Well," I said, "that I cannot do."

I was adamant. I knew only too well how easily my friends in Moscow could have their lives ruined by this ruthless organisation, though the KGB probably had their names already. Although I did not quite realise it at the time, Sokolov's demand showed that I had been down-graded: the few poor Russians I knew could have been of very little interest to the security organs. Sokolov was angry about my refusal, but there was nothing he could do, except except glare. The train had hit the buffers.

I thought for a moment, and made one last effort to salvage the situation. I had to presume that the KGB knew the exact date of my proposed marriage – since a foreigner was involved, it would certainly have been reported by the Palace of Weddings. If they decided that I was of no further use to them, they could easily cancel my visa and prevent registration. As far as I was concerned, the marriage was all that mattered. Perhaps I could come to some sort of compromise with them, tell them a very little about my harmless friends, and then warn the friends? The situation was desperate.

"Well," I said to Sokolov, "despite our disagreements, I still intend to get married to Ludmila Bibikova. If you can ensure that this goes through, I might be prepared to come to another agreement with you. But I would need proof of your good intentions first."

The familiar half-smile appeared in his cruel eyes, and I knew it was hopeless.

"Mervyn," he said, "you have a long way to go to get married."

I got up and left the room without saying anything more. Somehow I knew that I would not be seeing him again, either. But I telephoned him a day or two later, in the faint, faint hope that he might still help. Far from it, he only repeated his demand for information about my friends. "Your position is very grave, Mervyn," he added. "You must give me the names of all your acquaintances in Moscow. The KGB wants either to imprison you or expel you, and will do one or the other shortly. If you tell me what we want to know, I may be able to help you. But marriage is out of the question."

I put the receiver down feeling more despondent than ever.

Four. Wedding Day

S okolov's hard line boded ill, and sure enough, barely a few days after I had refused to inform on my Russian friends, the KGB moved against me. When I got to Mila's flat on the evening of the 24th May, she told me that there had been a telephone call from the Palace of Weddings asking us to go there urgently. It could only mean trouble. We went next morning, and our worst fears were confirmed. A robust lady by the name of Aleksandra Efremova, head of the Central Registry Office, which was located in the Palace, informed us in a throaty contralto that our application to get married was 'being taken off the list' because I was 'under investigation' by the militia.

There was no point in arguing with so authoritative a figure, and we were both so upset that we could hardly speak to her. There were no tears, though; Russia was a country of tragedy and we both knew it. In practical terms, what was to be done? As we sadly left the Palace, we had an idea. Was Efremova's action fully legal? Had she, under KGB pressure, broken the law? And if so, could her decision be contested?

In Moscow at that time legal advice could be obtained from *yuriskonsultanty*, legal consultants who charged a few kopecks an interview. They were at the very bottom of the legal hierarchy, and offered a service truly for the masses. We went to see one, queuing with a dozen or so silent and worried Russians in a dingy corridor. Anything less like the panelled splendour of the Palace of Weddings was difficult to imagine. When we at last entered the dingy office, we found we had lighted upon a young lawyer who was obviously sympathetic to our case (though he knew, of course, nothing of the background). He assured us that even a person awaiting trial had the right to get married, and since foreigners were married on an equal footing, no exception could be made for them. The matter of being 'under investigation' was therefore irrelevant.

We left his office feeling slightly gratified. Obviously, the Soviet legal consultation service was no match for the KGB, but we thought we should at least try once again at the Palace, objecting to the decision on legal grounds. Next morning we returned there, and although we had no appointment barged into Efremova's office, ignoring the protestations of her secretary. We demanded that she re-book us for the 9th as there were clearly no legal obstacles in our path.

"There's nothing I can do about it," she said, angrily, but no doubt truthfully. "There are regulations, regulations."

"What regulations? Where are they published?"

"Go and ask the British Embassy," she exclaimed, "they'll tell you!"

She knew as well as I that the British Embassy was just about the last place on earth where we could find out about her secret regulations. They almost certainly contradicted the law, which is precisely why they were not in the public domain. Efremova did, however, make one small concession:

"If the investigation is called off," she said, "then your application will be valid for the date given. Meanwhile your papers will stay here at the Palace."

★

As if things were not bad enough, another worry appeared at the Embassy, unhappily one of my own making. I had called to see Brimelow about the Certificate of No Impediment, and he asked me, as a matter of course, whether I was having any problems with the marriage arrangements. The best answer I could have given would have been 'No', but I was reluctant to do so: I have always been burdened with a naive tendency to tell the truth. Beyond that, I nurtured a hope that the Embassy would be more sympathetic, and more helpful, if they realised the pressures I was under. So I said 'Yes'.

Brimelow froze, and asked me to go down to the basement, where (as I knew) they had a booth supposedly secure against listening devices. When we were inside (it had air-tight doors and was exceedingly stuffy), I outlined the situation. Brimelow listened quite impassively, and made no positive suggestions, as I had half hoped. I immediately regretted having told him.

Worse, the thought occurred to me that the Russians might have some sort of X-ray surveillance there, and would know that I had gone into the booth. That could only raise the suspicion that I was collaborating with the Embassy and (in my small way) double-crossing them. I asked Brimelow about it.

"It's quite possible the Russians know who goes into the booth," he said, airily. "Yes, quite possible!"

Although I was sure I had gained nothing by telling him, except the likelihood of interference from another quarter, I soon came to doubt whether it really mattered. The KGB may have presumed that the Embassy knew, anyway. Naturally enough Sokolov had never mentioned it.

★

Then, quite unexpectedly, a gleam of real hope appeared. Mila heard on the radio that Harold Wilson (then leader of the opposition) and Patrick Gordon Walker, the shadow Foreign Secretary, would be in Moscow for face-to-face discussions with Nikita Khrushchev. I contacted the Embassy and found that the distinguished visitors intended to take up the cases of forty-four Soviet citizens who wanted to leave Russia. These were mostly, I imagined, the wives of British military personnel stuck there since the war, or Russians with relatives in the United Kingdom. In any case, I could hardly believe our good luck: this was a golden opportunity to get intervention at the highest level, from a potential socialist Prime Minister. The Soviet government favoured British socialists. Was this the answer to our problem?

The visitors were to stay at the National Hotel, which stood at the bottom of Gorkii Street, close to the Moskva where I met Sokolov. On the 31st May, the very evening the delegation arrived, I went there to look for them. The National was a prestigious establishment, where Lenin had set up office before moving into the Kremlin directly opposite. I did not take Mila, because I thought it would be easier for me to get in alone. Foreigners (usually obvious from their dress) had no difficulty in getting past the doorman, whereas Soviet citizens could be stopped. Having entered the elaborate hall, with its large, Grecian-style statues, I strode over to the reception desk and asked for Harold Wilson's room. I thought there would be extra security, but the receptionist was quite off-handed, and sent me straight up. The duty-woman at the end of the corridor, sensing that I was a foreigner, did not stop me either. I knocked on the heavy, half-glazed door, and heard a voice with a slight Yorkshire accent, familiar from radio broadcasts, inviting me in.

There was the usual small interior hallway. The room behind was dimly lit, but there was no mistaking the man who stepped forward. Harold Wilson looked at me questioningly.

"Who are you?"

"Mervyn Matthews, a British post-graduate."

"What do you want?"

"I'm trying to get married to a Russian girl. Can you help?"

I went on to explain the situation as quickly as I could, and asked whether he could intervene with Khrushchev personally on our behalf. But the quick-witted Wilson was immediately on the defensive.

"The best thing for you to do is to see my press secretary," he said hurriedly – and ushered me out. Yet another door closed on me. Again I was bitterly disappointed, yet puzzled, too. Why his press secretary? Was that simply the first person he thought of? The press secretary would know little about Russia, and nothing at all about handling the KGB. I decided on the spot that there was no point whatever in trying to see him.

As I left the hotel, however, I reflected that perhaps all was not lost. Patrick Gordon Walker was closer to such matters, and might be a little more responsive. I went back to Mila's, and after another long discussion I wrote him a letter. I called in at the National on my way to MGU and left it for him at reception desk. In it I outlined the facts of the situation again and asked if I could see him. I would return to the hotel the next afternoon, after he had had time to consider things.

Another brief, disheartening meeting awaited me. When I knocked on his door he came out into the corridor, a big man, with, I thought, a rather insensitive face. It was immediately clear that he had read my letter, and wanted to have nothing to do with me. "I suggest you get in touch with the Embassy," he said, and turning on his heel, walked quickly away. I will always remember the back of his expensively tailored jacket. I imagine that he had consulted the Embassy, and had been advised to keep out of the picture.

★

With the 9th of June now fast approaching, I was desperate. Life had turned into a nightmare which even the lovely Moscow spring could not dissipate. How different from the excitements I had known when I first lived there! Now when I walked towards Starokonyushenny along Gogol' Boulevard I hardly noticed the welcome greenery, the scent of new grass, or the relaxed babushkas gossiping on the benches. My thoughts centred on the KGB, the Palace of Weddings, the Embassy and Mila's future. The fact that I was trailed by goons only deepened my feeling of depression.

To make things worse – were that possible – I discovered that the KGB had started pressurising Valerii Golovitser with regard to our friendship. He was warned, under conditions of great secrecy, not to say anything about it, but he told Mila, who passed the news on to me. The KGB had called him in to the Lubyanka a few weeks after the Vail' provocation, and interviewed him for no less than six hours, mainly about me.

They started by trying to gain his confidence and praising his personal qualities. After a time, however, they came to the point: would he, Valerii, be prepared to fulfil his patriotic duty and help them? He asked them how, but they would not say: they wanted to get his consent before divulging their dark intentions. Like most people in a similar situation Valerii tried to avoid saying 'No' outright, so as not to provoke their ire. I was doing the same thing in my meetings with Sokolov.

At the end of the interview, having got nowhere, they told him to go away and think about it. In fact another two or three long meetings followed. The atmosphere deteriorated, and the last interview was conducted by a fellow Jew, who might more easily have gained Valerii's confidence. When Valerii finally refused to cooperate without knowing what was required of him, the KGB resorted to threats. "You have been trying for some time now to get a visa to visit your sister in Italy, haven't you? If you help us, we'll help you to get one! But if you don't, you'll never go anywhere, not even to Poland!"

It seemed likely that the KGB hoped to inveigle me, with Valerii's help, into some criminal or compromising situation, although the words were never uttered. Of course, it would have been quite easy for him to assist the KGB, for example, by giving me a drugged drink. In the event he stood by me, though at considerable risk to himself. The proof of the pudding was in the eating: he never invited me back to his room in suspicious circumstances (as Igor Vail' had done), and visa applications he made to visit both Poland and Bulgaria were indeed refused. True, I had not seen much of him, as I now tended to go straight to Starokonyushenny pereulok without stopping at Ryleeva Street: but I think he would now have avoided me, anyway, so as to make us both less vulnerable. As I was to find out later, Valerii Shein was also interviewed once, though the officers did not go so far as to mention me directly. He was less useful as an informant because he did not know me so well.

Having entrapped me with the speculation and anti-Soviet propaganda charges (or having me in their grasp, regardless of charges) why should the KGB have tried to pin more on me? Did they want to disrupt my emotional ties with Mila? Did they think I would respond in a more servile fashion if I were under greater threat? Or was it just a question of the operation, having been started, rolling forward under its own momentum? These questions were never answered. But the KGB, thanks entirely to Valerii's bravery, did not get anywhere on that particular front.

★

Naturally, as we ate sturgeon of an evening at Mila's tiny table, the burning question of 'getting registered' dominated the conversation. Mila was no less determined than I that the marriage had to go through. It was a matter of profound personal affection, with no trace of desire merely to win a battle. Neither of us had wanted this symphony of frustrations. And in the background was the image of the Canadian-Russian couple, several years our junior, who expected their marriage to take place without any problems whatsoever. Mila, as a Soviet citizen, was in an even more vulnerable position than I: would she be prepared to take the risk of trying to force the marriage through?

"We will have to go the Palace of Weddings on the ninth and try and get registered on the spot," she said, without hesitation. It was what I wanted to hear. The main risk was official reprisal against her: but given the fact that the KGB had so far left her in peace, it was a risk that she would take.

But what leverage could we get on that dreadful place, realistically? The options were extremely limited. The Embassy would not act: I knew that Georges Nivat had obtained some support at a diplomatic level, but I could hope for less. Harold Wilson and Patrick Gordon Walker, possibly the government-to-be, had refused to intervene. Sasha Vasin, Mila's brother-in-law, had considerable influence at the Ministry of Justice, but that was a different world. We thought that he could hardly help us, otherwise he would have done so already.

Our best chance, we decided, was a last-minute threat of scandal at the Palace itself, reported in the world press. The Khrushchev regime was anxious to open up Russia – a little at least – and the Soviet authorities did, on occasion, shy away from unfavourable publicity. The presence of critical journalists might just tip the balance in our favour. True, getting married was a long way from getting Mila out of Russia: but it would at least be a positive beginning.

I knew hardly any foreign journalists – from the point of view of students they were almost as undesirable as diplomats, and best kept away from. Most of them knew no Russian, and were closely supervised by the KGB. They could also be quite unscrupulous in their desperate search for stories. The doyen of the community, a certain Henry Shapiro, who had lived in Russia for years, was notorious. However, I did know the *Daily Express* correspondent, Martin Page, a reliable enough chap, and through him I contacted one or two others. Among them was the mysterious Victor Louis, who was to play a strange role indeed.

Despite his French name (he claimed an ancestor had come to Russia with Napoleon) Victor was a Soviet-born journalist who had performed the truly miraculous feat of getting himself accredited as Moscow correspondent of the *London Evening News*. The word 'miraculous' is apposite because the very idea of a Soviet citizen working for a capitalist newspaper was normally unthinkable. Victor Louis' ascent to this position may have been facilitated by the fact that he had an English wife who lived with him in Moscow, but this was unusual, too. His employment status brought with it unheard of perks, not least a fine flat, an English bank account, and access to foreign currency.

Of course he must have had KGB clearance for all of this, but some people thought he may even have been a staff officer. He claimed, on the contrary, that he had spent seven years as a dissident in a prison camp. It was rumoured that he was expected to slant news stories somewhat in Russia's favour and inform on other journalists: but no one in the London office would have been worried by such Moscow gossip, even if it reached their ears. In terms of knowing Moscow and getting news stories he was streets ahead of the average foreign correspondent, who knew no Russian and could hardly use a telephone.

In the circumstances I decided that he might be just the person to help, and indeed when I introduced myself over the phone I was very pleased with his reaction. He agreed to come to the Palace of Weddings to cover the event: it was a good story, and he had a professional interest in reporting it.

Finally, there was the small matter of the wedding ring. I was now under the closest-ever observation by the goons, and did not want to give the KGB any further hint of our intentions on the day. So I gave Mila money to go out and buy a gold wedding ring, unobtrusively, by herself. It must have been one of the saddest rings ever purchased.

*

I anticipated that the day of the wedding, the 9th June, 1964 would be one of the most difficult days of my life, and I was right. It dawned fair and sunny, but both of us were tense and we slept very little: I had stayed at Starokonyushenny to avoid any last-minute hitches with transport, or outside interference. The evening before there had been some nonsense with the wedding dress, a simple, beige garment made by Mila's friend, Galya Galadzheva. Galya was a skilled theatrical costume-maker, but had not got it finished on time, so Mila had to do it herself. Not that it mattered all that much, but it was another small problem to add to the pile of big ones. As for me, I just shaved and went as I was.

We had decided that we could not possibly go to the Palace with a regular wedding party of friends and relatives, as there was no knowing what would happen and they could all get arrested. We did, however, require witnesses, so we chose two of the most faithful people we knew – Valerii Golovitser and Mila's sister Lena. They were well aware of the danger of persecution which faced them if things went wrong.

Taxis were easy to find in Moscow in those days, so Mila and I took one. We arrived at the Palace just before the appointed hour of eleven: Valerii and Lena were already waiting outside, quiet, nervous, and in anything but a festive mood. I had expected to find a couple of correspondents there, but was amazed to see a small crowd of eight or nine. Only then did I realise what a big story this would be.

We all trooped in. The Palace produced an even stranger impression on me than it had when we first went there: although it functioned in a proletarian state it was used exclusively by an elite with bourgeois pretensions. In the hallway some expensively dressed young couples preened themselves in front of a large square mirror. Mila and I asked to see Efremova, but we were told she was not there. Instead Comrade Pokhomov would receive us, so Mila, I and the journalists all went into his office. It was a large room and most people could find somewhere to sit. Pokhomov presided at an imposing desk at one end. Just as proceedings were about to begin Pokhomov's secretary rushed in and told him, in a whisper, that there was an urgent telephone message for him. Mila just caught the words. He went out for a moment or two – perhaps to get direct instructions from the KGB – and then returned. Mila and I went up to his desk and he looked at us questioningly. We knew this was our last chance.

"I have a card here," I said, "which indicates that our marriage can be registered today at eleven o'clock."

"You have already been informed," said Pokhomov, "that that is not possible." He seemed completely aware of what had happened.

"Why should that be?"

"The appointment has been removed from the list. You were told."

"There was no proper reason for it".

"I gather that you are under investigation."

At this point Victor Louis, who was sitting in front, joined the argument, and in a surprisingly supportive manner.

"Are you refusing to register this marriage?" he asked. "If so, you must give a full legal explanation! What's the problem?"

"You can ask him," said Pokhomov, pointing to me. "He'll tell you." The remark irritated me no end.

"I don't know," I said stoutly. "Why should I? You are legally obliged to register the marriage."

Clearly, truth had no place in this tragi-comedy, and I certainly had no intention of going into detail in front of a crowd of uncomprehending newspapermen. Beyond that, I believed that even now there might be some advantage in keeping the role of the KGB under wraps: perhaps my discretion would be appreciated on the Lubyanka and yield benefits later.

"Either register the marriage, or provide a proper explanation," said Victor.

It was apparent from the questioning glances that hardly any of the journalists knew Russian, so Victor Louis had to translate for them. He argued with Pokhomov for some time, while the latter repeatedly referred him back to me. In practical terms we could get nowhere. Pokhomov was simply refusing to register the marriage, evidently according to instructions he had received, regardless of the foreign press. Mila sat beside me, calm and collected throughout. Efremova, we were told, should be back before the Palace closed at four o'clock. After half an hour of repeated refusals we decided to leave the office. Outside the corridors were teeming with grey-faced men, goons bussed in to handle trouble, no doubt. Mila and I decided to await Efremova's return in the unkempt little garden alongside the Palace. One of the journalists suggested that we sat down on a bench together, and as we sat there he photographed us, smiling sadly at what was not to be. We told Lena and Valerii, who had kept very much in the background, that they had better go home.

Four o'clock came and went with no sign of Efremova. It seemed obvious that she had been instructed to keep her distance. As the crowd of journalists drifted away, I decided that the best thing to do was to take a taxi to the British Embassy, (leaving Mila at the Palace in case Efremova appeared), and ask them if they could help us quickly. Perhaps an urgent note could go in to the Ministry of Foreign Affairs. But when I got to Sofiiskaya naberezhnaya I found no one in authority who could talk to me, and I was told, I think over an internal telephone, that nothing could be done at a ministerial level. An official enquiry might be possible at the Palace of Weddings – but not today.

Moscow, 1959, on the balcony of our Embassy flat – as it was all just beginning

В лоханке с толстыми боками
гниет рассольник с потрохами.
Нам говорят, что это — ил,
а в иле — нильский крокодил.

ЗВЕРИНЕЦ

Photograph of Pasternak's early work, taken in the Lenin Library

Central Asian trip: Vadim Popov in the market place at Bukhara, November 1959

Siberian trip: on the ice, Lake Baikal, with the chairman of the local collective farm, April 1960

In my Co-op overcoat, photographed by Aleksei on board the cutter on the River Ob' in Siberia, April 1960

June 1960: a day trip from Gagri – *left* at the lakeside; *right* Vadim admires a waterfall

Aleksei Suntsov, just as I knew him, and *right*, a corner of Moscow University

Mila at work in the Library, Moscow 1963

Spring 1964:
at the Vasin
dacha outside
Moscow; and
right Lena and
Sasha Vasin
with Mila

Mila with samovar at the Vasin dacha

Return to England, Heathrow 21 June 1964

Campaigning from my study, Nottingham University

A moment's reflection in Fleet Street

When I got back to Griboedov Street Mila was waiting for me anxiously. Nothing had happened there during my absence.

"No luck," I said. "They're not going to do anything, or at least, anything useful."

There was nothing more to be done at the Palace. We took another taxi back to the flat, just the two of us, knowing that our strongest card had been played. But there was still one niggling doubt. Should we have refused to leave Pokhomov's office until he registered us? Perhaps we weren't tough enough with him?

*

Clearly, the presence of so many journalists at the Palace of Weddings more or less guaranteed widespread publicity abroad. That had been part of my plan, and it evidently succeeded – though without the orientation we hoped for. We would have reports of distress, without a happy ending.

I knew my long-suffering mother in Swansea would get the news immediately, and would probably be besieged by journalists. The neighbours would be rushing in as well. I needed to contact her with a word of reassurance, albeit unfounded. She had no telephone, and although Jack, my half-brother in London, did, ringing him from Moscow would have meant a long wait at the Central Telegraph Office. So the same evening I telegraphed my mother: "ADMINIS-TRATIVE MUDDLE HOPE TO SORT OUT SOON AM WELL MERVYN". My mother replied to my university address: "CHEER UP LOVE TO BOTH AM WELL AWAITING NEWS MOTHER"

As I was to learn later, she was already in the tender grasp of the *Daily Mirror*, which 'always got the mother'. She was quoted as saying "I am frightened in case he might be clapped in prison for defying the Russians". She was having a hard time of it, poor thing. I could just image her reactions. Nobody in our family had ever been in the news, let alone accused of 'crimes against the state'. The only minor exception was my elderly Auntie Doris, who had been fined for shoplifting in her dotage.

*

The next day I went to my room at MGU and saw David Shapiro, the *starosta* of the British students. He had a scholarly approach to everything, and had made a point of keeping up with the foreign press, mainly through Moscow correspondents. Actually, he was quite good at it. He assured me that the incident at the Palace of Weddings had been written up in all the national dailies, sometimes as a small article on the front page. The picture taken in the garden had been printed in some papers. Most of the correspondents dressed it up as an administrative muddle which would be sorted out – and make pleasurable reading – later. Russia was still an isolated and mysterious country, so a Russian-British marriage was newsworthy, even without intriguing complications.

This was my first immersion, at long distance, in the world of publicity, so different from university life at Manchester and Oxford. For writing a dissertation, logical thought and accuracy were essential: the popular press, on the other hand, went for immediacy, emotion, and local colour. The odd clutch of factual errors which (as I discovered later) appeared in many pieces didn't seem to matter. Victor Louis's version of the events on Griboyedov Street for the *Evening News* positively bristled with them:

> After waiting for hours at Moscow's registry office today to marry a Russian girl, an Oxford graduate [wrong] found himself still baffled and bewildered by Soviet red tape. He is Mervyn Matthews... now working for three years as a research fellow at Moscow University [wrong]. His bride to be (or so he hopes) is Ludmilla Bibikova, 30, a dark-haired student [wrong] at the Institute of Marxism Leninism. The couple applied for permission to marry six weeks ago and today was named as the wedding day.... Today he and Ludmilla, wearing a pearl-embroidered linen dress, with her relatives and 20 fellow students [wrong], turned up at the registry office in Moscow's Griboedov Street for the wedding. [Victor evidently could not distinguish between an English student and a goon]. But when the couple were called to sign the documents [wrong] the deputy registrar said that their official papers were not there. "They had," he said, "been withdrawn. An argument followed but with no effect.... Early this afternoon the couple were still unmarried. And the bouquets of flowers carried by the wedding guests were beginning to wilt [wrong].

Victor's own role at the Palace remained, of course, a mystery. Why had he pressed Pokhomov so hard on our behalf? Did he think that by putting the arguments cogently he could really help? Did he know that it was hopeless, yet want to create an impression of concern? Was he actually working *against* the KGB?

★

Mila and I had to go on trying. Over the next few grief-laden days I lived mostly at Starokonyushenny, visiting MGU but intermittently.

I hardly saw any of the other students, though they must have known what had happened. It didn't matter, anyway. Mila and I penned elaborate letters of appeal to Gromyko, Khrushchev, and his secretary, a certain Shuiski, knowing all too well that it was time wasted. We decided that it might be worth visiting some institutions in person. I trailed around the dreary offices of the Supreme Soviet of the USSR, the Supreme Court, the Procuracy, the Central Committee of the Party and even the Moscow Palace of Weddings again.

I went to the 60th Militia station in the Maly Mogiltsevski pereulok, behind Smolensk Square, where I had been taken after the incident at Vail's. I thought I would try and elucidate the exact state of the so-called investigation. Mizurev, who had been in charge when I was arrested, was not there, so I spoke to Todorov, head of the criminal investigation section, instead. He made no secret of the fact that he had no documentation on the case or interest in it. Before I left, however, he telephoned a superior and asked me to return for an interview at 12 o'clock next day. When I got back to Starokonyushenny and told Mila her response was immediate.

"Don't go back under any circumstances," she said fearfully. "They'll only pin something new on you." I thought about it, and decided that she was right. How could it be otherwise? No good was to be expected from that quarter. Perhaps I should not have returned there at all.

I did a lot of telephoning, speaking to persons of influence in the Soviet hierarchy, unseen and unknown. Martin Page gave me the telephone number of an official called Vinogradov who worked in Ministry of Foreign Affairs but was said to have close KGB connections. No help available there. I spoke to someone in the Department for Surveillance over the KGB (established as a 'liberal' measure in April, 1956) but the voice admitted quite frankly that the case was outside its competence. I tried to get into touch with Aleksei a couple of times – I still had his number, of course – but I was always told dismissively that he was not in Moscow.

In a search for some kind of normality, I suppose, I explored the possibility of taking a translation job in Moscow. If by some miracle the marriage problem sorted itself out, I could consider staying on to live with Mila at Starokonyushenny pereulok. The Progress publishing house, on Zubatovski Boulevard, was a prestigious institution which specialised in translating approved Soviet texts into English. A few shadowy Englishmen, mostly Moscow-based communists, made a living by working there. A job like that might be quite a good option for me, at least in the short term, and would obviate the immediate problem of getting an exit visa for Mila. I had heard that the editor, a man called Tsetsenko was always on the look-out for good transla- tors, so one morning I went along to see him. He said he liked the sample of work that I showed him, and might be able to offer me a job. As I left his office, however, I found I was being followed even more closely than usual, this time by a young and malevolent goon. There was precious little chance that the KGB would tolerate me as a permanent resident.

Mila and I also went to Victor Louis' flat to find out whether he had anything more to suggest – he may have genuinely tried to help at the Palace. The stories of his Western-style living were basically true: he had a double flat (two knocked into one) in a privileged block not too far from the centre; it was comfortably furnished, diplo- mat-style, with plenty of room to move. I was particularly struck by his sleek modern telephone, so different from the clumpy instruments one usually saw in Moscow. Both he and his wife were charming, but it soon became clear to us that there was nothing more he could, or would, do.

Mila's brother-in-law Sasha Vasin now tried to assist us as well, even though the power he wielded in the Ministry of Justice was not relevant to our circumstances. He had, for instance, helped one or two ne'er-do-wells escape prosecution, thereby earning their life-long indebtedness. He had also managed to keep a family member out of an unpleasant murder case after she had been called in as a witness. But assistance at a court level was not what we needed: and like all his close colleagues, Sasha was (as Mila told me) mortally afraid of the KGB.

He did, however, have a friend the Moscow division of the organs, a man called Misha Kazakov, who came from the same village. Misha's dacha was close to Sasha's, and indeed one day, when Misha was observed approaching the gate, I was bundled into a back room, so that he would not see me: the presence of a foreigner in the local- ity would have embarrassed him. But I was told that Misha's good will and connections could be used in specific, and relatively unimportant, matters.

Sasha asked him if he could request the details of me from the Moscow files section, to see how things stood. Misha apparently did so, but he was told, perhaps inevitably, was that there was no record of a Matthews at that level. The 'bulging dossier' Aleksei had talked about was evidently kept elsewhere. Sasha also considered bribery, a sure way of solving many problems in Soviet Russia. The matter was discussed in the family, and he certainly had someone in view, but I was told not to part with any money unless the person did something.

In the event it turned out that he did not want to get involved.

Finally a member of the family passed to me (in clear violation of the Soviet secrecy laws) an internal telephone listing of the Soviet Procuracy, the office which was supposed to ensure the implementation of justice. My first thought on seeing the booklet had been: "How can I get this to London without harming anyone in Mila's family?" My patriotic inclinations were still undented by the shabby treatment I reckoned I was getting from Her Majesty's Government. Unfortunately, the listing did not seem to contain the names of any people who might be able to help. And since I had no means of copying it quickly, back it went.

★

I was spending more and more time in Mila's room – somehow or other she managed to get time off work by claiming to be ill (which, given the stresses of the moment was not far from the truth). Apart from the fact that we were together, Starokonyushenny was much more homely than MGU. The day-to-day noises of life in the communal flat – the shuffle of slippers on the worn floorboards, the occasional altercation in the kitchen, the sound of the lavatory cistern – had a calming effect, even though the goons were roaming outside.

The peaceful atmosphere was, of course, fragile, and soon to be disrupted. On the morning of the 17th June, a week after the wedding fiasco, the telephone in the corridor rang, and one of the neighbours picked up the receiver. She came to Mila's room to say it was for 'her friend' – no one had ever, it seems, learnt my name. When I went to the instrument I heard, to my horror, an English voice on the line: a call from a foreigner would have all the neighbours agog. It was someone from the Embassy who had evidently got the number from one of the students, as I had never given it to a diplomat. Anyway, the voice requested me to go to the Embassy immediately. Again, it boded ill.

So there was another taxi ride to Sofiiskaya naberezhnaya, while Mila waited anxiously at Starokonyushenny pereulok. Another ride to disaster, I thought, as the taxi passed the red brick walls of the Kremlin. I glimpsed the golden cupolas of the churches inside, and the massive yellow facade of the Great Kremlin Palace where I had attended a reception when I worked for the Embassy. Past the old goon den about which I had told Aleksei, now being used as a storage depot, or something. The taxi stopped outside the embassy compound and I hurried in.

I was awaited. Two branch-A officials, Brooke-Turner, Head of

Chancery and a Secretary called Sewell, together with Kirby, the Consul, came to meet me in the vestibule. There may have been a fourth, I am not now sure. They were all obviously ill at ease and seemed concerned only to get me out of Russia, regardless of the consequences for my fiancée.

"The Embassy has been informed," said one of them, "that you have been accused of impermissible activities, including anti-Soviet propaganda and economic speculation. Your visa has been annulled and you have forty-eight hours to leave the country. The Embassy has made arrangements for you to take a flight to London."

"If you would like to, you can bring your fiancée to our flat for dinner, before you leave," said Kirby. "You can stay overnight, too. In fact it might be dangerous for you to go back to the university."

This no doubt was intended as something between a helpful gesture and a frightener, cleared by the sage folk in Chancery. I did not reply. Kirby did not seem to understand that if there was anything I could not do, it was take Mila to a foreign diplomat's flat. Moscow was not London. And if I were in danger of arrest, what about her? Never was the gap between embassy perceptions and Moscow realities wider.

"Leaving now is the only option," one of the diplomats added.

"Thank you," I said, "I'll consider the matter."

There was an uncomprehending silence: they must all have been thinking 'What can that mean?' The idea that I might not take valuable Foreign Office advice had, I am sure, never entered anyone's mind. We were now on the portico, watched suspiciously by the militiamen at the gate. At this point Sewell played what the Embassy no doubt considered to be two trump cards.

"There's some good news for you," he said, with an engaging smile. "We've heard from St. Antony's that your Fellowship is still open, they will be glad to have you back."

"That's not good news," I said, "it's exactly what I expected. I'm supposed to be going back anyway. Why should they stop me?"

Sewell looked at me meaningfully.

"There are indications that your fiancée is a 'plant'," he said.

I was shocked and speechless. Obviously, this was not an ad lib remark on his part – as an experienced official, Sewell was no doubt fulfilling an instruction, dutifully passing on a message from on high. The Embassy was not to know how immersed Mila was in this night-mare, or how outrageous the suggestion was. At that moment I had no means of knowing where it had come from: the fact that Sewell expressed it meant nothing. As far as the Foreign Office was concerned, I thought bitterly, it was just a matter of getting me home, by hook or by crook, so that the whole affair could be safely forgotten.

In one of the proudest moments of my life I turned away from them and walked slowly out of the compound. When I got to the gate I glanced back and saw they were still standing there, silent and perplexed. They could give advice, but not, of course, oblige me to take it.

★

My visa was due to expire on the afternoon of the 19th, if the timing were to be taken by the hour. For the rest of that day nothing much happened. I thought it might just be worth telephoning the Ambassador, Sir Humphrey Trevelyan, to see whether any high-level, last-minute intervention was possible. Normally he would not have come to the telephone, of course, but mine was obviously a special case, and perhaps he felt vulnerable. He answered in a wooden voice that he could only advise me to return to England immediately. I lost my temper.

"If you cannot do better than this," I said, "you should go back to England yourself."

And I put the receiver down: it was, I thought, an excellent suggestion. When my composure returned I contacted David Shapiro at MGU. He told me that a couple of questions about the case had gone down in the House of Commons. Also, there had been some sort of reception at the Embassy, where Henry Shapiro (no relation of his) had been looking for me desperately among the guests. That could only mean that Mila and I had become hot news. I spent the night at Mila's.

The following morning we were no less depressed and anxious. The fact that my visa had been annulled meant we could expect only another catastrophe. It came towards midday, with a ring on the door-bell. Some of the neighbours were at home, and I believe it was Maria Ivanovna who opened the outer door. A moment later there was a tap on ours. We looked at each other in alarm.

"What is it?" said Mila, opening.

"It's two foreigners," said Maria Ivanovna, in a tense voice. "For your friend." I went out into the corridor, past the two family rooms with doors ajar. Everyone wanted to know what was happening. When I got to the threshold I saw, to my dismay, not one but two embassy creatures, who shall remain nameless. Coming to a real Soviet flat must have been quite an adventure for them.

"Mr. Matthews? We have been asked to deliver a very important letter from the Embassy."

"You should not have come here, you know. This is a Soviet flat. The people here are afraid of foreign diplomats."

"Would you please accept this letter. It's urgent."

Should I take it or not? Reluctantly I did so, and closed the door. I simply did not have the self control to thank them for their delivery service. I imagine, though, they felt relieved to have fulfilled that delicate mission. No doubt they would have liked to be invited in, to have a look around: they would never have been inside a communal flat.

The actual letter did not worry me much, I could more or less guess what was in it. What did concern me were the possible consequences of the visit for Mila. The embassy officials simply did not understand the implications of their appearance on the doorstep. The neighbours had lived in Stalin's Russia, and were still, I was sure, subject to all sorts of wild fears. They would be resentful about having a foreigner there, anyway, afraid of KGB interference, of being called in to inform. The obvious reaction, in a Russian communal flat, was to take it out on the person concerned, that is, Mila.

Beyond that, if the KGB was looking for a pretext to deprive Mila of her Moscow residence permit, the British Embassy had provided one. Perhaps people like Brimelow did indeed understand: but they ignored such consequences so that the Embassy could fulfil its 'proper' procedures, and report back to London that it had done so. A telephone call to the flat, reading the text to me personally, would have been safer for Mila, and just as effective.

I took the envelope back to Mila's room and we opened it together.

"The Embassy," wrote the Consul "has now been informed officially that the time limit of 48 hours set for your departure from the Soviet Union has expired and that you must leave without delay. I feel obliged to warn you that we have received indications that the consequences for you if you do not leave now may be serious. It is possible that the Soviet authorities may put you by force across the frontier; a more serious possibility is that you may be arrested and brought to trial on the charges outlined in the Ministry's statement on June 17th. I should be grateful if you would at once get in touch with me, either at the office or at my house, Sadovo Samotechnaya 12/24 Flat No. 42 (Tel No. 95 56 58). K. Kirby H.M. Consul."

I looked at Mila.

"I can't stay here now," I said. "It's too dangerous for you. I'd better get back to the University."

No sooner had I uttered the words than there was another ring at the front door bell, this time long and imperious. I jumped up, went to open the door myself. This time a militiaman and a plain clothes man were standing on the threshold. The embassy staff were certainly under surveillance, and this call was timed to follow their visit. The militiaman asked me to identify myself, and explained that he was accompanied by a 'volunteer helper'.

"We have reason to believe that you are living here without permission," he said, "and we request you to accompany us now."

With scarcely time for word with Mila, I was led out to a car waiting in the street.

This was the second time I had been arrested, and again I had no idea what was going to happen to me. There was not much traffic in the Moscow streets, so the journey was fast. We drove down the Arbat, past the Lenin Library, where I had retrieved so much Pasternak: along the broad Mokhovaya Street, up the Prospekt Marksa into Dzerzhinski Square, where, behind the imposing statue of the infamous Chekist, stood the imposing granite building of the KGB. I thought for a moment that this was our destination – I was being taken there for further questioning or incarceration. Though I was not much accustomed to dangerous moments (despite a little experience of them in Russia) I felt strangely calm, with no hint of panic.

The car, however, did not slow or turn into the sinister entrance at the side. We drove past and went straight up Chernyshevski Street, turning into Potapovski pereulok, where, in a formerly picturesque villa, the Moscow visa office, or OVIR as it was known, was located. I knew the street from past visits, and Olga Vsevolodovna's flat was there too. I was taken inside and told me that the deputy head wished to speak to me. Then I was led into an inner office and greeted brusquely by a small, dark-haired man. There was no discussion, just an instruction: "You must leave the Soviet Union at the earliest possible moment."

I was then asked to wait until someone came from the Embassy. It turned out to be a bespectacled individual, one who had come with a colleague to deliver the letter at Mila's flat. We obviously irritated one another in equal measure, so no time was lost on pleasantries. He confirmed that I would have to leave the country as a matter of urgency, and the Embassy had been asked to facilitate my departure. I demonstratively ignored him and spoke to the officials only in Russian, so the poor devil had to get everything I said translated into English. Unpardonable rudeness on my part, of course, but it seemed pardonable to me, given the inflexibility of the Embassy from the beginning. The diplomat declared, however, that despite the difficulties the Embassy had managed to find a seat for me on a very crowded plane to London next day. This didn't seem like help to me because I did not want to go: but the Embassy no doubt thought otherwise.

The game was now definitely over, and there was no way that I could stay in Moscow with Mila. I would clearly be arrested if I tried. I went at once to the flat to tell her, in the deepest despair.

*

Word had got around among the foreign journalists that I had 'disappeared' in Moscow. As I was to find out a day or two later, there wasn't much other news, and the British newspapers had gone for it in a big way. I was the front-page story in the *Daily Mirror* on Saturday, 20th June, with a screaming headline: 'Deported Briton Vanishes in Moscow'. Once again, the reporting was less than accurate.

> Oxford don, [wrong] Dr. Mervyn Matthews, who was ordered out of Russia after being banned from marrying a Russian girl, vanished in Moscow last night. He disappeared as the regular B.E.A. Comet flight to London – the last one before his expulsion order expired – left Moscow Airport....
>
> The mystery of where he is deepened later when British Embassy officials announced they had been unable to trace him, [wrong]. Earlier, Dr. Matthews indicated that he might not catch the flight. "I have not made any arrangements for my departure yet," he said. "I am trying to explore all possibilities for getting my marriage through. I haven't quite given up hope." [In fact I have no recollection of speaking to a journalist – I tried to avoid them.] "Then on Wednesday Dr. Matthews was given forty-eight hours to leave Russia. He was accused of 'impermissible activities', hostile propaganda and economic speculation.

The *Daily Express* of the same day provided further detail, unknown to me at the time.

> In London the Foreign secretary Mr. R.A. Butler rapped Russia over the expulsion order. The British Ambassador has delivered a Note 'expressing concern' at the expulsion. Mr. Butler said "this expulsion must have an adverse effect on the student exchanges between the countries. Mr. Matthews is the second British student ordered out in seven weeks. The first was Mr. Peter Reddaway, of Cambridge, accused of trying to persuade a Russian family to emigrate.

And, inevitably, a pungent quote from my mother:

In Swansea, Mr. Matthews' widowed mother, Mrs. Lilian Matthews, aged 52, said, "He is a stubborn fool. He ought to know better."

★

The Embassy had managed to book me onto a very full Pakistani flight which left Moscow Airport at 2.15 pm the following afternoon, that is, on Sunday, the 21st June. There was no time for me to go back to MGU and pack my belongings, not to mention getting them through the customs. In any case, I would not have wished to spend my last precious hours in Moscow in so trivial a manner. I contacted some of the students in our group who said they would liaise with the Embassy and do it for me.

I cannot remember how Mila and I spent the last evening together, but it was certainly in grief. On the Sunday she came to Vnukovo to see me off, and as we embraced she was absolutely distraught. Perhaps, inwardly, she heard echoes of the awful night in her early childhood when her mother, screaming, had been torn away from her: it was something I never asked about, as I did not wish to re-awake such painful recollection.

As I walked across the tarmac I was photographed several times by a Russian photographer who seemed completely indifferent to my distress. It was highly unlikely that any report of my departure, let alone a picture, would appear in the Soviet press, so what he was doing there? Perhaps he had been sent by the KGB to get a final photograph for my 'bulging dossier'? I tried unsuccessfully to hide my face from him, but when he approached within a few yards I threw my briefcase – the only thing to hand – at him. It missed and bounced on the ground. "You'll pay for that," he shouted, as I retrieved it and stepped off Soviet soil.

When I got on board I found the plane was indeed packed – maybe the Embassy had had to persuade someone to get off so that I could have a seat. That was the sort of thing they were good at. As the engines started I burst into tears – it was the first time I had cried since I was a boy. Fortunately, nobody seemed to take any notice.

Another ordeal awaited me when we touched down at Heathrow, though it was minor compared to the others. Following the 'disappearance' stories a press conference had been organised in the VIP lounge, and I was photographed profusely as an unfortunate who had returned from Russia 'without his love'. A television producer invited me to record a two-minute interview, but suddenly put me on live. I was taken aback, but two minutes is not very long. Afterwards, when asked by a BBC reporter whether I thought that the government had done enough, I said "No". I was reported on the news later that day as having said 'Yes'. Obviously the gentleman had misheard me. Two reporters from the *South Wales Evening Post* were there to find out if I would be returning to my rainy homeland. I was not too surprised when, next day, the *Daily Mirror* gave me much of its back page, with a full-length picture.

But the story faded quickly: I was safely back in England, and my little tragedy lost its news value. My first concern was to find somewhere quiet where I could lick my wounds. Before I left Moscow I had managed to send a message through the Embassy to my old friend, Michael Aidin, who lived with his mother and father, a medical consultant, in Worthing. "You do realise," the F.O. official had warned them, that he was rude to the Ambassador!" Nevertheless Michael had replied by telegram, saying I could indeed stay with them. I had first met Michael when we were in hospital together (in my Hafod days) and his family had always been very kind to me. So Michael and his father met me at the airport, together with my half-brother Jack and his family. As soon as I had finished with the press and television I was whisked off to Worthing in the Aidin car.

Five. Picking up the Pieces

The Aidin's guest bedroom, with its partially sloped cottage ceiling and neat oak suite, was about as different as you could imagine from Mila's tiny cell on Starokonyushenny pereulok. But as I lay in bed next morning, listening to the birds in the garden, my thoughts were far away, in Moscow. Despite the surrounding calm I felt very restless. It seemed to me that this was the beginning, rather than the end, of the story. The KGB had won a battle, but the war would go on. To be realistic, I thought, I would devote several years – perhaps five – to waging it. And only then, if it still looked hopeless, would I give up, to live the rest of my life as best I could. At least it would be in the knowledge that I had done everything possible to get Mila out of Russia.

I was so concerned with the future that I was unable to perceive, with any coherence, the strange course of events behind me. It was only years later that I came to analyse their sequence – and wonder why I had not been expelled earlier. If Sokolov had finished interrogating me – or more accurately, had given it up as hopeless – in the middle of May, why did the KGB not expel me forthwith, with the usual forty-eight hours' notice? They could easily have done so. Why did they restrict themselves to blocking the marriage, while leaving me to roam Moscow, which only involved more surveillance work for their goons? My visa was not due to expire until the 4th July.

Several possible answers came to mind. Firstly the KGB were in the process of expelling another member of our group – Peter Reddaway – on a ludicrous charge of encouraging a Soviet family to emigrate. Perhaps they thought two expulsions within a few days would be too disruptive of the student exchange. Secondly, Harold Wilson, a socialist Prime Minister-to-be, was due to arrive in Moscow, and two such cases would not help the visit. Thirdly, the KGB could not have anticipated the fuss that I would create at the Palace of Weddings on the 9th June. And lastly, there may have been some hope in the organisation that I would voluntarily renew contact, come crawling back, as it were, though that does not seem likely, given the way they rebuffed my attempts to reach Aleksei.

Beyond that, the fact that the KGB took over a week to expel me after the fiasco at the Palace of Weddings was also puzzling. Perhaps in this instance there were purely technical difficulties – the matter was one for several hands, the KGB case-officers may have had more important matters to deal with, or there may have been some element of bureaucratic lassitude. Perhaps, perhaps....

★

After breakfast I surprised my hosts by saying that I would have to go back to London. They were very kind, and Worthing was idyllic, but I needed to be in the capital to attend to various practical matters. The strands of my life had to be picked up, one by one. My half-brother Jack's house was out in Barnes, but it was still London, and on the London telephone network. So I went to stay with him for a few days. I phoned St. Antony's College, and William Deakin, the Warden, asked me to meet him urgently for dinner.

The Warden had scarcely noticed me previously, but I could understand his interest now. I had committed the scarcely pardonable sin of getting the name of the College onto the front page of a populist news-sheet, and I suspected that he wanted to know whether the College was vulnerable on some other score. Perhaps I had indeed committed a crime in Russia, or was involved in other unsavoury matters. Above all, the intelligence implications had to be considered

We met at a posh fish restaurant near Piccadilly. Bill, as he liked to be called by his equals, was a small figure, but imposing in any surroundings – a ducal type, as it were, who overawed me without any difficulty whatever. From the perspective of an upbringing in the Hafod he seemed to have absolutely all the aces – a fine family background, money, a titled wife from Rumania, and an exquisite, upper-class pronunciation of English. He had taken virtually every undergraduate history prize in Oxford, and became a history don at Christ Church. He had associated with Winston Churchill personally, and had been parachuted into Yugoslavia to establish contact between the British government and Josef Tito. Being dropped behind German lines required personal courage, which he had in good measure.

The restaurant was crowded and surprisingly noisy, and the dinner was not of the quality of Aleksei's offerings. But the Warden showed his companionable side, and was very easy to talk to. He had read the letter I left covering my earlier contacts with the KGB, and he wanted to have a detailed update from me personally. I told him all that had happened – that is, in the security sphere.

"Well," he said earnestly, downing another whiskey, "I think you should have a talk with the security people, don't you? There may be things they want to ask you. When I went to Hungary to get so-and-so out, I went to the Ambassador first." Obviously, we approached these things from different angles. I was most impressed by his readiness, after we finished the meal, to shower ten-shilling tips on all who served us: ten shillings was a lot of money then. He had no ZIL awaiting, but called a taxi to get back to another part of central London, where he had parked his car.

★

The next day a letter came from my long-suffering mother.

> Thank God you are back in Britain, son. Try not to worry and vex too much, and for God's sake rest and relax.... How can I thank Dr. and Mrs. Aidin at Worthing. I thought you looked tired and worn on TV.... When it was announced on TV Friday evening that you had not turned up at the airport in Moscow and that you had disappeared, I thought I would have died. [After that, on several occasions, she accused me of murdering her, – "not many boys have murdered their mother!"] ...For my sake Mervyn give up the idea of going to Scandinavia to see Khrushchev... he is moving about with a terrific bodyguard and you might get shot.

She knew, either from Jack or some comment I had made to a reporter, that I had another plan in mind, desperate or ridiculous, depending on how you looked at it. Nikita Khrushchev and his wife Rada were imminently expected on a state visit to Sweden, and it seemed to me that this was a golden opportunity to get the Soviet leader to intervene. He would be physically within reach (which was not the case in Moscow) and might not wish to court unpopularity in the Swedish press by refusing to help two ordinary young people to get married. The fact that my story was unknown in Sweden, and that any appeal could be dismissed out of hand, hardly entered my mind. So on the 23rd June I sat down in Jack's back bedroom and penned two heartfelt pleas in Russian, one for Nikita and one for his spouse. I hoped to hand them over in person.

The trip had to be organised in a tearing hurry, as Khrushchev was only staying for a very few days. I took a plane to Gottenburg in the hope of catching him there, but landed at Toslanda airport a few minutes after he had taken off for Stockholm. The police knew I was coming – perhaps from some press comment, or because they had a list of potential trouble-makers – I never bothered to find out. Anyway, they were immensely pleased that I had missed him, if only because it was one problem less for them. When I asked where he was I got only a satisfied smile. "Khrushchev gone," said the Swedish plain-clothes officer, pointing to the evening sky.

I went into town and contacted the local paper, the *Göteborgs Handels och Sjöfarts Tidning*, and found they would be very happy to do a story on my quest. The editor even asked me out for dinner. Presumably Gottenburg was not a very vibrant place, so when Khrushchev disappeared they were glad to have something more to write about. But having missed Khrushchev, what was I to do? It seemed pointless just to return home. The chances of meeting the Soviet leader were (I could now see) infinitesimal, security was too strict. But could I at least get an interview into the Stockholm press? My intentions would be made public, and that was better than nothing.

I travelled to Stockholm on the night train. Sweden no doubt has its charms, but viewed through a train window in the falling dark it seemed a sad sort of place, watery, with gloomy forests. Stockholm, despite its open, pleasant aspect, looked empty. Apart from that, staying there was fearfully expensive, and after paying the air fare, I had little money left. When I arrived I put up at the Hellman Hotel in Bryggargatan, the cheapest I could find. Once in my room I set up the tea-making equipment which was to serve me well in the future – a mug, a little electric spiral and a perforated teaspoon. I also had my own plate, knife and fork. I knew my food would comprise mostly snacks bought outside, restaurant meals being beyond my budget.

With regard to the newspapers, I was not disappointed. Two of the main Stockholm dailies, the *Stockholms Tidningen* and the *Avtonbladet* confirmed that although Khrushchev was unapproachable, they would both do large articles on me, with pictures, and they kept their word. Having got that little ordeal out of the way I spent a sad evening at an amusement park on one of the city's islands, watching dozens of young couples dancing. Curiously, they had to pay separately for each number: I thought of Mila and me going through the turnstiles together.

I had to return to England next day, before my money ran out altogether. The adventure was not quite over, though. About three o'clock in the morning I was awaken by a knock on the door of my room. I opened it to find a balding man aged about thirty on the threshold. He introduced himself as Des Zwar of the *Daily Mail*. I was not overpleased to see a total stranger at that ungodly hour, and my first impulse was to send him packing, but he was used to dealing with difficult customers, and persuaded me to let him in – he was, I thought, only trying to do his job, and might even be able to help. We had a long chat, sitting on my bed. "The office thought there might be a good story in it," said Des, "so they sent me over. But they couldn't tell me where you were, and I've been around every hotel in Stockholm looking for you." He was rather proud of his own persistence.

Des was a colourful character who loved golf and beautiful women, probably in that order. I asked him how intelligent correspondents like him could write the nonsense people read in the popular press. "I deliberately keep myself ignorant," he replied, "so as to see things like the man in the street. I've got a friend at the *Mail* who's so sharp we're afraid he'll cut himself"... "The best headline ever," he told me, "hasn't been used used yet. But they have it ready in the office. 'Queen rushed to Palace in Dramatic Sex Change'."

The story he wrote after speaking to me was significantly more dramatic than the situation warranted, but the *Daily Mail* ran it on the 26th June.

> Dr. Mervyn Matthews, the 31-year old research student who was refused permission to marry a Russian girl, was in Stockholm tonight waiting for his chance to see Mr. Kruschev tomorrow. He arrived last night from Gottenburg to make a desperate appeal to the Russian Prime Minister.... Earlier today he wandered around Stockholm's city centre with a letter to Mr. Kruschev in his pocket. He said 'I won't give up.'...
>
> A few hours later Mr. Kruschev left with his guard of 500 police, commandos and security men to spend the night at the Swedish 'Chequers' at Harpsund, 18 miles south of Stockholm. If Dr. Matthews tries to break through the cordon of machine-gun carrying police he runs the risk of being shot dead. Security men, nervous since the reported threat to kidnap Mr. Kruschev, are in the trees, lining the roads and even on horseback, with orders to shoot if there is a sudden move to get near the Russian leader.

Needless to say, I did not get anywhere near the great man. But I learnt a little more about the practices of the British press.

The trip to Sweden was followed, only a few days later, by another to Bonn in West Germany, in an attempt to meet Aleksei Adzhubei, Khrushchev's buffoon son-in-law. I thought this time I would try and hand over a letter unobserved, without any press backing, so I arranged the journey as unobtrusively as possible. One of my college friends put me in touch with a woman called Carola Stern, who worked for a German publishing house, and she kindly provided all the necessary information about Adzhubei's movements, including a private address where he was to attend a small reception.

I was only in Bonn for a few hours, but I went to the house and managed to approach Adzhubei. There was virtually no security. I found him surrounded by sycophantic German directors and managers hoping to break into the Soviet market. He took my letter, but instead of reading it passed it on, without comment, to an embarrassed aide. With so many eager businessmen around it was useless trying to speak to him. My impression, as I left, was that discreet approaches would not help either. My hurried journey to Bonn had surely been a complete waste of time.

★

Another letter from my mother was awaiting me on my return to London. "Apart from throwing money away, Mervyn," she wrote "flying after Khrushchev and family, you are undermining your health and your fanatical behaviour is bound to react on your career. I think you would be well advised to consult a psychiatrist without delay. Hope you are having enough to eat. Love, Mother xxxxx P.S. If you can find time between flights to come home please let me know when."

She was right about my career. I was also handling a small publishing catastrophe, in so far as I had to stop production of a book I had written before leaving for Moscow. Entitled *Khrushchev and Soviet Youth* it was already in page proof, and the American publisher had great hopes for its success. My experience of living in Russia was rather uncommon, and the text contained a lot of original material on how young people were controlled by the regime. But I was frightened that its appearance would provoke reprisals against Mila, and I wrote to the publisher asking him to abandon publication. For someone like myself, who was thinking of an academic career, it was a heavy blow, self-inflicted.

The publisher came to London on other business, and we had tea in the Rubens Hotel, just opposite the Queen's Mews in Buckingham Palace Road. Although abandoning the book meant a loss of thousands of dollars for him, he graciously agreed to do it. Looking back, I am sure that publication would have made no difference whatever – the book, though critical, had no intelligence connotations, and meant little, compared to the fuss I was making elsewhere.

★

Behind this flurry of activity lay my main concerns – contact with Mila and her well-being. In this respect, happily, there were some positive developments. I got her first letters just after my return from Sweden: at least the postal channel was open. The first was dated the 24th June.

"Today we are starting a new life, a life of letters and struggle," she wrote. "I feel very bad without you, it is as though life has stopped... In the three days since you left I have lost a good deal of strength, health, and nerves. I know you will be angry, but I could not do anything with myself. I am sleeping very badly, I keep on thinking that you must return, and that I should be waiting for you, I jump at every sound. My friends try and support me.... Everybody who is honest and sensible thinks [our separation] is stupid, inhumane, vicious, and shameful." And next day she wrote: "I live only with my grief, the world outside has ceased to exist for me."

"I am very sorry I let you go," she wrote on the 3rd July. "We should have waited longer. Everything is a thousand times harder now, the loneliness is unbearable. At the Institute all the women feel sorry for me, [and when talking among themselves] they think that you deceived me. They say "Will he go on trying?" I tell them that you certainly will, and that we love one another very much. They all run to the library to read the *New York Times*. A lot of people liked your photo.... I try to get home as quickly as possible and not see anyone. My mother reacted very badly [to your departure]. She says she thought that would happen! You are a foreigner."

Another encouraging fact was, in one sense, a lack of news: on the Soviet official front everything seemed to be quiet, and no reprisals had been taken against Mila. The Palace of Weddings responded in writing (albeit negatively) to her application for a review of their refusal to let us get married, and the Ministry of Foreign Affairs formally acknowledged letters she sent to Kosygin and Gromyko. The neighbours at Starokonyushenny had not been provoked into any unpleasant activities, and she was still in a job. The horrors of her mother's ordeal were evidently not to be repeated.

True, a few days after my departure, a problem arose at the Institute: a party meeting (Mila was not in the CPSU) decided that she should be asked to leave. But even here the outcome was positive: the Director got her transferred without loss of earnings to the Central Library of the Soviet Academy of Sciences, which was also an 'élite' institution. There she spent most of her time translating articles from French learned journals.

I telephoned her sister Lena early in July, and soon Mila and I established a system of fortnightly telephone calls. It was not convenient for her to use the instrument in the flat at Starokonyushenny, as all the neighbours would be listening. So she would go to the

Central Telegraph on Gorki Street and wait for me to reach her there. We would talk for a few hurried minutes – the time was expensive, had to be ordered in advance. Not much could be said, but they were golden minutes indeed.

"Mervusya, how are you?"

"Fine. Any movement in Moscow?"

"No, none at all. And in England?"

"Well, I'm trying my best, but nothing to report at the moment. Don't lose hope, though. How are things at work?"

"Normal"

A few more comments, reassurances, words of affection, and then we would fix the time for the next call. It was always a very nervy business.

I had no interest whatever in clothes, but Mila was soon asking me to send garments which in Russia were expensive and difficult to get. It was all very constrained, because parcels had to be handled by a single specially licensed firm called Dinnerman. So I trailed around the ladies' clothes shops in London, and periodically telephoned Dinnerman's, while Mila responded by sending me endless packets of books from the Moscow bookshops. Soon there were literally hundreds on my shelves.

★

Following my meeting with the Warden, various people had to be seen. The idea, I suppose, was to 'de-brief' me, though there was clearly little of real interest that I could say. Someone, perhaps the Warden himself, suggested that I wrote a report for MI5 on my contacts with the KGB. I did so, including the outline I had written before departing for Russia in September. The report comprised altogether ten closely-written foolscap sheets.

One of the first people I saw was David Footman, a Fellow of the College and my (quaintly-named) 'moral tutor'. He was the person who got me admitted to the college, and was supposed to extend a helping hand when necessary. I think, in fact, he developed a warm spot for me. Tall, gaunt, with thin, carefully combed hair, he was impressive in all respects, like the Warden, in a way. Now half retired, he lived in a cavernous basement flat in Chelsea. David had a stupendous memory, a Military Cross from the First World War, and an effortless intellectual superiority to match. He disdained showy things and always dressed in a careful, but somehow shabby manner. When I first got my Fellowship he told me I should call him 'David', but never once did he call me 'Mervyn' in return. His condescension was subtle, though in fact I rather enjoyed it. I was certainly no match for him.

I knew dimly that he had intelligence connections, though his name had never been mentioned in Moscow. If you asked him about his past, David would blandly tell you that he had worked in the Levant Consular Service, and had then retired to a Fellowship in St. Antony's. Only after his death some years later did I discover that he had headed a department in MI6 and left for unexplained reasons after the Philby affair. In his brief autobiography *Dead Yesterday* he covered his years at Marlborough School and travels in the Balkans, but wrote no word about his intelligence work. The sympathetic reader learned that he had come from a modest background – his parents could afford only two servants.

In his flat that afternoon, over rather weak tea in cracked cups, he exhibited an easy acceptance of all that had happened. Young people were supposed to get into scrapes, he had got into a few himself, it was part of life. But then, with a little common sense, one got out of them again. He had had to leave Oxford before graduating because he lost too much money betting on horses. And he would always prefer to have a secretary who had had 'a tumble in the hay' rather than a staid type, she would probably be less tense and easier to work with.

David listened to my story with great attention, and I had the impression from some of his questions that he would be discussing it elsewhere. There was, of course, no hint of blame in his response.

"I think," he said, as my tale came to an end, "that you should have a word with Battersby, in the Foreign Office Security Section.... They would be interested."

He re-filled his pipe and passed his hand over his distinguished brow.

"You're not reckoning on getting her out, are you? That would be a bonus. You've got to be realistic about these things."

★

On the 19th August I telephoned the Foreign Office, and somehow got through to both Youde, the man who had returned my article to Moscow, and the mysterious Battersby. Youde had nothing to add, but I was able to ask Battersby about the 'plant' story that Sewell had quoted on the embassy steps. "Oh," he said, "you may presume that this was a precautionary presumption, there was no other source." As far as the Foreign Office was concerned, that was the end of the matter.

My last intelligence meeting took place a few weeks later. MI5 arranged for one of their ghosts, a certain Mr. M.L. McCaul, to come up to Oxford to interview me. When he arrived, late one afternoon, I found he was a rather fat, deliberate character, with a sergeant-major bearing. He seemed to speak with bated breath, and I wondered vaguely whether he suffered from asthma. But he kindly proposed that we went out to dinner at The Bear, the famous hotel in Woodstock. I formed the impression that in the framework of MI5 activities dinner in an old country inn was something of a treat, though he had to drive up from London to enjoy it. Mr. McCaul referred to Aleksandr Fedorovich and Aleksei as 'your friends in Moscow' and 'that pair'. The object of the meeting evidently was to check that I had no further information to impart, and perhaps to get a personal assessment of me.

"We've read your report," Mr. McCaul said. "I can tell you that the copyright on it has already been breeched. We liked your phrase 'using an aura of friendship for purposes of recruitment' so we put it into one of our things."

I had no means of knowing what 'things' it had gone into: but I enjoyed the feeling that I had made a contribution to MI5 literature.

"We would very much like to fix the identities of the people you have been dealing with," he continued. "If we send you on some photographs, can you tell us if they correspond?" I agreed. The dinner came to an end and Mr. McCaul disappeared into the night, never to be seen again.

A few days later a couple of photographs arrived. I was horrified when I saw them. One was of Victor Popov, a Russian scholar who had actually spent a year at St. Antony's before I went to Russia. We met frequently in Oxford and his identity presented no problem whatever. He had not, of course, associated with me in Moscow. How could MI5 make so crude an error? I remembered Aleksei's comment on how badly they worked. The other photograph was of a youngish man in spectacles whom I could not recognise. I sent them both back, as requested.

The unseen researchers, however, kept at it and eventually redeemed their Service. On the 2nd March, 1966 an MI5 officer showed me, during a quiet meeting at Charing Cross Station, a picture of an elegant figure with a broad, handsome face, swept-back hair and a grey streak above the temple. The image was unmistakable, and the officer revealed that the surname was Suntsov. It was the first time I had ever heard it: in Moscow Aleksei had named his boss (truthfully or not) but never himself. I never dared ask him about it, lest he thought I wanted to pass it on to the British side.

The summer in Oxford was warm, the surroundings green and blissful. Yet I felt downhearted and ill at ease. The best thing I could do was to set aside my academic work and garner support for my cause. I was well placed to do so: St. Antony's specialised in political studies, and the College was extraordinarily well connected. Perhaps I could persuade some of the people who were known there to help me.

No less a personage than Aleksandr Kerensky, Prime Minister of Russia for a few months before the Bolshevik coup, came to Oxford to write an account of the Revolution. His sight was very poor and I was asked to help him with his research. A spidery little man, with a shock of white hair and thick glasses, he was deep into old age, but fully *compos mentis*. He listened to my tale with great sympathy, but there was nothing he could do. For him Russia was a distant and totally hostile land, and his contacts were with the older generation of émigrés, anyway. Even so I took great pleasure in his company, not least because he had such a refined and delicate mode of expression. "Rasputin?" he said one day. "Oh, yes, he was very strong, very strong!"

I built up a register of people who might help. A few were pro-Soviet left-wingers, but that did not deter me. To quote the old Russian proverb: 'Be glad to get a tuft of wool from a lousy sheep'.

First among people I approached was Professor Leonard Schapiro of the London School of Economics, an eminent critic of the Soviet Union. He suggested a few sympathetic MP's, and also that I wrote a letter to Sir Humphrey Trevelyan apologising for telling him to go home. My advice to Trevelyan had, in my view, been of the best that I had ever given, but he occupied a key position in officialdom and had indeed protested the manner of my expulsion. The Foreign Office in London had also done a little more than was reported in the *Daily Express*. As Rab Butler, the Conservative Foreign Secretary, told Neil McBride, my mother's MP, the day the Soviet note had been received in Moscow (the 17th June) the Embassy had sought further explanations and had requested an extension of the time limit. So somewhat mollified, I wrote to Trevelyan saying that although, to my mind, he had made an error of judgement, my rudeness was unjustified. He sent a note graciously acknowledging my letter.

My mailing list soon included the great and good of the day, mostly now forgotten. There was Lord (Bertrand) Russell, the popular philosopher who pleased the Russians by going anti-nuclear in his old age; Selwyn Lloyd, the former Conservative Foreign

Secretary, who 'got on well' with Gromyko; Sir Frank Soskice, a Labour Home Secretary who was of Russian extraction; Sir Isaiah Berlin, influential Russian philosopher of All Souls; Lord Thomson, the Canadian millionaire; George Woodcock, General Secretary of the influential Trades Union Congress: Commander Anthony Courtney, the combative Conservative MP who wrote a book about his Russian mistress and subsequent embroilment with the KGB. I had a good friend in David Floyd, who wrote on Russia for the *Daily Telegraph*. I re-established contact with Patrick Gordon Walker, and now, all too late, found him supportive. The letter-writing, telephone calls and visits demanded an enormous amount of time and effort.

I also tried to do something through the Soviet Embassy. Soon after my expulsion I wrote a letter to the Ambassador, Aleksandr Soldatov, and got a response from his private secretary, who agreed to meet me. I put on my best suit and went to the Ambassador's splendiferous residence in Kensington Palace Gardens. I was received by a pleasant young man of about my own age, who led me into a grand, old-fashioned sitting room on the first floor. But it was evident after a moment or two that he had nothing positive to say, and could do nothing to help. The meeting was a sheer formality, perhaps intended to calm me and discourage me from making a fuss. In any case, all the applications for entry visas which I made over the next few months were turned down.

My contacts also included Frederick Cumber, a businessman, who, of all the people I approached, tried hardest. Our association began in December, 1964 and went on into the spring of 1966. His business interests in East Europe had prompted him to cultivate Soldatov, and he was apparently a welcome guest at the Embassy. Our story had touched him deeply. He lived relatively close to Oxford, in the Cotswolds, and after an exchange of letters he invited me down for a chat. The drive through the rolling countryside on a bright winter's morning was filled with hope, and I shall never forget it. His house was delightful – stone-built and nestling in a hollow.

Middle-aged but spritely, Mr. Cumber clearly knew what was what. "I've looked into this carefully," he said after shaking hands. "I've cleared you with Interpol. No problem there." It soon transpired that he had also discussed my case with his friend the Ambassador. "He had your file on his desk," said Mr. Cumber. "It looked pretty thick to me!" He thought that I should use all means to get Mila out, and suggested that she try and get a exit visa to go to East Germany. But I had my reservations on that score, as it might provoke KGB intervention. I had already suggested that she apply for an exit visa to England. On learning about this Mr. Cumber asked me to tell her to wait until he had had time to take it up with Soldatov. By the middle of February he actually thought that something was moving. One morning I was delighted to have a letter from him: "Will you please advise your fiancée to apply for an Exit Visa to come here?"

My joy was overwhelming – but lasted only until I had opened a letter from Mila which came by the very same post. Something was definitely wrong in Moscow. "Thank you for your letter," I replied to Mr. Cumber, "but I gather from Mila that she has been followed sporadically, starting about three weeks ago.... At the time when she wrote, however, just under a week ago, it had stopped." Nevertheless, the fact that Mila had been under surveillance, even for a short time, was unnerving.

Weeks went by without any visible movement, until finally, at the end of April, an official in the Soviet Foreign Ministry contacted Mila and told her that her request for an exit visa had been refused. It was quite clear that Mr. Cumber had either been misled by the Embassy, or had over-estimated his influence there. Being very practical, he suggested that I apply for Soviet entry visas elsewhere in West Europe (presumably in the hope that one would be issued in error). But with no movement in Moscow it seemed rather pointless, and I set the idea aside, at least for the time being. Eventually, in August, 1965, I wrote him a final letter, assuring him that I had not told anyone about his involvement, and thanking him for his kindness.

*

It was in April, 1965 that Russian activities against a British citizen again made headlines, and on a far greater scale than in my case. On the 26th of the month the national newspapers splashed news of the arrest in Moscow of a young English lecturer called Gerald Brooke. I knew him because he had been a post-graduate student with me at MGU in 1959, and had also spent some time at Oxford.

It was the sort of spy-heart-throb story which could not but make a big impact. He had been picked up at a flat belonging to an agent of the NTS, the small anti-Soviet organisation I had learnt about at Oxford. Gerald had delivered NTS propaganda to the flat the day before, and when he returned KGB officers were waiting for him. He was arrested in the company of his wife Barbara, but she was released and sent back to England almost immediately.

Of course, there was considerable public sympathy for him, but there were reasons why his arrest was of particular relevance to my own problems. I contacted Martin Dewhirst as soon as I heard about it. "Oh yes," said Martin, "didn't you know? He was recruited by Georgii Miller at Oxford, the chap who approached you." I recalled Miller's earnest outpourings in my rooms at St. Antony's: there, but for the grace of God, I thought, go I. At least I had avoided that disaster.

But more, much more, was to follow. After a few weeks Gerald was given a show trial and sentenced to five years' imprisonment as a 'spy'. The Soviet press used the case to promote anti-Western xenophobia. Among several Westerners mentioned during the trial were Martin Dewhirst, now accused of anti-soviet activity, and Peter Reddaway, who had been unfairly expelled about seven weeks before me. As far as I was concerned, it was a question of the dog that did not bark in the night. If Brooke, Dewhirst, Reddaway, whom I knew personally, why not Matthews? Perhaps the decision to exclude me was taken to avoid implicating Mila in what could have been a very serious matter.

The KGB was known to be extremely protective of any personnel captured in the West. Rumours soon began to circulate in Moscow that the Soviet authorities were proposing to swap Gerald for two genuine Soviet agents, Peter and Helen Kroger who were serving twenty-year prison sentences for espionage in England. Gerald was certainly not of that ilk, but the Soviet authorities had no hesitation in claiming that he was. It was clear that the five-year sentence was nothing short of blackmail, with all sorts of negative implications for the safety of Westerners in the USSR if other Soviet agents were imprisoned. But could any advantage be derived from it for Mila and me?

"There is already talk," I wrote to Mr. Cumber on the 6th August, "of a Kroger-Brooke exchange, which means two K's for one B. I personally think there are a number of excellent arguments for getting Mila tagged on to this. The Russians would regard it as a negligible concession, and they are certainly anxious to get the Krogers out.... As a first step I am considering an approach to Sir Frank Soskice, whom I knew.... These months of separation are weighing very heavily on both of us, and not a day goes by without my giving a great deal of thought to the problem in hand. We live, so to speak by letter. I have now received some 430 from Mila, and sent her about the same number (not to mention postcards)."

By this time Mr. Cumber had evidently decided that there was nothing more he could do, and he stopped answering my letters. Nevertheless, I continued to regard him as one of the brighter figures on my horizon, someone who did his very best to help. As for a spy exchange, the British government indicated that in no way would it consider one. But I was not so certain. "Dear Mrs. Brooke," I wrote to Gerald's wife on the 21st September "I was indeed distressed to hear of your husband's misfortune, though somewhat relieved to read the reports of negotiations for an exchange.... Now that the matter has been raised in this form I am sure that some solution will be found before long... today's reports, despite the many obvious differences between our cases, have awakened a new, faint glimmer of hope...."

★

The Foreign Office still offered the best hope of leverage, but again I was unlucky with personalities. The supremo at the 'Northern Department', which covered Russia, was a certain Howard Smith, who was said to be a mathematician by training. No doubt a wizard at advanced calculus or numbers theory, his handling of affairs of the heart (mine, at least) left much to be desired. After my return to London I contacted him a number of times: his unconcealed impatience over the telephone and brief letters invariably evoked feelings of despair. Everyone in the Foreign Office seemed to regard the case as hopeless, and me (at best) as a troublesome ne'er-do-well. As far as they knew I might even have betrayed my country.

The official Foreign Office stance had been passed on to me through Mr. Laurie Pavitt, M.P., who wrote to Michael Stewart, the Foreign Secretary, on my behalf. Mr. Stewart's comments were not without a trace of exasperation. "Dr. Matthews' case," wrote the Foreign Secretary "is one with... which we are very familiar. He has been told repeatedly in interviews and correspondence with officials and Foreign Office Ministers alike the reasons why we do not consider it right to single out his case for official representations... [i.e.] in view of the past history of this case there is really no possibility of a favourable reaction to official intervention." The furthest the F.O. would go was to promise that Mila would be eligible for a British entry visa, should she ever need one.

The nadir in Matthews-Foreign Office relations came one evening in Oxford, when Howard Smith and a group of Foreign Office officials came to the College for a dinner. Knowing that the gentleman was in the Senior Common Room, I asked Fred, the college Steward, to ask him to come up to my rooms. When he appeared in the doorway I was so agitated that I rather lost control of myself, and expressed an earthy view of his person. "He came back down to the Common Room visibly shaken," a friendly colleague, Harry Willetts, recounted afterwards. "He told everyone in hearing that you had been sprawled in an armchair and called him 'the shit of Smiths' when he opened your door. His cigar had gone out". My own recollection was that I had only called him 'a fart', but I imagine that in the circumstances his reporting was accurate. Perhaps I had even used both terms.

A Dean of Christ Church, or Warden of All Souls' could easily have got away with an apposite fecal reference, especially if it were rendered in good Latin. But not, alas, a lowly research fellow like myself. The incident was the final nail in the coffin of my Oxford career, if one were needed. Actually, it may have been finished after my appearance on the front page of the *Mirror,* though the disruption of my research activities did not help either. Smith's discomfiture was quickly reported to the Warden, who called me to his house next day for what every member of the College dreaded most – an admonitory glass of sherry.

"Rude and totally unacceptable," said Bill Deakin in his impeccable tones as he poured it out. "And he was a guest of the College, too. We cannot possibly put up with that sort of thing. Have you heard anything more about the job going at Glasgow? Perhaps it would be better for you to go up north, and get away from things." Max Hayward came to my rooms a little later, to find out more. He was himself of modest background, and we had a good laugh about it. Years before, Max had had trouble with the Foreign Office himself, through getting drunk in Georgia. But for me the die was cast: soon afterwards Harry Willetts gently confirmed the news over half a pint of beer in the Lamb and Flag on St Giles.

★

The academic year rolled on, autumn 1965 was approaching, and with it my departure from Oxford. I accepted an appointment to teach for a year at the University of Nottingham, a pleasant, academically respectable institution, with a very nice head of department. I was fortunate, I suppose, in having had a good training, with good prospects. But with the portals of Oxford closing on me, and Mila still in Russia, an impenetrable sadness enveloped my whole life. I got a pass to visit Wytham Woods, and on sunny days I would drive there and wander along the paths alone, gazing over the green fields of Oxfordshire. Fourteen months of effort to get Mila out of Russia had brought no success whatever.

But before leaving the city of dreaming spires I thought I should again attempt to shift matters. Orthodox methods seemed to be getting me nowhere – perhaps something more adventurous might do the trick. An opportunity presented itself in the unlikely form of attendance at the Twelfth International Historical Congress in Vienna at the end of August. The College indicated that they might cover the travel costs – quite a generous gesture, in so far as I had been doing little serious work on Russia, and had no paper to present.

One day, after I had raised the matter, Theodore Zeldin, one of the long-term Fellows, came up to me in the corridor.

"If we give you money to go, Mervyn," he said meaningfully, "you won't be up to any funny business, will you?"

There have been moments in my life when acute necessity has over-ridden my concern for truth. This was one of them.

"What 'funny business' can I get up to in Vienna?" I asked innocently. Theodore gave me a knowing look and passed on: but a few days later the authorisation came through.

I arrived in Vienna at the beginning of September and put up at the Auge Gottes students' hostel. The Congress itself turned out to be a lavish affair, with endless lectures and meetings. It included a stand-up banquet in the city hall, certainly the largest expanse of delicious food I had ever seen, but the number of guests was huge, and the great platters emptied with astonishing rapidity. You had to be quick to get anything at all. The only Russian influence I could detect in the city centred on a small restaurant called the Feuervogel (or Firebird). It was owned by a very fat Russian who worked as his own waiter and gave you vodka even if you had not ordered it. I dined there a couple of times while a Bulgarian guitarist sang mournful Russian songs and bickered with the owner.

As soon as the congress finished I got down to the "funny business" I had in mind. It involved taking a train to Prague (which was only a hundred and fifty miles away) so as to get behind the iron curtain. The more I thought about it, the more apprehensive I became. On the eve of departure I passed a sleepless night in Auges Gotte, the dirges of the Bulgarian guitarist echoing in my mind. This would be my first visit to KGB-controlled territory since leaving Russia, and if they knew about it, given the trouble I was causing them, they might well try a Brooke-type snatch. But the modest task I had set myself could be accomplished only by spending a day where Russia ruled.

I got to Prague on the 6th September. The so-called 'golden city', was indeed beautiful, but like the Hotel Slovan, where I stayed, badly in need of a coat of paint, if not extensive re-gilding. My only experience of life behind the iron curtain had been in Russia, and it was interesting, in the few hours at my disposal, to compare the Czechoslovak capital with Moscow. Despite the language difficulties

(Czech is barely intelligible to a Russian speaker) the Czechs seemed more ready to associate with foreigners, and the talkative doorman at the hotel quickly put me to shame over my ignorance of some of our wartime figures.

A stroll around town at dusk revealed that there was much more in the shops, and I even found a small night club, which was unthinkable in Moscow. It functioned behind an iron gate which was locked every time a customer went through. Yet the Soviet-style administration of the city was evident from the overall greyness and the fact that large areas of cobbled roadway had been raised for long-term repair, making the streets impassable for vehicles. This would hardly have been tolerated in a western capital. My fears about surveillance were in some measure confirmed. As I returned to the hotel from the night club, I detected a shadowy figure lurking in the street behind me. Yes, just as in Moscow, I was being followed, though I had no means of knowing whether it was on a chance basis, or because the local security services were aware of my presence. The feeling of unease was all too familiar: would they try something on?

Back at the hotel I settled down by the light of a dim reading lamp to deal with the main object of my visit. I composed a long, 'brass tacks' letter to Aleksei, setting out the propaganda advantages of releasing Mila – and offering a 'substantial' sum of money if they would do so. I pointed out that there had already been a few cases of East Germans East Germans, Poles and Romanians purchasing their freedom on an unofficial, but legal basis. Although I had little money myself, benefactors could be found. The British government offered major tax concessions to people who gave money for charitable causes. The sum could go towards some worthy cause in Russia.

"Can we find a common language on this basis?" I wrote. "It would solve the problem, help Russia, and help my fiance, who has done nothing wrong. A good starting point would be a letter from myself to the Russian ambassador in London, though I can be reached by letter in Oxford.... We are about the same age, Aleksei, and can talk seriously and honestly. Please help!"

But even as I pondered my own words I realised that they lacked a key proposal, namely, an offer of full collaboration. That was out of the question – and would probably not have been accepted, anyway. The KGB had a good idea where my true allegiance lay.

It was important to dispatch the letter through one of the Soviet satellite states, so that both Aleksei and I could be sure that it was truly confidential. If it came to the notice of MI5 or MI6, they might decide to scupper my initiative. Hence the journey to Prague. I posted the letter in a registered envelope next morning, and went straight to the Czech airlines office to get a ticket to London.

★

My next attempt to get things moving came at the end of the month, shortly before I was due to leave for Nottingham. Some British newspapers carried reports that the Soviet authorities had again raised the question of exchanging Gerald Brooke for the Krogers. But now there was a new twist to the story. The man representing the Soviet side was a certain Herr Wolfgang Vogel, the East Berlin lawyer who had handled the exchange of the American U-2 pilot Gary Powers for the veteran Russian spy Rudolph Abel in 1962. He also, it was said, arranged the 'purchase' of East German citizens by relatives in the West. "Last night," declared *The Sun* on the 22nd September, 1965

> it was revealed that he [Vogel] slipped into Britain within the last month to try and open the way for an exchange of the Soviet agents Peter and Helen Kroger for two Britons jailed behind the Iron Curtain. The British Government is bitterly rejecting all suggestions of a swap, now or in the future. They consider that both Gerald Brooke, jailed in Moscow for subversion, and Arthur Wilbraham, awaiting trial in Berlin for 'violating East German law' are both being held to ransom.
>
> But this reaction has not apparently deterred Herr Vogel.... On Monday night... his green and cream Opel had been waved through Checkpoint Charlie [at the Berlin Wall] without the usual close scrutiny of papers.... Yesterday he was back again for a meeting with Mr. Christopher Lush, a Foreign Office man who is the top legal adviser at the British Headquarters in West Berlin. The rendezvous was in lawyer Juergen Stange's plush office suite at no. 39, Schluter Street. Later Herr Stange said the talks had been about Arthur Wilbraham. He said: "I can't say too much about negotiations. Indiscretion would cause damage." British security chiefs are now adamantly opposed to any swap.

It never occurred to me that anything could be done through specifically legal channels, using men of law, but the new avenue had to be explored, and quickly. On the 26th of September I was on a train bound for Berlin. I reached the beleaguered city after a very cold night's journey across East Germany – for some reason the heating was switched off. Like most visitors, I suppose, I was saddened by glimpses of watch towers and barbed wire from the train window.

I put up, as usual, at the cheapest hotel I could find, which happened to be the Pension Alcron in Lietzenburgerstrasse. When I asked the hefty German matron who ran it about crossing into the Eastern Sector, she looked at me with suspicion. What could this lone Britisher be up to? Strange things happened in the city. Anyway, with the help of Carola Stern I contacted Herr Stange by telephone, and made an appointment to see him. He asked me to write a detailed account of the case and bring it along. I had a day free before the meeting, and used it to enter the Soviet-controlled part of the city. The contrast with West Berlin was striking – there were still many ruins, and everything seemed grey and tense. I was glad to get back to my Pension. I also managed to fit in a visit to West Berlin's famous Zoo and relaxed a little, watching the monkeys.

The next morning, a little before the appointed hour, I made my way to Herr Stange's office. It was indeed opulent, but the owner, a youngish man, was very relaxed and welcoming. There was no problem about my identity or the seriousness of my intent, because of Carola's introduction, but I took a sheaf of newspaper cuttings with me, anyway. The outline of events which I had typed for him made no secret of KGB involvement. Probably he was not too surprised, given his association with Vogel.

"I can certainly arrange a meeting with Herr Vogel," he said, after he had looked through the papers. "He comes to West Berlin sometimes. Perhaps tomorrow evening, when the working day has ended. I usually meet him in a small place called the Baronen Bar, before he returns to the Eastern sector." Herr Stange gave me an address. "Can you be there?"

★

I got to the bar just as dusk was falling. It was a small, elegant establishment, frequented, it seemed, by professional businessmen. I was very struck by the appearance of the barman, a tall imposing fellow with impossibly large shirtcuffs and extravagant links. I imagined that they were designed to inveigle customers into giving him larger tips. Herr Stange was there, and we had not been seated very long before Herr Vogel appeared. He was a round-faced, bespectacled man with an agreeable manner, and was carrying a medium-sized suitcase. Herr Stange introduced me, and we quickly launched into our discussion. It was not very easy, because I only had a reading knowledge of German, while Herr Vogel had no English. His grasp of foreign tongues, he said, was limited to Latin and Greek, which he had learnt at school. So Herr Stange helped.

Vogel made some of the usual generalisations about improving relations, but naturally uttered not a word of criticism with regard to Russia. As might have been expected, he was very positive about exchanges of living souls, and quite sympathetic towards Mila and me. He said perhaps the Russians would let Mila, or Mila and some other person, go in exchange for one of the Krogers. My first thought was that this was (to say the least) unlikely, but on the other hand Vogel was experienced in these matters, and his opinion could not be ignored. Anyway, he said he would look into it, and let me know. It was all very up-beat.

We finished our drinks, and Herr Vogel declared that he would have to be off. His car was standing outside. I jumped up.

"Let me help you with your suitcase," I said, but when I grasped the handle I found it was so heavy that I could hardly lift it. "What on earth has he got in here?" I thought, but said nothing. I managed, with great effort, to hoist it into the boot, and he drove off in an easterly direction. The mystery of the weighty contents was never solved.

The next thing to do was to telephone Christopher Lush, the local representative of the Foreign Office, and tell him about the meeting, so that any developments could be given official status. Lush said he would see me next day. I also sent a letter to the Foreign Office in London asking for an appointment on my return.

I met Lush at the Western Allies' Headquarters. He seemed to be a reasonably pleasant person, but very much an F.O. official, too. I told him what had transpired, and expressed my hope for some sort of exchange. Perhaps, I said, he could take it up with London quickly, so that he could meet Vogel while I was still in Berlin? My presence might be needed.

Lush replied that he would have to discuss it with his colleagues: but next day, over the phone, he was quite dismissive. I set down what he told me in my letter of the 1st October to Herr Stange. "I cannot refrain," I wrote, "from reproducing here some of the remarks which [Lush] made, but please treat them in confidence. 'This problem [he said] does not concern Berlin.... We don't want to become a channel for this sort of thing ... we don't want everyone coming here'." When I spoke to Lush a little later I found that he had not sent a telegram to London on my behalf: instead he suggested I got into touch with the Foreign Office myself.

I was well used to disappointing responses from Foreign Office personnel, but even so this turn of events upset me. Was there really no one in that organisation who understood? I returned to England hoping for some sort of a breakthrough, with Vogel's help; but the weeks went by, and nothing happened. Perhaps Vogel, for his part, was waiting for an initiative from the Foreign Office. In December I wrote to Stange asking him to name his fee, but he generously ignored my letter.

★

Mila and I were constantly thinking of ways to meet, although nothing could be said over the telephone, and little written. Normally a Soviet citizen who had enough money could join a tour to one of the People's Democracies. This course of action would at least have allowed us to have a few days together. But alas, it was not practicable: any application for travel abroad had to be backed by a 'clear' personal recommendation from the applicant's place of employment, and Mila could not possibly get one. Everybody at the library knew she wanted to marry a foreigner, and her superiors would not dare write anything positive, knowing it was destined for perusal by the KGB. Such an application, moreover, might even lead to her dismissal as a potential trouble-maker.

Given the failure on all fronts, it was, I suppose, inevitable that I should have started to consider illegal means of getting Mila out of Russia. Bribery was an obvious route: was there any Soviet official who could, at this stage, be quietly bent? It had not been possible when I was in Moscow, but now that I was in London.... A nice new car for a responsible KGB officer?... Alas, the KGB people who had dealt with me directly would never go down that path, and I had no idea who else could be approached. And if my marriage was being tied in with the Gerald Brooke case, bribery would be impossible, anyway. Vogel's silence also suggested that he had not been able to shift anything in that sphere.

Another way would be for Mila to make a so-called 'fictitious marriage', registering a union of convenience with, perhaps, some innocuous African who could take her abroad. Fictitious marriage was used in Russia for all sorts of things, particularly the protection of rights to living space. Unfortunately, in our case, it was as much out of the question as a trip to the People's Democracies or bribery. Not only was the idea itself distasteful to both of us, but it would inevitably have involved Mila going back to the Palace of Weddings, and more KGB intervention. Also, the details, if publicised, would cast an unpleasant shadow over our whole campaign.

Yet another idea came to me one day as I happened to flick through my passport. What about forging one for her? I had no knowledge of printing, but it seemed to me, on looking though the heavily-stamped pages, that some minor modification of the personal details was entirely possible. All I had to do was get a legally issued passport from someone who did not need it, and alter it. The original name could, of course, be left in.

Photographs of Mila presented no difficulty, and reproducing the official FCO stamp which covered part of the bearer's photograph need not be much of a problem, either. The stamp was a simple oval which contained the words FOREIGN OFFICE – LONDON – and a date. Several firms made desk-top presses, and any block could be fitted to them. Obviously, I could not order a replica of a Foreign Office stamp as it was, but it would be easy to order two or three innocuously worded blocks, with FOREIGN, OFFICE, LONDON, and the date on them. Having got the various blocks together I would then only need to file off unneeded words, and position the modified blocks over the passport photograph, as required.

A more tricky operation would be to alter the year of birth, but I reckoned that with a little practice I could do it. The other task involved reproducing the Soviet entry-exit visa stamp and the official emblem of the Soviet Embassy. For this I would only need to send in photocopies to a block-maker who did not know Russian. Getting passports proved to be easy. I asked Mrs. Dorothy Morris, the mother of an old friend, who never intended to go abroad, to apply for one, and Mrs. Pat Utechin, my friend Sergei's wife and a person of impressive probity, to tell the Passport Office that she had lost hers. Both ladies promptly broke the law on my behalf, and I ended up with two blue booklets.

It was only after I had spent several days enthusing over the scheme that I realised how impracticable it was. Firstly, a one-way Moscow-London air ticket would have to be purchased from Aeroflot in Moscow, and this would require, no doubt, some kind of official authorisation. Secondly, there was my ignorance of behind-the-scenes practice at Soviet passport control points. Did they have prior notice of the visas which had been issued? If so, they would immediately spot an unnotified document. Thirdly, I was not sure that Mila was capable of taking the terrible risk, for if she were caught the penalty would be long years of imprisonment. So I abandoned the idea.

My other machination took up more time and effort. One day I lighted upon a report about an unnamed Russian who, during the Second World War, had decided to walk to China. The account was somewhat garbled, but the gist was that he had walked and walked until finally he came to a non-Russian village. To his surprise, it was inhabited not by Chinese but by a darker, Indian-like people: he had misjudged the direction and ended up in Afghanistan. What interested me, though, was the fact that he had actually crossed the Afghan frontier without noticing it. Apparently guards were then few and far between. This prompted me to examine a few maps of the southern borders of the USSR. The distances in the south were too great, but could not something be done elsewhere?

My thoughts were propelled a little further in December, 1965, by a newspaper report about a young Russian called Vladimir Kirsanov who had actually managed to get over the Russian-Finnish frontier, traverse Finland, and obtain political asylum in Sweden. He could not stop in Finland because the authorities there would have repatriated him under the terms of some bilateral treaty.

I thought this should be explored, and with the help of Peter Reddaway, who was now teaching in London, I managed to locate Kirsanov. He was, it appeared, staying at the house of a certain Frau Rally in Frankfurt-am-Main, but was understandably sensitive about contact with people he did not know. Peter prepared the ground, and I wrote to Kirsanov, ostensibly to ask whether he would be prepared to discuss student affairs in Russia. He replied in the same vein, and said he would be happy to meet me.

At the end of March, 1966 I went to Frankfurt especially to see him, this time by sea and train. I have only a dim memory of our meeting, but I think we had nothing more than a cup of coffee in a bustling coffee-house. Vladimir was his mid twenties, well-built and outgoing, indeed, one of the most pleasant Russians I ever met. I explained my problems on a confidential basis – it seemed highly unlikely that he was a Soviet agent, and he did not have Mila's name, anyway. But after listening to his story for a very few minutes I realised that illegal frontier crossing was not only highly dangerous (as I had presumed) but quite out of the question for Mila.

For him it had involved a trek of several days through the Soviet frontier zone with its forests, streams and bogs. When he got close to the frontier he was faced by two ten-foot fences. He was just able to crawl under one, and swing over the second after climbing a pine tree. There were dogs, soldiers, near-misses. I had always thought areas between fences were heavily mined, but that was evidently not so, at least where he crossed. Even so, it all required considerable strength, fortitude – and good luck. Mila had no experience of surviving in forests, and was partially disabled, whereas Kirsanov had done a great deal of trekking and camping.

Having gone to such trouble to meet him, I wrote a secret letter to Mila telling her about it, while realising that this was no solution for us, either. But what was I to do next?

Six. Back to the USSR

In the autumn of 1965 I loaded my chattels into my clapped-out Ford and headed into the Midlands, or 'North' as I called it. Leaving St. Antony's was as much of a wrench as I expected. I had spent five years of my life there, and my belief in the intellectual superiority of Oxford and Cambridge was unshakable. But in my heart I knew I did not fit in at Oxford too well, either: since I had vastly irritated the Warden, there was no question of continued association with the Senior Common Room, and my battle with the Soviet authorities almost precluded new research. My reluctance to speak at seminars (stemming, I suspect, from cultural deprivation in the Hafod) did not help. Even so, it irked me to think that a few intellectual dead logs would still be floating around the college after I had gone, awaiting the chance of permanent posts. Despite his brilliance, the Warden sometimes seemed unable to distinguish between academic worth and academic mannerism.

My destination was not exactly Nottingham, because tutor's accommodation was not available at the university (that came later). I had taken a small flat in the little town of Long Eaton, a twenty-minute drive to the south. No doubt Long Eaton had its happy residents, and wonderful meat pies were certainly baked in the locality: but it turned out to be one of the dreariest places I ever lived in. I was no drinker, and did not frequent pubs, so there was little by way of recreation. The most exciting spot of an evening was the local laundermat, where a bright light burned until late, and you could watch people's garments swirling wildly behind glass portholes. Characteristically, the sole contraceptive shop announced its closure a month in advance, so as to give the slower-witted customers time to stock up.

I bought little in the way of furniture, because I did not intend to keep the flat for long. My main problem was not upholstery, but electronics: how to get a telephone, so that I could ring Moscow. This was no easy matter, because Long Eaton, it turned out, was full of people desperate for telephone contact with the outside world. Eventually I got through to the local telephone manager, and explained my unusual situation.

"Sorry, I just can't help," he said. "There's a long queue. It will take several weeks."

"I can see the problem," I replied. "if you have a lot of people waiting already. I won't be here very long, either. There's nothing more I can put on the table. Of course, I know Sir Frank Soskice, the Home Secretary, but I would be very reluctant to write to Sir Frank over such a small personal matter."

"Really!" said the manager, "sorry I can't be of more help."

Sure enough, but a few days later, technicians came to install an instrument, and the boredom was relieved, at least occasionally, by sound of Mila's voice.

★

Happily, lecturing at Nottingham turned out to be less fearsome than I thought, so there was no problem on that front. I still spent most of my free time looking for people who could help, and writing letters. Then, all of a sudden, a correspondent from the *Guardian* contacted me to say there had been movement in Moscow: and next day, on the 25th January, 1966, a startling news item appeared in its columns.

'Russian May Come to UK to Marry' ran the heading. "Reports from Moscow last night indicated that Ludmilla Bibikova, a librarian aged 30, had been given permission to come to England to marry her fiancé, Mr. Mervyn Matthews.... Mr. Matthews said he was surprised to hear the news, but was very pleased." *The Daily Sketch* ran a similar piece on the 27th, with Mila's picture.

Other papers contacted me by telephone to find out more, but I could tell them nothing. There was a letter of congratulation from Mr. Cumber. Of course I was delighted – but profoundly puzzled as well. Why had not Mila contacted me urgently with the good news from Moscow? I wrote to my mother to advise caution. Surely the problem had not disappeared overnight? When I finally managed to get through to Mila, a day or so later, I found she had heard nothing. The English correspondent must have made his own enquiry at the Ministry of Foreign Affairs, and been given totally inaccurate information. But clearly he was only trying to help.

When it had all blown over, with no perceptible change in the situation, I went down to the Soviet Consulate in London to try and find out what had really happened. Was it simply an error, or did it betoken some impending solution? The Consul, Stanislav Roshchin, had nothing to lose by talking to me, and he was slightly helpful. He suggested that I complain personally to the editors involved, and that Mila send a letter to the Ministry of Foreign Affairs, confirming that she was not responsible for a wild rumour.

A month later another gleam of light appeared, very faint but at least indicative that positive things could happen. On the 27th February the newspaper *Pravda* – the most authoritative organ in the country – published a large article on the Kharkov Tractor Works, which had been providing machinery for Soviet agricultural development since the thirties. That was where Mila's father had worked before moving on to a party secretaryship in Chernigov. And now, on the *Pravda* page, his efforts were lauded.

> "I spent the day with the worker Chernoivanenko," wrote the correspondent. "We talked about what is going on in the factory, but our thoughts kept on going back to the thirties. We recalled people who worked in the Works, what they were like.... Bibikov, the party agitator and mass organiser, a cheerful sincere comrade who could, not merely by order, but by the strength of his passionate conviction, rouse young people to overcome difficulties by storm – glaze a roof in record time, tar [!] a floor, set up machinery. ('And they weren't just ordinary people,' said Chernoivanenko in a hoarse, restrained voice, 'they were giants.'). Chernoivanenko himself came to the help build the factory in 1931, when he was seventeen"

Boris Bibikov had been 'rehabilitated' about ten years earlier. I found the mention of him in *Pravda* in 1966 intriguing, and thought it might be taken as a sign of flexibility somewhere or other. The writer of the article must have been instructed to include him, and the reference to 'hoarseness' suggested clearly to the Soviet reader that his fate had been tragic. The correspondent could scarcely have known about Bibikov's daughter's plight, and the matter was too marginal to affect us directly. But it was in its way ironic, and could add weight to our appeals for help.

★

I did not have to wait more than a few weeks for the next bolt from the blue, though it was of quite a different order. On the 10th May I spent rather a busy day in London, with a fruitless visit to the Soviet Consulate. In the early evening, my tasks completed, I went to an Indian restaurant, had a curry, and then proceeded to King's Cross Station. The trains to Nottingham were not all that frequent, and I found that I had half an hour to spare. I went into the cafeteria, which was rather crowded, took a tray and queued up at the counter to get tea and a cake. Then, unaccountably, I felt rather strange:

reality seemed to be receding and returning in waves; there was no pain, except a strange headache. My vision seemed to falter. Then I blacked out.

The next thing I remember was a rough, cream-painted brick wall, voices, and clattering noises. As I regained consciousness I found I was lying, fully clothed, on a stretcher. I turned my head and perceived a hospital environment, with nurses and doctors. I was in an emergency ward, no doubt. My scalp was sore, and on touching it I felt a large lump. I had evidently struck my head, perhaps I had fallen in the cafeteria? A moment later a young doctor was leaning over me.

"Where am I?" I asked.

"University College Hospital Casualty Department," he replied. "You had a black-out."

I was silent for a moment, my thoughts slow and leaden.

"At King's Cross, I suppose."

"Yes," said the doctor. "You've been unconscious for some time." I raised my hand and looked at my watch. About an hour had gone by since I was in the cafeteria.

"I've got a lump on my head," I said. "Perhaps that's got something to do with it."

The doctor smiled with embarrassment, and examined it. The medical staff had not checked, and it was a possible cause of my lengthy loss of consciousness. But not of the incident itself.

"It must have been some sort of fit," he continued. "Perhaps you hit your head as you fell. We'll have to have some X-rays, and we'll keep you in overnight. Have you had any epileptic episodes before?"

"No," I said. "Never."

I was discharged next morning, and returned to Nottingham feeling distinctly the worse for wear. On the 16th May I had further tests at a local hospital, but they were inconclusive. I was seen by a consultant from East Europe who may have been slightly mad.

"Do you have any epilepsy in the family?" he asked nervously.

"Not to my knowledge."

"Any history of migraines?"

"Yes," I said. "I had a few nasty ones when I was in my teens, with vomiting."

"Your electroencephalogram does not show epilepsy," he said. "But that does not mean very much. You certainly had a fit. It could happen again. I can't say more at present."

With all the problems on my plate, that was the last thing I wanted to hear, and I confess I had to hold back a tear. But perhaps it would not be too bad: epilepsy, if I had it, need not necessarily impede me in my battle. What had brought it on? Was it caused by the tensions of my daily fight with Soviet intransigence? I rushed to the university library and looked it up in a couple of medical encyclopedias. Fortunately, it seemed, epilepsy tended to recede with age. I decided that only a strongly optimistic outlook could keep me going. And from that day on, regardless of the news from Russia, I always made a point of going into the classroom with a cheery smile on my face.

★

In the summer of 1966 I finished work at Nottingham and accepted a post at Battersea, the well-known Polytechnic, having just obtained its charter as the University of Surrey. There were other possibilities of employment, but I chose this one because it was located in London (our department functioned in a disused warehouse in Clapham), and because I liked the configuration of the courses. The university would only be moving as far as Guildford, when the new buildings were ready, and I could easily commute there from London. My struggle with the Soviet authorities made it imperative for me to be near the Soviet Consulate, the Foreign Office, and Fleet Street. I found a mortgage and bought a small, two-roomed flat in Belgrave Road, Pimlico, where, as I hoped, Mila would one day set foot.

Some two years had passed since my expulsion from Russia, and there was no progress whatever. From time to time I thought about ways of getting back to Russia, albeit for a few days, to see Mila again. Nottingham is not the best place in the world for travel information, but in London I discovered that it might be possible to cross the Soviet frontier – the Baltic shore, at least – without a visa.

Obviously, the matter had to be looked into with great care. I wrote to my former secretary Fay, who was now living in Helsinki with her American husband. They made one or two enquiries on my behalf, but could not elucidate the crucial question of the documents needed for entering the Baltic ports.

I went to the Finnish Tourist Office in Haymarket. They told me that a Helsinki tourist agency called Kaleva indeed ran one-day tours to the Estonian capital Tallinn, and no visas were needed. The facility was intended primarily for Finnish citizens, as Russia regarded Finland as a 'friendly' state. There were also, apparently, short, visaless trips to Leningrad. I had to make several visits to the office to extract all the information required, and by the time I finished the hapless girl I dealt with guessed that something fishy was going on. She got thoroughly alarmed and began disappearing whenever she saw me coming through the glass doors. But no matter, she had told me enough. Had I found a way into the Soviet Union?

Presumably, Mila could get to Tallinn easily enough during her summer holiday. But since neither of us had ever been there, the first thing to do was find a precise spot where we could meet. I regarded this as a purely academic problem: writing a thesis on Soviet employment had its boring moments, but it engendered useful research skills. An afternoon at the British Museum sufficed: I quickly located a large, 1892 map of Reval (as the town was then called) and a pre-war German guide book. After some thought I decided that the Oleviste Kirik (St. Olav's Church) would be the best place, as it had a tall, easily recognisable spire, and was not too far from the harbour.

I included a series of covert instructions, little by little, in letters I wrote to Mila at the beginning of August. Would she be taking a holiday in the Baltic? How nice Tallinn was said to be... on the 26th and 29th of August I might well have to be in Scandinavia for medical reasons... had she heard of St. Olav's Church? She understood, of course, and indicated that she could be there. I hoped we could meet on one of the two days I mentioned. I could hardly wait.

★

Despite the apparent legality of my plan I had no doubt it could get me into trouble – surely any foreign vessel entering a Soviet port would be under some sort of KGB surveillance? So, on 22 August, before setting off from London I wrote a letter addressed to the Foreign Office and and sent it to my friend Boris Thomson, with a covering note. It was designed to explain the situation if I did not return.

> Herewith the letter I have written for the fools in the Foreign Office. My main hope at the moment is that it will not have to be dispatched. I shall be away for about a fortnight (from tomorrow) but I cannot give you many details of my whereabouts, because I have no fixed programme. I shall get into touch with you by the middle of September: if I do not do so, or there is a hell of a lot of fuss and it is clear that something has gone wrong (which Heaven forbid), then please send the enclosed letter off.
>
> I shall try and go over to Tallinn on the ferry from Helsinki next Saturday (27th August) or Sunday, and also the weekend after. I am not sure whether I will try the other method which I mentioned to you, or not.
>
> Please note (in case there is any fuss) that I shall not have in my possession a single paper which might be construed as in any way hostile to the USSR.... I am most grateful for your help.

The letter I enclosed for Mr. Stewart, the Foreign Secretary, dated the 6th August, 1966 was forthright.

> At the end of the month I am going to make one or two attempts to return to the USSR, in order to see my fiancée. I shall almost certainly try to go over to Tallinn and see her there (it appears that this is possible on day trips run from Helsinki, no visa being required) and I may, in addition, try to procure a Soviet visa in Denmark by submitting a new passport to the Soviet Embassy in Copenhagen and making certain inaccurate statement on the application forms.
>
> There is some chance that I will end up in a Soviet prison.... I wish to make it clear that if I am seized by the Soviets I do not wish to have any assistance from any Foreign Office employees in the USSR, and I must tell you categorically that none of your people are to make any attempt to contact my fiancée. I hope that statement leaves no uncertainties in your mind.

And after some detailed references to Foreign Office sin and failure, as I perceived them, I concluded grandly: "I regret having had any dealing with your office whatever, and want no more."

I went to the Soviet Consulate on the morning of the 24th August, which was also the day of my departure, to tell them (quite truthfully) that Mila had just sent me a private, notarized invitation to come to Moscow, and to enquire how I should handle it. I was slightly gratified to be received by the Consul himself. Comrade Roshchin was, of course, very cautious, but said I could make another application for a visa at the Consulate, enclosing Mila's letter. The application required a detailed 'life history', Soviet style, and it took a couple of hours to complete: but I finished it and got it back to the Consulate before they closed, telling them (in case there was a rapid response) that I would be 'abroad' for about two weeks. The application was a mere formality – but the fact that it was accepted raised another faint hope.

★

My journey to Helsinki was circuitous for economic reasons – a cheap night flight to Copenhagen, passage by boat to Stockholm, with an overnight stop there, and then again by boat to Helsinki. By now I had abandoned the thoughts of trying for a visa in Denmark, as referred to indirectly in my letter to Boris.

On the last lap of the journey I was astonished to run into a pleasant young couple I had known in Oxford. They were both very religious, and had been attempting to get nearer to God by studying the Bible in Hebrew and Greek, the texts had been lying open on their kitchen table when I visited them. We were very happy to meet up in the middle of the Baltic, though they refused to join me at the ship's smorgasbord. "I don't think we should have any of that, darling, do you?" They gently dissuaded one another. "It's too greasy. It'll upset your tummy."

Regardless of their culinary prejudices, I was glad to have their company on my lonely journey. "We're on our way to Leningrad," they said, "the agency in London couldn't reserve accommodation for us, so we'll join a Finnish group and go in from Helsinki." They were rather worried about the absence of bath and wash-basin plugs in Russia, and wondered how on earth they were going to manage. I wish, I thought, my worries were of the same order: but I listened to their travel plans with interest, while remaining silent about my own. When we got to Helsinki we went our separate ways. I had little money, as usual, and Scandinavia was fearfully expensive. So it was a question of lining up at the tourist accommodation bureau and taking a cheap room in the suburbs.

★

Next morning I went to the Kaleva Travel Agency in Snellmaninkatu to try my luck. I found a small nondescript office, where the staff had no interest, as far as I could see, in anything except in selling tickets. It was Thursday and I ordered one for the day-trip to Tallinn on Saturday.

I had a day to spare, and I used it to look around Helsinki. I had spent a few hours there on my way to take up my post at the Embassy back in 1958. I took the ferry to a fort on one of the off-shore islands, and wandered among the old cannon, mostly Russian. I sat down on a parapet and wrote Mila a letter. During the trip I continued to write to her daily, though I mentioned nothing of my plans, lest they come to the notice of the censor. I asked her to send letters to me poste restante in Stockholm and Helsinki, where I would pick them up at my convenience. "More interesting than the artifacts here are the natural surroundings," I wrote. "I just can't find words to describe the local beauty. The open sea with great bays and islands, smiling in the sun, and lovely white yachts sailing in the calm sea. The island I'm on now, incidentally, is called Seaborg."

Later in the day I returned to the agency with some trepidation: would they really issue a ticket to a non-Finnish passport holder? I need not have worried. A few moments later I emerged with the valued prize in my pocket: a little pink voucher for a one-day tour to Tallinn on the motor ship *Vanemuine*, and no questions asked. I was told only that I should take my passport with me, which was natural enough. The ship would be leaving at ten a.m., and passengers were to be at the Southern Harbour an hour before.

I was on board well before she sailed. The weather was clear and cool, with some puffs of cloud, a typical Scandinavian day. The sea was calm, so there was no danger of sea sickness – or cancellation of the voyage. As the ship moved out into the Gulf of Finland I watched the funnel rock slowly to and fro against the sky. Two hours to cross to Soviet waters. What would the day bring?

We had not been at sea for very long before my internal alarm bells were pealing. A dark-suited and rather ominous Russian was going around collecting everyone's passports. Although no visa was needed, personal documents evidently had to be checked – and before landing. The man was evidently a KGB frontier guard in plain clothes. When I handed him my British passport, he gave me a strange sort of look, which evoked the all-too familiar feeling of unease. He could not do anything in international waters, I thought: but would he stop me getting off the ship in Tallinn? It was to be another cliff-hanger.

There were not many people on board, perhaps because Tallinn had no great appeal for Finns. Eventually the low-lying Estonian coastline hove into sight and we were sailing up a broad estuary, in which a few old cargo ships were moored. Men were fishing from small wooden boats, they all looked poor, rather as in Russia. Passengers could move about the ship freely, so I went up to that part of the bridge which was open, and gazed at the spires of Tallinn as we approached. Spires are not part of traditional Russian architecture, and the old town, as I had read, was fairly Germanic in character, though Peter the Great had done some building there.

When we finally docked everything on the quayside seemed to be relaxed, with only a couple of frontier guards standing by nonchalantly. But what about the passports and landing procedure? The Russian reappeared with a box of passports, and started handing them out. As the owners' names, all Finnish or Swedish, were called, I got increasingly nervous. Would my mine be withheld, and with it the right to land? In the event, my name was the very last on the list: but my passport was indeed returned to me, and without comment.

The gangway went down and I was one of the first passengers off. Of course, I was in anything but holiday mood. Would the KGB know about my arrival, despite all my precautions? And Mila? Would she be there? I had hardly stepped ashore when a pleasant surprise awaited me. Someone called my name, though it was not Mila's voice. I looked around, and to my astonishment saw Nadya, whom I had last met beside the samovar at the Vasin dacha. She was radiant.

"Mervusya, it's you. How wonderful! But such good luck, too."

"Good luck?" I said, thinking about all my carefully-laid plans.

"Yes," said Nadya, "we were expecting you tomorrow! We only came down to the docks by chance, to do a trial run. Thank heavens you were standing at the front of the ship, otherwise we would have missed you. When we saw you we could hardly believe our eyes."

I swallowed hard.

"There must have been a misunderstanding in the letters, it wasn't easy. Where's Mila?"

"She's gone off to wait for you at the Oleviste Kirik, just in case I couldn't get you here. Or in case the KGB tried something on. Everything seems OK, though, no operatives. Come on, I'll take you there."

We made our way past the Customs House towards the bastion of the old town: as far as I could see there were indeed no goons. Then a silly event occurred, one which stuck in my memory. As we drew near St. Olav's I saw a woman waiting nearby, her face partly muffled in a kerchief. "Mila!" I called, only to perceive, to my intense embarrassment, that it was someone else.

"There she is, over there," said Nadya, pointing to a small, familiar figure at the church entrance. I cannot describe my emotions at that moment. It was clear that two years of separation had changed nothing, the regular contact by letter and telephone had kept us together. I found the same kind eyes, sympathy, common concerns. We knew we had only a few hours together, as the ship was leaving at six o'clock. Nadya said she would keep an eye on us from a distance, warn us if she thought there was any KGB surveillance, and buy some Russian newspapers for me, as I requested.

Mila and I spent most of the time wandering through the old medieval streets, mostly quite shabby and run-down, though we had no time for sight-seeing. Arm in arm, we discussed what was to be done next. I told her about the two-day trips from Helsinki to Leningrad, and we arranged to meet there, if possible. I would telephone in advance from Helsinki to confirm it. Mila had a Russian friend in Tallinn who was married to an Estonian seaman, and we called in to see her for a quick glass of tea. As for the girls' stay in Tallinn, it was not, they said, very congenial, because the Estonians did not like Russians, and had no way of knowing whether they were sympathetic to the Estonian cause.

The day advanced. We had already turned our steps slowly back towards the port, when suddenly we heard the blare of the ship's hooter. I looked at my watch: it was much later than we thought.

"Hurry," cried Mila, thoroughly alarmed, "the ship's leaving! You'll be left here without a visa!"

We broke into a run, Mila limping heavily beside me. In a few minutes we had passed the bastion and reached the open area around the harbour. The ship was about to cast off, but the gangway, thank heavens, was still down. There was just enough time for a quick hug. I boarded the ship, the engine-room bells rang, and the mooring ropes were cast off. The *Vanemuine* edged out into the fairway. Nadya had by now reappeared and stood with Mila. I waved at the two women as they wept on the quayside. The parting had been dreadfully rushed, but perhaps it was better that way: separation was inevitable, anyway. It was a moment of mixed feelings, unutterably sad, yet hopeful.

"Well," I thought, "we did meet, after all, and were together for a few short hours. So has there at last been a little progress, after two years' struggle? Can we meet again in Leningrad, or somewhere else? Has Mother Russia opened her creaking gates enough for me to squeeze through? Let's see what happens next."

Dusk was falling, and the motion of the ship became ever more perceptible as she moved into deeper water.

★

I had several days to fill in before venturing to Leningrad. Accommodation was an on-going problem. I had started off with a sympathetic Swedish landlady, but lost the room when it was booked by someone else. After that I moved from one cheap hotel to another, and ate snacks in my room to avoid the breath-taking restaurant prices. I went for walks on the Helsinki islands, tried to enjoy the sunshine, and spent some time in the University Library, which possessed great charm. It was a pre-revolutionary establishment which had received a copy of every book published in tsarist Russia, so there were interesting things to read.

But Helsinki was not a very exciting place for a lone foreigner, and its initial charm soon faded. I had not tried to contact Fay, because I thought my travel plans might cause some embarrassment, given that her husband worked in an embassy. I preferred to keep them secret, anyway. "Thank God," I wrote to Mila on the 3rd September, "that my stay in Helsinki is coming to an end. The boredom is getting unbearable. I have so much on my mind – our struggle, my career in England – that I can hardly work." I found a restaurant called the Marienbar, where I had dined on my way to Russia in 1958, and I treated myself to a good steak.

Travel to Leningrad was handled by the Lomamatka Tourist Bureau on Yrjonkatu. My inquiries there quickly revealed that I could in all probability follow in the footsteps of my religious friends. The tour offered by the bureau included two nights at sea, going and coming back, plus two days and one night in Leningrad, sleeping aboard ship. No, I was told, no visa was needed. I might be able to spend two days with Mila in Peter the Great's capital, hopefully unnoticed by the KGB. I presumed that I would be joining a group of Finns on what was effectively a boozing trip – many went only for the cheap vodka.

At 6.00pm on the evening of Sunday, 4th September, I stepped aboard a Finnish passenger ship called the *Kastelholm*, moored in Helsinki harbour. She was a small, old-fashioned vessel with a reciprocating steam engine that clicked like a sewing machine and was audible on all decks. I had developed a great love of steam engines during the war, when I was evacuated to Gwendraeth and I spent a lot of time in the engine houses of the local collieries. There was more motion than on the *Vanemuine*, but not enough to trouble me. The party was led by a nice, middle-aged, and completely sober Finn who collected our passports himself. This suggested that there was no Soviet official on board – which was also a little reassuring.

Next morning, when I went up on deck, we were already chugging our way down the Neva river towards Leningrad docks. The morning was quiet, except for the sound of the engine and the ship's wash. The sky was clear, and the spire of the petrine Admiralty building was just visible in the far distance. St. Petersburg had been Peter the Great's 'window on Europe' and I was climbing through it. After breakfast on board the tour leader returned all of our passports without any hitch. So by the time the ship pulled into a jetty, and the mooring ropes were out, I was sure that I would at least step onto Soviet soil. If anyone on the *Kastelholm* had wanted to stop me, he would have done so already.

On this occasion the passengers surrendered their passports to a smiling and rather embarrassed young soldier at the foot of the gangway. The documents were kept in an open box, to be returned when people went back on board. Much as in Tallinn, it was a typical dockland scene, with warehouses and lorries. There was no customs control, and we were told that we would have to make our own way to the centre of town. Again it all seemed very relaxed: but the absence of formalities was no guarantee of peace and quiet over the whole visit.

Yes, Mila had come, and was waiting for me beside one of the vehicles. There were no warm embraces in public. As she told me later, she had made her way to the docks as unobtrusively as possible, fearing that the KGB might be watching her: perhaps they wanted to catch me on Soviet soil. Also, on this occasion she was alone, with no one to help. We slipped off quietly together, careful not to attract the attention of other passengers, or less friendly eyes.

For the better part of two days we wandered around the elegant, if slightly faded, squares and streets of Peter the Great's capital – there was not much else to do. Again we were lucky with the weather – no rain. The inhabitants of Leningrad have always been proud of their monumental marsh-built city, but I always found it rather provincial, compared to Moscow, with fewer shops and restaurants. Mila had an uncle (Sasha's brother) there, but she thought it better not to visit him. It would have taken up valuable time, and his family would have been wondered why she had come. They would have been frightened to know she was meeting a foreigner. We spent some time at the famous Russian Museum, and for a few worrying moments lost one another by wandering into different halls. Fortunately, the incident was quickly over. We could not face the splendours of the Hermitage, which we had both, of course, visited before. We had a couple of very mediocre meals, including some catastrophic duck, in a restaurant on the Neva Prospect.

We would have much preferred a friendly corner to the wandering and sight-seeing, but there was nowhere. Mila managed to book a room in a hostel belonging to a branch of the Academy of Sciences, and when the evening of the first day came she smuggled me in for a few hours. Yet there was no peace and quiet there, either: I had hardly been there an hour before someone started banging at the door. We thought my presence may have been detected, and the management, the police, or the KGB had come to haul me out.

But it was a false alarm, the wrong door, and the unknown visitor soon went away. There was no question of my spending the whole night there anyway – my absence from the ship would have been noticed. The hours we spent together in Leningrad were as tense as they were happy. But how could it be otherwise? I kept on wondering whether I would be able to get away before the 'organs' discovered that I was in town. And could we meet in Leningrad again?

On the second day I got back to the ship well before it was due to leave, anxious to avoid the near-miss we had in Tallinn. Mila came to the harbour to see me off. She said a quick goodbye and skipped off behind one of the parked lorries: it would, we thought, be better for her not to wait at the quayside. Our parting was less sad than at

Tallinn: the visit to Leningrad had been, in its way, successful, and we thought that some element of hope might be creeping into the situation. Not only had we now met twice, on Soviet soil, but there was also the relatively benign response of the Soviet Consul in London.

As the ship sailed down the Neva I went down into my cabin and wrote a short letter to Mila for posting in Helsinki:

> So I'm on my way back to Helsinki, over the darkening Baltic waters. I have just spent my happiest ever two days during our two years of separation. It was wonderful, mentally and physically. I hope I did not say anything hurtful when we were together. I looked back as I was getting on board, and I saw your slight figure and legs disappearing. I felt very, very sad. I still love you and we will continue our struggle for happiness. Now I have the impression that everything will improve quickly. You'll see.
>
> In fact I'm just starting my journey back to England. When the ship arrives in Helsinki tomorrow morning I'll go to the post restante to get any letters that have been forwarded, have something to eat, and then get the boat to Stockholm.

"After our meetings in these northern towns," I continued in my letter of the 8th September from Stockholm, "my life has again begun to acquire a meaning.... I think that things will never again be as bad as they were, so whatever you do, don't get downhearted.... I'll go and have some tea now. I have to be at the port terminal by eight."

Mila, for her part, carefully avoided any mention of our meetings in the letters she sent from Moscow, apart from wishing me well "on my travels in Finland". She had another fright on the 8th October when she read that a Norwegian ferry had sunk in the Skageraak, but a look at an atlas had convinced her that I could not be on it.

★

The next opportunity to do something positive came in London just over a month later. It was announced that Gennadii Voronov, a member of the all-powerful Politburo of the USSR and President of the Russian Federation, would shortly be making an official visit to Great Britain. His standing was modest in the wider context of Soviet foreign policy, but from the perspective of the Palace of Weddings on Griboedov Street he was a very big fish indeed. It was soon clear from conciliatory statements in the Soviet press that the Russians wanted Voronov's stay to be as sweet as possible.

What with my two uneventful, clandestine visits to the USSR, the favourable mention of Mila's father in *Pravda*, and the more benign atmosphere in the Consulate, I thought things might be softening up a little. If Voronov could be induced to give some sort of public undertaking that he would facilitate the marriage, then things might really start rolling.

I went along to the Consulate and told them in mellifluous Russian that I wished to make Comrade Voronov's visit as pleasant as possible. Perhaps I could even get some nice notices about him in the press. The Consul responded by saying that the Consulate itself did not have any objections to my marrying a Soviet citizen, everything was decided in Moscow. I did not tell him that I intended to see Voronov myself, if humanly possible.

In fact, press reports indicated that security would be tight. I imagined this was at the insistence of the Soviet side, since no one in England (except myself) could possibly have had any interest whatever in Voronov's presence. He would be staying, it was said, at Claridge's, the hugely expensive hotel in Mayfair. Rather than chase after him in the street, I thought it would be simpler to pay the money and book a room in the same establishment. A day or two before his arrival I went there to have a preliminary look around, taking Martin Dewhirst for moral support. We ordered coffee in the lounge. It was served by a middle-aged footman in ludicrous eighteenth-century garb who was rude when I gave him a small tip. Initial impressions were not encouraging.

On the morning Voronov arrived I packed an overnight bag and went to the hotel, though I hoped to contact the eminent visitor before I actually moved in. The clerk in reception gave me his room number without ado: but when I found it, the reason was clear. Unlike Wilson's room in Moscow it was guarded by a muscular young spook in a smart suit. He told me that there was no way that he would let me knock on Voronov's door, even to hand him a letter.

There was nothing to be done for the moment. But hardly had I got to my own room when the telephone rang and I was called down to the vestibule. A small crowd awaited me there, resembling one of the vocal groups in a Gilbert and Sullivan opera. There was a plain-clothes officer from the Special Branch, a dapper hotel manager, a Soviet diplomat, and one or two serving folk. I think I caught a glimpse of the footman glowering as he passed.

"There are objections to your presence here, Mr. Matthews," said the manager in an easy tone of voice. "We think it would be better if you left. Claridge's would be happy to refund the cost of your room."

"I came here to meet to Mr. Voronov," I said. "Surely there can be no objection to that?"

"We will not allow it," said the Special Branch man imperiously. "Mr. Falin here is representing the Soviet visitors, and you can talk to him. Better than trailing in the gutter."

How easy it was, I thought, to insult people if you have a Special Branch card in your pocket. I would not, however, allow myself to be fobbed off with Falin.

"I will only see Comrade Voronov," I said.

Glances were exchanged, and there was a brief discussion in the corner: the upshot was that Voronov would see me for a few moments, just to accept a letter. He appeared shortly afterwards, a middle-aged, affable sort of man. Yes, he said, he would look into the matter when he got back to Moscow. So I left Claridge's feeling that all the nonsense had not been in vain. I contacted my friend David Floyd, who covered Soviet affairs at the *Daily Telegraph*, and he got a couple of carefully-worded paragraphs into the paper next day: "One man agreeably surprised by Mr. Voronov's reception of him," wrote the editor of the Day by Day column (or David himself) on the 22nd November, "is Mr. Mervyn Matthews, who... on his departure from Moscow in 1964 had to leave behind his fiancée... When Mr. Matthews approached Mr. Voronov he received a very polite hearing and an undertaking that the matter would be looked into. Should the Russian leader become a matchmaker everyone would be pleased."

I was anxious to get a small piece into the *Daily Mail* also, but when I phoned them a voice in the editorial office adamantly refused to give me even of an inch of space. I took a short letter along to Viscount Rothermere's residence close to St. James's Palace, surely one of the most prestigious addresses in London. The impressive front door was opened by an equally impressive butler, who accepted my missive, but it had no effect whatever. Such (I thought ruefully) is the manner of newspapers, they splash you half a front page when you don't want it, and begrudge an inch if you are desperate for mention.

I wrote to Mila to tell her what had happened, and ask her to contact Voronov herself. "I'll take some advice on that," she replied cautiously. "He is very elevated here, and it might not do us any good."

*

As the weeks went by it became clear that Voronov had not helped – either he had not tried, or not been able to. The end of the year was approaching and I was getting restive. After the relatively successful, if fraught, trips to Tallinn and Leningrad, I thought it might be worth trying to get back to Russia again. Best apply for an entry visa in some country where I was not known to the Soviet consulate, I thought. Mr. Cumber had suggested it earlier, but the idea had long been in my mind.

Belgium would be a good choice: it was close, French-speaking (I knew French) and almost certainly had travel agencies offering tours to Moscow. There was one other advantage: I had a couple of friends in Brussels who might help me with accommodation while I made the travel arrangements. On the 12th December, 1966 I took a cheap cross-channel flight from Southend to Ostende, and completed the journey by train.

Brussels has three railway stations, and I had no reason to choose any particular one. Descending at the Gare du Nord I quickly discovered that I was in the brothel quarter, but at least the brothels offered cheap lodging, and could be (as I discovered) clean. I spent a night above a noisy bar, with a fat negro snoring loudly in the next room. The ladies in the street had little attraction for me.

Next morning I located a suitable agency – Belgatourist – in the rue des Paroissiens, and booked a five-day trip to Moscow, with departure on the 22nd December. I would have liked to have left sooner, but that was not possible. It would take at least four working days to get a visa, I was told, and the trip had to be paid for in advance. So I would be sadly out of pocket if things went wrong. I knew my mother would be disappointed that I would not be going to Swansea for Christmas, but that had to be tolerated. Of course, I did not tell her of my plans.

I hoped to have some friendly contact in Brussels while I waited, so I telephoned my old friend Jean-Michel, whom I had met when we were students. He had heard something of my mishaps, and on his way to work he dropped into the brothel to see me.

"Delighted to see you," he said in his beautiful French (he worked at a radio station). "Why don't you come and stay with Jean-Pierre and myself while you're waiting for the visa? There's room in the flat."

"Excellent," I replied. "But if you've got any free time over Christmas the two of you might like to stay at my place in Pimlico. It's empty."

So we decided there and then to do a swop. It would mean a lonelier wait for me in Brussels, but since the two Jeans were keen to go to England I felt I could hardly do less than invite them. They had two large, elegant rooms in an old house some way from the centre, with an extra room upstairs which they put at my disposal. There were creaky wooden floors, large mirrors and elaborate fireplaces. "The rooms here," I wrote to Mila in my daily letter, "are beautifully furnished – perhaps over-furnished – with French and Flemish *objets d'art*. In a corner by the door there is a polished wooden stand with dozens of old tumblers, glasses and goblets."

Jean-Pierre admitted to me that he had a liking for glass which was faulted and bent in the wrong places. The morning after I moved in I came down to the kitchen earlier than expected to find my hosts stripped to the waist and boiling eggs; stripped up to the waist, I mean. I retired soundlessly. Their unusual cooking methods were, of course, no concern of mine, so nothing was said about the matter. Later in the day they left for London.

The weather in Brussels was grey and cold. After their departure I had nothing to do except sit in the flat or wander around the uninteresting streets. There was no contact with the neighbours. But at long last Monday the 19th arrived, the day the visa was supposed to be issued. I rushed down to the travel agency, bracing myself for another refusal.

"Here you are," said the girl behind the counter nonchalantly, pulling an envelope out of a drawer. "It's all ready. Passport and visa, air tickets, hotel vouchers. You'll be staying in the National Hotel, right in the centre."

I sat down for a moment to steady my nerves. The visa was indeed there, a separate document, as usual. Either I had suddenly become *persona grata* (which seemed highly unlikely) or it had been issued by mistake. Perhaps the Soviet Consulate had not bothered to clear my name with Moscow, or (less probably) had cleared it in a cyrillic transliteration which did not match the KGB records. On the visa itself my surname had been spelt quite differently from the form used in London – 'Matthews' can be rendered by at least twenty variants in cyrillic. So it seemed that from the KGB point of view I would be going to Russia as a different person.

I had two full days to wait until departure, and I spent most of them waiting for a telephone call from the agency asking me to return the visa. But I heard nothing, and at 11.00 a.m. on Thursday, the 22nd of December I flew off to the Soviet capital via Amsterdam and Stockholm. It was a relatively slow journey, and I arrived about ten o'clock in the evening, Moscow time.

★

The National Hotel was completely unchanged. It was the first time

I been there since I made my unsuccessful attempt to speak to Gordon Walker. For someone interested in an unobtrusive meeting, a less suitable spot could hardly be imagined: the presence of numerous foreign tourists and businessmen made it a hive of KGB activity. Official cars with dark windows were invariably parked outside, and plain clothes men lurked everywhere.

Shortly after arrival I went out and telephoned Mila from a booth in the street. I presumed all the internal phones were monitored, and I feared that the KGB might intervene before we had even met. As a matter of fact, Mila had just sent off her daily letter, and was amazed to hear my voice. There was no certainty that I would get to Moscow, so I had not forewarned her. We decided that since I would be watched as a foreign visitor at the National, and since we would be going around together anyway, further attempts at concealment would be pointless. She said she would come around to the hotel early next morning. The doorman might stop her if she tried to get into the building, so we arranged to meet outside the entrance. I shall never forget the joyful moment, or her smile, as she ran up to me over the snowy pavement.

After a few words on how I had got to Moscow we turned to the central, long-standing problem. Might things go well, at last? Was there any chance that the KGB might not mind my returning to Moscow, if and when they found out? That was obviously the key question of the moment. The marriage application I had lodged at the Soviet Consulate in London in August had so far yielded no reply – which meant no refusal. Walking slowly through the Moscow streets, we decided that my stay could be best used to restart marriage proceedings. Mila took me back to her room on the Arbat (like the National, it was unchanged in every respect) and I wrote a letter to Voronov, asking if he could help while I was there. Then we telephoned the Palace of Weddings (open, naturally enough, on Saturday), found that Madame Efremova would be in her office on Monday. We would try and see her again.

Sunday was Christmas Day, perhaps the most peculiar I ever spent. Mila and I passed most of the time sitting in the flat. Life outside carried on as usual – there were no religious holidays in Russia, and the Orthodox Christmas was two weeks off, anyway. It was very cold, but not snowing. In the afternoon we went to the Central Telegraph Office and I sent my mother a telegram with a few words of hope and reassurance.

On Monday morning, as soon as it opened, we were back at the Palace of Weddings. I shall never forget our meeting, brief though it was, with Efremova.

"Do you remember me?" I asked, rather needlessly, as Mila and I trailed into her office.

"Yes, yes, I do," she cried, obviously very much on her guard. She must have been surprised to see us, having had no official indication that we were coming, but she tried not to show it. With regard to registration she was entirely noncommittal, and referred only to 'the normal procedures'. We interpreted the fact that she had admitted us to her office as a neutral, or possibly hopeful, sign.

It seemed wise to contact the people at the British Embassy, who might even agree to lend a hand. So although it was closed for the Boxing Day holiday, I telephoned. Much to my surprise, the voice that answered the phone was distinctly friendly: it turned out that both the Duty Officer, a Mr. Hall, and the Vice Consul, a Mr. Brown, were anxious to help. There was not much they could do at that moment, they said, but they promised they would see whether any official documentation could be issued when the Embassy opened on Tuesday. I went to the Aeroflot desk at the hotel and asked them to change my ticket, so that I could stay a few days longer: they were not sure whether it would be possible. Then, since there was little more to be done, Mila and I went for a long walk in one of the outlying parks, to get some fresh air. I was still fairly sure that we were not followed. Perhaps things were looking up.

But they were not. When I went out into the street on Tuesday morning my inward ear immediately picked up a strident discord, such as is heard in horror movies. Yes, there was no doubt about it, I was now being watched closely by all-too-familiar goons. At last the KGB had swung into action. What would they do? I did not have to wait long to find out. When I returned to the hotel in the early afternoon there was an urgent message waiting for me. The main Intourist office, which happened to be just along the street, requested me to go there as soon as possible.

The official who received me was a fellow of about my own age, and seemed a little sympathetic. But he was under instructions, he said, to tell me that my visa was being annulled and that I would have to leave the country. He could not say why it had been issued in the first place. I returned, disconsolate, to the National. Mila appeared shortly afterwards, and on hearing the news was terribly upset. "Mervusya, we can't do anything now. If they've annulled your visa there's no legal basis for you to be in Russia."

That afternoon, about 4.30, I was summoned to OVIR, the gloomy visa office in Potapov perelok for an unnerving repetition of my previous visit. The deputy head was waiting for me. He uttered the same sentence twice, and said no more: "You must leave Russia as soon as possible, today or tomorrow, on the first available plane."

Mila and I decided that this time I had no option but to go – if the KGB turned nasty I could easily end up in prison with Gerald Brooke. The Krogers, after all, were still incarcerated in England. Intourist changed my ticket to fly out at seven o'clock on the evening of the 28th, and Mila saw me off for the third time in five months. Unlike the other two visits, this one had ended in disaster.

I telephoned her from England on the 30th December, and sent her a letter the following day. "Life has stopped again," I wrote. "Your voice yesterday was very sad, but we have had a lot of sad news, and we can live through this as well. I just can't understand why things are turning out in this way. Oh God, how difficult it all is. How can I help you at this difficult time. I will go on trying...."

★

After a few days I decided there might be some advantage in getting my misadventure into the press, so as to keep the publicity pot boiling. In fact the Foreign Office had received a protest about my visit from the Soviet Ministry of Foreign Affairs – which would have made the story more newsworthy – but they did not tell me about it. On the 27th January, 1967, David Floyd helped out again by getting a short piece into the *Telegraph*.

> Mr. Mervyn Matthews, a lecturer in Russian, revealed yesterday that he was expelled from Russia last month for the second time in three years when on a visit to his Russian fiancée. He stayed at a hotel in the centre of Moscow and made no attempt to conceal his identity. On the fifth day he was summoned by the authorities and ordered to leave on the first plane next day.

The *South Wales Evening Post*, faithful as ever, wrote to ask me whether there were any other developments they could report. The *Western Mail* in Cardiff, which was also very supportive, invited me to do a half-page feature for them in the light of the forthcoming visit of Mr. Aleksei Kosygin, the Soviet Premier. "Kosygin should have sufficient authority to put this matter right," I wrote hopefully. Des Zwar (who had reported the Stockholm escapade in 1964) wanted to do a big article for *The People* on how to enter Russia illegally. I turned that down flat.

Strangely enough, the Christmas fiasco did have one positive result – through David Floyd's article. A day or two after it appeared my telephone rang. "Mr. Matthews?" It was a man's voice, with a slight cockney accent.

"Yes."

"My name is Derek Deason, and I was given your number by David Floyd. I read his article on your expulsion from Russia."

I waited expectantly.

"I was expelled from Russia myself in October, 1964, just before I planned to get married. I've been trying to get my fiancée out ever since."

"Well, let's meet," I said, unhesitatingly. "We can compare misfortunes."

And indeed we got together shortly afterwards at Victoria Station.

Seven. The Great Paperchase

Derek turned out to be about the same age as I. He had a pleasant face, and I took an immediate liking to him. We had a cup of coffee together. Intelligent and fair-minded, he would have done well at a university, had he had the chance to attend one. In fact he came from a poor East London family and worked as a 'scaleman' at Ford's motor works in Dagenham. I had never associated scales with car production, but Derek said they were essential to some processes and a specialist mechanic had to be on hand if any went wrong. Normally he had little to do, and he was active in a small scalemens' union.

He knew something of my problems from the papers, but I had never heard of his. They seemed bizarre, even in the context of Soviet bureaucracy. Derek had never been involved with Russia, and knew no Russian. Some four years before, when holidaying on the Black Sea coast, he had met a girl called Eleonora Ginzburg, fallen in love with her, and asked her to marry him. She was a perfectly ordinary Jewish-Russian girl, a teacher of English in Moscow, with no security connections. They did not anticipate any trouble.

The ceremony was to be in Moscow in October, 1964, and Derek went back to Russia with some days to spare. However, Eleonora could not put him up very easily – she shared a cramped flat with her sister – so he decided to go down to Sochi, alone, and pass the time there. Whilst he was at the resort some Russian acquaintances offered him a stag supper. He got drunk on vodka – understandably, because he drank little – and became obstreperous. The militia were called in, and though no one had been hurt, he was quickly bundled onto a plane for Moscow. There he was put onto another, bound for London, without being given a chance to telephone to his fiancée. She was astonished to have a call from him in England. Although the incident seemed to be utterly trivial, Derek had never been allowed to return to Russia to get married and had been refused an entry visa nine times. His MP – as it happened, Patrick Gordon Walker – had tried to help him, but to no avail.

I gave Derek more details of my own particular plight, and we quickly found a common language. He respected my experience, such as it was, and for my part I thought he could be an excellent companion-in-arms. In fact, that's exactly how things turned out: there was never a hint of dissension between us, and never once did we let one another down. We exchanged Mila and Eleonora's addresses, so that they could contact one another in Moscow. Derek lived out in Leytonstone, so we sometimes met to discuss progress, or more accurately, the lack of it, at two Edwardian pubs in the centre – The Audley in South Audley Street, Mayfair, and The Albert on Victoria Street. We also kept in close telephone contact, updating one another on relevant items in the press.

At that time Derek was trailing Lord Fenner Brockway, a doddery old socialist who claimed to have a special relationship with the Soviet Embassy, and soon after we started cooperating Derek took me to meet him. The occasion was the peer's eightieth birthday party, celebrated in a public hall in Camden: you had to pay to go in, and the money was used for some good cause or other. I will always recall the horrified silence when the birthday boy turned to a famous actress among his guests – I think it was Vanessa Redgrave – and addressed her as 'Constance Cummings'. But even in his less forgetful moments, Lord Brockway could not help, either.

Derek was was profoundly frustrated by Soviet intransigence, but he was also a very positive person and a spirited fighter. My friendship with him was one of the few – very few – benefits of my struggle with the KGB. Beyond that, there was no doubt that he had more to lose by associating with me than I with him, for he had no background of confrontation with the Soviet authorities, and his case was clearly much easier.

★

The abrupt reaction of the KGB to my Moscow visit prompted the thought that I needed some completely new initiative, preferably outside Russia. Aleksei Kosygin, the Soviet Prime Minister, was due to arrive in England early in February, 1967, and an audience with the Queen was included in his programme. I decided to write Her Majesty a letter asking for her help. After explaining my circumstances, I wrote: "I hope your Majesty will be able to help me, and other persons in a similar position, when you entertain the Soviet Prime Minister at Buckingham Palace this week ... I believe that an expression of interest from our Monarch could well be a deciding factor in prompting the Russians to adopt a more humanitarian attitude."

The Queen has always been famed for her graciousness, and sure enough, a few days later, an envelope bearing the royal emblem dropped into my Pimlico letterbox. Her Majesty did not reply in person, but a certain Edward Ford did so in lieu. "I am commanded by the Queen," he wrote, "to thank you for your letter of the 5th February, the contents of which have been noted by Her Majesty." That kind thought was the closest I ever got to Royal favour.

★

Kosygin's visit was to last an entire week, from the 6th to the 13th February. My failure to get anywhere with Khrushchev in Stockholm, Adzhubei in Bonn, and Voronov in Claridge's prompted me to try again, rather than give up in despair. I prepared a letter for the great man, and managed to place one or two pieces in the press, so as to register my existence, as it were. *The Daily Telegraph* published my letter under its own headline 'Waiting for Marriage: Kosygin's chance to Improve Goodwill', and the *Western Mail* in Cardiff, which also continued to take a benign interest in my affairs, gave me half a page. I wrote my own article which they entitled 'From Russia – But Without his Love'. I did not, of course, mention the machinations of the KGB, which had never been publicised. As for my plans to hand the letter over, I decided not to involve the press – if there were to be more failure of that kind it was better not brought to public notice.

Matters would be greatly eased, I thought, if I had the assistance of the Special Branch, which would be guarding him. They had, after all, allowed me speak to Voronov. So I telephoned them and arranged to see one of their officers. When we met I was impressed enough by the man's mild manner to tell him all about the Kosygin letter. Perhaps the Branch could suggest a time and place for me to hand it over, or help in some other way? Much to my chagrin the response was entirely noncommittal, and shortly after the meeting, after Kosygin arrived, I found, more to my amusement than anything else, that I was actually being followed in the streets of London.

The failures, tedious and probably inevitable, followed in due course. I went to Downing Street, open to the public in those days, hoping to hand the letter to Kosygin as he came out of Number 10. A couple of KBG security men were on the pavement, and I asked one, by way of ingratiation, when Kosygin would appear.

"I should not try and approach him," said the goon, helpfully. "Your English police may arrest you!"

Hence to the Houses of Parliament which the Soviet leader was also due to visit. A small crowd had assembled outside one of the entrances, and, paper in hand, I told a nervous, grey-haired inspector of my intention.

"You can't do that," he said.

"But I am not breaking the law, or doing anything wrong."

"If you step out from the crowd," said the inspector, "we will take you back to the station and pin something on you."

I was appalled: like most children of my generation, I had been taught to respect the police. In a flash that respect disappeared, to be replaced by life-long scepticism.

My third attempt to reach Kosygin was made just after he and Harold Wilson had visited an exhibition (devoted, I believe, to Anglo-Soviet cooperation) at the Victoria and Albert Museum. I did not get close enough to Kosygin to speak to him, and he was driven off, leaving Harold Wilson standing in the front of the building, waiting for his own car. This was a chance to confront the British Prime Minister, if not his distinguished visitor. I darted up to him, for some reason unaccosted by his guards. "What about our fiancées, Mr. Wilson?" I said. He turned towards me, startled, but there was a gleam of recognition in his eyes, too. "I know you!" he said. A brief moment later his car drove up and he, too, had gone. Happily, neither the police nor the security guards took any notice of me afterwards. Kosygin was due to leave for Scotland the same day, so I decided that there was nothing more to be done during his stay in the U.K.

★

A few days after Kosygin had departed, a more fruitful idea came into my mind. Perhaps I could offer the Russians something they would love to get their hands on, something which could serve as a bargaining counter, and induce them to let Mila go? The question was, what? Any dealings would have to be above board and legal, so as to obviate the danger of trickery on the Soviet side.

Could I not find some of Lenin's writings, the so-called Leniniana, in the West, buy them, and offer them to the Soviet authorities in return for Mila's departure? Lenin had lived in western Europe at various times between 1900 and 1917, and scraps of his copious effusions might still be scattered around. So I started the Great Paperchase, involving no less than four overlapping initiatives.

I rushed off to the manuscript division of the British Museum to see whether they had any originals of the great man's handwriting. His massive collected works contained facsimiles, but all I could find were in Cyrillic, and I wanted if possible to familiarise myself with the Latin hand which he might have used abroad. In any case, it would be interesting to see some originals. The British Museum did indeed have a copy of his application for membership (under the name of Jacob Richter), which I ordered up and fingered thoughtfully. The lettering was nondescript, without as far as I could see any strong, distinguishing characteristics. Regretfully, I returned the papers to the issue desk – if only they were mine!

Paris seemed to be the best starting point for my quest. In the past it had housed a large Russian émigré population, though much of it comprised pre-revolutionary intelligentsia. I spoke to one or two Russians in London, including Victor Frank, who worked for Radio Liberty, the American-sponsored station in the West. He sent me the address of the Russian émigré artist, Georges Annenkov, who had known Lenin, and had done a famous, and hopelessly flattering, sketch of the bald head. "I'm interested in the life of Lenin, and would welcome the chance to discuss it with you," I wrote to him. I also wrote to Georgii Viktorovich Adamovich, the wonderful teacher who had led me through the by-ways of Russian literature at Manchester University. He was a fine writer himself, robbed of his readership by the Revolution. I thought he might also be able to give me some useful leads.

★

I obtained some research money to work at the Radio Liberty Institute in Munich, and arranged to stay in Paris en route. When I arrived in the French capital on the 4th April I lugged my suitcase and typewriter to a cheap hotel on the Left Bank, and set up my tea-making equipment. I would be staying for a few days. "How strangely travel affects you, Milochka," I wrote on arrival. "I have become absolutely indifferent to the place I find myself in. Everything seems to look the same. Perhaps it's because I only travel in Europe, where there's a kind of sameness... I hardly know anyone here in Paris. There is one person I know from my university years [I was thinking of Georges Nivat] but I don't like contacting him without warning." I thought it premature to tell Mila about my proposed contacts with émigrés, or for that matter, my real intentions: I did not want to raise false hopes.

★

Annenkov received me in his spacious studio lit by a vast, square window – the 'northern light' prized by painters in the past. He was a wizened little man, suspicious and unhelpful. I was interested in Lenin in the West? Yes, he had written a book about him, but he

159

would not lend me a copy. He did not say why, but I imagined that it was because he wanted me to buy one. A slight trace of coolness quickly crept into the conversation, and I realised that I would not get anywhere with him. I left his studio soon after. It was one of many failures.

*

Georgii Viktorovich Adamovich was, by contrast, very helpful. He was a small man, with a strange, sallow complexion and black hair which he kept beautifully parted. He dressed meticulously and took enormous pride in concealing his age, which could have been anything between 40 and 65. In the Paris telephone book he described himself as 'un homme de lettres', which meant that he scraped a living helping old ladies with literary pretensions. Although he had laboured for a time in the lecture rooms of Manchester University, his chances of employment in Britain were sadly restricted by his complete ignorance of English. He taught us in Russian and French.

When I saw him in Paris he was clearly at the centre of émigré life. We met in one of those vast cafés on the Boulevard Saint-Michel, with white table cloths, supercilious waiters and prices which destroyed any possible enjoyment. I was a little concerned about who should pay for the coffee, but need not have been, for he did. On that day he was in particularly good form. Every so often, catching sight of an acquaintance, he would rise from his seat, smile and bow. We had always thought, at Manchester, that his family had been close to the Russian Tsar: in any case, his manners were perfect. Before the morning was out he had given me two possible leads – an émigré family called Aleksinski, which was selling a political archive with bits of Leniniana in it, and a bookseller called Lambert, who was offering a manuscript said to be entirely in Lenin's hand.

*

The archive seemed to be the most promising line of enquiry, so I telephoned the Aleksinskis. They did indeed have some papers for sale. Grigorii A. Aleksinski had been a socialist deputy for Petrograd (as St. Petersburg was then known) at the Second Duma, in the spring of 1907. He knew Lenin personally and had also corresponded with the famous Russian Marxist Georgii Plekhanov. Aleksinski's son, also Grigorii, or Grégoire, confirmed that the archive was still available, and we arranged to meet. Grégoire was was an affable man

Mila in woodland near the dacha

Mila on holiday...

...and at work

The *Kastelholm* steamer: my transport to Leningrad

Just Three Russian Women . .

In Moscow . .   **In London . .**

LUDMILLA BIBIKOVA

and

ELEONORA GINSBURG
In five years no exit visa
not even to get married.

LUDMILLA SMIRNOVSKAYA
The Soviet Ambassador's wife at a
reception in Mayfair.

AN OPEN QUESTION

Two Russian girls, Ludmilla Bibikova and Eleonora Ginsburg, cannot get Soviet exit visas to come here and marry their British fiancés. *

Believe it or not, they have been trying for nearly five years!

All their applications in Moscow have been turned down.

The Soviet authorities expelled their fiancés on various pretexts in 1964, but refuse to give reasons for preventing the marriages (perhaps because in so doing they committed a clear infringement of Soviet law anyway).

Madame Ludmilla Smirnovskaya, wife of the Soviet Ambassador in London, has so far failed even to acknowledge the problem. She has not answered a single letter about it, though she has received many.

But silence will no longer suffice. The question is whether Soviet women do or do not enjoy the right to marry whom they please.

Who can answer this question better than Madame Smirnovskaya?

* Mervyn Matthews, 83, Belgrave Road, London, S.W.I.
Derek Deason, 19, Hillboro Court, Hainault Road, E.II.

Above leaflet for the press campaign; *opposite* some of the widespread coverage

THE BARTERED BRIDES

ELENARE GINSBURG.

LUDMILLA BIBIKOVA.

Permission deal over

SKETCH

Britons free to wed in Brooke

Britons free to marry

By A. Staff Reporter

Four Britons, who have been trying unsuccessfully for years to marry Russians, will now receive permission as part of the Brooke-Kroger agreement.

Mr. Stewart, the Foreign Secretary, told the Commons yesterday that, not later than October 24, three of them would be granted visas to enter the Soviet Union and register their marriages. The fourth, Mr. Michael Singer, "may have a Soviet visa at any time."

After the marriages, all the couples would be free to leave the Soviet Union if they wanted to, Mr. Stewart explained.

Beside Mr. Singer, the Britons are: Mr. Derek Deason, aged 39, an engineer from Leytonstone, London. Dr. Mervyn Matthews, aged 36, a lecturer in Russian at the University of ... instance, on the related questions of families who were separated by national boundaries were both level-headed and profoundly humanitarian in spirit.

Heavy

The Soviet prime minister has had no particular reason to interest himself in the question of difficult Anglo-Soviet marriages so far.

We must hope that Mr. Wilson, as his host, will now seize the opportunity of breaching this problem during their discussions.

Furthermore, this is a good opportunity to impress upon Mr. Kosygin something which might not have been very evident to him or his colleagues in Moscow—the fact that public opinion in Great Britain is genuinely concerned about the fate of individuals.

He must understand that official intransigence, even in such minor matters as these, can do much damage to the image of the Soviet Union in Britain. The hardship caused is quite unnecessary.

This is why I should like to see Mr. Kosygin, and if possible ask for his help. His

From Russia—but with love

By MERVYN MATTHEWS

JANUARY 21, 1964, is a date which does not mean much to the majority of people in Great Britain, ...

the Swansea-born lecturer who has fought for three years ... was a Russian research assistant.

Diary of a courtship

The brid... bartered w...

Brook

By DONALD Y...

FOUR Britons who had waited up to five ... marry their Russian sweethearts were ... wedding plans last night.

The four—three men and a woman—will be given visas to go to Russia before October 24.

Once there they can register their marriage intentions and the four couples will be free to leave the Soviet Union.

The "Bartered Brides' deal was part of the Brooke-Kroger package announced by Foreign Secretary Mr Michael Stewart yesterday.

Romance for one of the Britons, 39-year-old engineer Mr Derek Deason, blossomed during a Black Sea holiday at Sochi eight years ago.

There he met schoolteacher Eleonora Ginsburg. Mr Deason knew no Russian.

He flew back to Sochi the year after this graduation. On his third ...

Eleonora ... to ... was the Soviet ... ... ng our engage-

Expelled

Discreet

It was my misfortune that the sale of a sweater to a ... the couple were ... back in a fortnight. A few days later, we went celebrating with Russian "friends" ... arrested for a ... episode and ...

Russian ... age
At his hot... Road, Lexingt... to last night ... h my pleased. "Harsh— ... be charges which very lil... io to ...

... ... most kinds ... ding are com... selling a single ... a friend can tech... sidered as an ... ment of the law, i.e.

DEREK DEASON AND ELEONORA GINSBURG.

original misdemeanour was compounded. The charges, once made, were very difficult to shift.

So my fiancee and I were not allowed to marry, as we had planned, and at the end of June 1964 I was ordered out of the country.

When I got back to London I found that I was one of a small number of British citizens who, for one reason or another, had not over the years been allowed to marry Russians. Like them, I found myself in an extremely weak position, for having no legal ties with anyone in Russia I could not expect the Govern...

Just after the wedding

Outside the British Embassy by Moscow River, the Kremlin in the background

Eleonora, Mila and myself, photographed by Derek after the wedding, October 1969

Derek and Eleonora together before their tragedy, Summer 1964

Mila and I back in Moscow on a family trip, July 1979

in his mid-forties who worked, I believe, as a non-uniformed official somewhere in the French security or policing services. This was quite fortuitous, but it prompted me to ask myself why so many of my acquaintances had intelligence-linked jobs.

I sent Mila an account of the meeting, without explaining why it took place.

"First we drank an apéritif together. Then we went to have a meal at a 'cheap' restaurant, (but the bill for two of us was nearly three pounds!) That was with wine, which made my head spin. After that he took me back to his home where his wife was waiting with tea and gâteaux. Their apartment was luxurious, and they had three magnificent samovars. There was a lively conversation but my host kept on switching from French to Russian in each sentence, so in the end I did not know which language I was supposed to be speaking."

The main object of the visit was to meet Aleksinski senior, who turned out to be another tiny old man (all the Parisian émigrés seemed to be diminutive). But he was also very frail and clearly not destined to live much longer. The family showed me the archive in boxes, but did not allow me to examine any particular items. An official of the Soviet State Archives called Irina Minaeva had come to Paris to negotiate a purchase, but the old man was very anti-Soviet and would have none of it. Although Minaeva had talked with him for seven hours he refused to show her anything.

Afterwards Grégoire proposed that he and I went out for a walk in the Quartier St. Denis. The conversation was a strange mixture of business and social comment from an official perspective. "Look at those girls," he would exclaim, pointing at a group of young (and extremely attractive) prostitutes in a doorway. "Quite lamentable, isn't it. Poor girls. But it's part of life. Now with regard to the archives...."

After a while Grégoire admitted that he had also been approached by two American universities, but they "had not appreciated the value of the collection", so there had been no agreement. (In other words, he must have asked too high a price, I thought.) There were one or two items which his father wanted to keep, but most of it could go.

"So how much are you asking?" I asked.

"Fifty thousand francs," he replied.

Anyone dealing with Russia gets used to shocks, but I was not prepared for that. Fifty thousand francs! That was about £3,700, or my entire salary for over a year and a half! There was no way I could afford that sort of money. But my financial state would be of no concern to Monsieur Aleksinski, so I did not mention it.

"Could you send a full listing of the contents to me in England?" I asked. "I hope to take the matter further."

★

Despite the difficult financial implications, I was quite excited. If properly handled, this might be a golden opportunity to get Mila out of Russia. I decided to start right at the top of the ideological pyramid, and when I got back to London I wrote a detailed letter to Petr Nikolaevich Pospelov, Director of the Institute of Marxism Leninism. Ironically, he was Mila's old boss: he would certainly have known about her departure from the Institute and the reason for it. But I kept my cards close to my chest and did not reveal that he was getting a letter from her unfortunate fiancé.

"I know [I wrote] that Soviet historians make great efforts to seek out manuscripts of Lenin in West Europe and return them to the homeland of the great leader of the Great October Revolution." (I spent much of my working life reading this sort of drivel, so it flowed easily from my pen.) "I have recently discovered that the valuable archives of Grigorii A. Aleksinski, a member of the State Duma and close acquaintance of Lenin, are in Paris. They contain some cut-outs from Lenin's letters, photocopies of some of his lost letters, and some Plekhanov letters. I have a partial listing.... At the present time Mr. Aleksinski's son, whom I know well, is giving me the opportunity to buy his father's archives. I personally consider that Moscow is the proper place for Lenin's documents, and I would like to assist in passing them to Soviet historians."

To my absolute delight, there was a reply: Pospelov had, it seemed, retired, but he was replaced by one Petr Fedoseev, no less ponderous and important a dinosaur.

"Dear Mr. Matthews, (wrote Fedoseev on the 26th March) May I express our profound gratitude to you for sending us a short description of G.A. Aleksinski's library... we are mainly interested in the documents in the collection...." And he went on to give me a full-page listing of items he particularly wished to see, some in photocopy. I wrote to Aleksinski immediately asking for full details of his holdings, and what items his father wished to retain.

I thought this might be a good moment to improve relations with the Soviet Consulate, especially as my last application to return to Russia had remained unanswered. So I went to see them. I lighted upon an official called Grishin, who made it clear that he was going to be as unhelpful as possible. I guessed that my last expulsion from Moscow had soured their attitude, apart from which the Consulate had other functions, mostly subversive, and collecting Leniniana was not a priority.

The new Consul was not inclined to assist, either. By the strangest of coincidences it was none other than Ivan Shishkin, who with Wolfgang Vogel's help, had negotiated the Powers-Abel exchange in 1962. Shishkin was given the rank of First Secretary as an indication of his age and negotiating status: hitherto the Consuls had tended to be younger Second Secretaries. According to the British newspapers, he was also believed to head Soviet intelligence in West Europe.

When I found out who he was I thought it might help if I could actually see him – a meeting, if carefully handled, could hardly make things worse, and personal contact might help a little. Somewhat to my astonishment he gave me an appointment, perhaps under the 'know your enemy' principle. When I went into his office I found a thin, unresponsive bureaucrat, bespectacled and grey-haired. We were only together for a few minutes, during which he emphasised that "all decisions were made in Moscow". Clearly, he had no interest in solving blocked marriages, especially (I thought) if they could be used to further an exchange deal.

Subsequently my relations with him, and the Consulate in general, deteriorated badly. He accepted a few telephone calls from me but only, I am sure, because he enjoyed being nasty. "You cause me a lot of trouble, Mr. Matthews," he told me on one occasion in his awful guttural English. "And you cause me a lot, too!" I replied. I felt ill for the rest of that day. The only other significant development at that time was the appearance of Victor Louis, who was visiting the editorial office of his paper in London. We met briefly for a chat at the Regent Palace Hotel, just off Piccadilly. There was little he could say or do – but at least he took the trouble to meet me, perhaps because he regarded me as a potentially good story.

★

Despite the negative response from the Consulate, I decided to press ahead and seek funds for a possible purchase of the Aleksinski archive, if only to make things a little more realistic. The problem was that I did not know anybody wealthy enough to help, and the search went on for months. I began by writing to Isaiah Berlin, the well-known Russian philosopher at Oxford. He took an interest in Russian affairs and had married a lady who was said to be very wealthy. "Dear Mr. Matthews [he wrote back] I wish I knew of a rich person prepared to set aside a couple of thousand for this purpose; but I don't. Are you sure money will do it? I understand that you wish to go on – of course you must – but if it is really a matter of money, and you must borrow it, you need someone with a large bank account and a generous heart. It seems a terrible thing to say, but I know of no one in Oxford like that."

I wrote to my friend Priscilla Johnson in Harvard. She had been very close to Stalin's daughter Svetlana after she emigrated, and Priscilla had written a celebrated article about her. "To put it briefly" I wrote, "I read that Svetlana expects to earn vast sums of money from her publications, and give most of it away to trusts. I am wondering whether there is any point in my writing to her and asking for her help for Mila and myself.... The money can be advanced on excellent security, because if the scheme doesn't go through (and I think it has a 75% chance of success) the money will be repaid." In the event, Priscilla could not help either. I wrote to Rauf Kahil, a friend I had in Oxford. Rauf was a kind, Coptic Christian who owned so much land in Egypt he couldn't bear to think about it. He had also associated with the fabulously wealthy King Farouk. This flame, however, was untimely extinguished – I learned that Rauf had dropped dead at a podium while lecturing in Africa.

Finally, through my friend Michael Aidin, I got into contact with Lord Thomson of Fleet, the famous millionaire. I had some difficulty in obtaining an appointment with him (he was tied up with more significant matters), but at last, on the 27th May, 1967, I entered his plush office. I explained the situation to him and he came to the point straight away. "Don't pay out a large sum for documents before you know what is going to happen," he said. "Ask the sellers to give you an option. That won't cost much, and it will leave your hands free." Just at that moment his personal assistant (following earlier instructions, no doubt) dashed in and reminded his Lordship that he had to go off for another meeting. "Can I give you a lift?" Lord Thomson asked. "Which way are you going?"

We drove off in his grey Rolls, under the respectful gaze of the doorman and to the admiration of passers by. Lord Thomson had given me no money, but a very useful piece of advice.

*

My other iron in the fire was the Lambert manuscript in Paris. During my visit to Paris in April, 1967, I had contacted Monsieur J. Lambert, who owned the Librairie de l'Abbaye on the rue Bonaparte in the centre of the city. His shop was impressive indeed, with elegant, glass-fronted bookcases and rows of leather-bound volumes. When I went there a well-dressed old lady, evidently a client, was sitting at one of the antique tables looking through some volumes. Monsieur Lambert introduced himself and bustled off to get the Lenin document. As I waited I unthinkingly opened one of the volumes on the table.

"Oh, Monsieur," cried an assistant, alarmed. "Don't touch!"

Obviously, there was rigorous control of the stock. Monsieur Lambert returned holding a thin manuscript. I looked at it carefully. It was some twenty two pages in length, in French, and entitled 'Les tâches des représentants de la gauche de Zimmerwald dans le Parti Socialiste Suisse'.

"You see, Monsieur," said the proprietor, "Lenin knew the Swiss socialist Henri Guilbeaux very well. They met at a socialist conference in Zimmerwald in September, 1915 to discuss how the First World War could be turned into a struggle for socialism. The manuscript was confiscated by the police and lost for some time, but Guilbeaux went to great lengths to recover it. It is unique, and written entirely by Lenin, in excellent French, with very few mistakes."

"The price?" I asked.

Monsieur Lambert paused. "Thirty thousand francs" he said.

I thought, my God, this time it's thirty thousand! Cheaper than the archive, but still over two thousand quid!"

"Well, if it *is* Lenin," I said coolly, "I might well be interested. I imagine you have no client interested at the moment?"

"One never knows," said Monsieur Lambert, mysteriously, from which I gathered that he didn't.

"I shall give it careful thought, Monsieur," I said. "I return to England tomorrow, but I will write to you."

I withdrew from his hallowed premises to a small café nearby, so as to have a cup of coffee and a think. Given all the uncertainties of the Aleksinski archive, this variant seemed worth pursuing. Fedoseev might well be interested in it. There was nothing more to be done in Paris, but I had to look into the question of its authenticity.

As soon as I got back to London I spent more time in the British Museum, looking for references to the work and checking Lenin's genuine handwriting against the photocopy which Lambert had given me. My findings were not reassuring. The hand in the photocopy seemed very fluent and mature, but I still could not be sure that it was really Lenin's. Moreover, Guilbeaux was an uncritical admirer of the Soviet leader and may have been only too ready to publish a 'Lenin' manuscript without adequate authentication.

I wrote to Lambert telling him that in my opinion the authenticity of the manuscript was by no means proven. On the other hand, if it turned out that the Russians wanted to have the manuscript, believing it to be authentic, the problem of its actual provenance was secondary. The matter dragged on, Lambert insisting that Guilbeaux would not have gone to such trouble to find and publish it, had he not been certain of the authorship. Most important, Lambert did not want to reduce the price. He merely offered to put the manuscript aside for me until the end of January, against a deposit of £100 which he would keep if the deal fell through. I had no intention of doing that, so my initiative fizzled out.

★

At the beginning of June a third possibility surfaced. In 1963 a French scholar called Georges Haupt brought out a collection of letters that had passed between Lenin and a certain Camile Huysmans, in his day a well-known socialist. When I found out about this I wrote to Monsieur Haupt, who informed me that Huysmans was not only still alive, but also had papers to sell, among them, apparently, some Leniniana.

I went over to Brussels again in the beginning of July, and spent a convivial evening with the two Jeans. They helped me arrange a visit to Huysmans, who was living with his young wife in Antwerp. I say 'living', but as I soon discovered, 'dying' would have been a more accurate term. When Jean-Michel and I were taken into his room we found a very old man, thin and worn, lying prostrate on a couch, doing a close imitation of a corpse. He could hardly move, or hear anything, though his eyes were lively and he was mentally very alert.

"Bonjour, Monsieur Huysmans," said Jean-Michel in French. "This is my friend Mervyn Matthews, I think Madame Huysmans told you about him. Could you tell us about your correspondence with Lenin?"

Mr. Huysmans smiled and launched into a long response directed at the ceiling. Unfortunately, it was in Flemish and I could not understand a word. Not having heard Jean-Michel properly, he spoke in his native tongue. After a little shouting my friend managed to get him to speak French.

"Ah, yes," said Huysmans, "I knew Lenin, we corresponded... my archives? Well, I don't know, ask my wife about them.... Yes, we know some people of influence in the Soviet Union, I will write to them, I am sure they can help your friend.... Sorry, I feel rather tired."

Obviously the old man could not be pressed. He did not say whom he had in mind, and neither did his wife. When I spoke to her about the archives, she was distinctly evasive.

"I can't help you much at the moment, I'm afraid," she said. "No, the documents are not here, they're being sorted.... But let me assure you that they will not be sent to Moscow without benefit to you."

I could only make the best of a disappointing response, and arranged to write to her from London. In fact the correspondence continued into August, but nothing more specific was said about the archives, or Huysmans' letters. He died shortly afterwards.

★

July saw me back in Paris, trying to make some progress with the Aleksinski archive. I arranged to meet Grégoire at a little restaurant near his home. When I got there I sat down at a table on the pavement, ordered a coffee, and waited. A long time passed, unpleasant on account of the hubbub of other people's conversation and the traffic noise. Where could he be? Suddenly I felt a hand on my shoulder and looked up. He was standing there, not welcoming, as I had hoped, but tense and annoyed. "How long have you been sitting here?" he asked. "I've been waiting for you at another table for half an hour."

If the meeting started badly, it got worse as it proceeded. I decided to tell him something of the background to my story, to gain his sympathy: but as a result his manner only became more off-handed, and it was clear that he had down-graded me as a client. He ordered some onion soup (which was dreadful), and seemed anxious to get the meal over as quickly as possible.

The glow of the Aleksinski archive faded further on the following day, when I visited the Maurice Thorez Institute. Thorez had been a prominent French communist, and was much lauded in the Soviet Union. The institute named after him specialised in Marxist studies, and naturally investigated any material bearing on the activities of Soviet leaders in the West. I had difficulty in getting into their building – security was strict and the place had obviously been bomb-proofed, like the headquarters of the British Communist Party in London. But once inside I met their expert on Lenin, a cheerful, heavily bespectacled gentleman by the name of Lejeune. I wondered why so many Western communists had thick glasses, perhaps reading the voluminous outpourings of their mentors damaged their sight.

I told Monsieur Lejeune about the Aleksinski papers, and asked his opinion. He seemed to be right on the ball.

"Ah yes," he replied, "I know, Aleksinski has been trying to sell them for a long time. The notes in the margins? I've seen them, no, that's not Lenin's writing, not at all."

He seemed absolutely certain about it, so I left his office feeling that I had made yet another firm step backwards. But I was still a little puzzled. Why hadn't Fedoseev, Director of the Institute of Marxism-Leninism dealt with Lejeune, the main specialist at the Thorez Institute, directly? It seemed the obvious thing for him to do. There were probably two answers: it was more advantageous for Fedoseev to authorise a paid trip to Paris for a member of his own staff (Minaeva); and he was so interested in the archive, whether it contained genuine Leniniana or not, that he wanted to deal with the Aleksinskis through his own channels.

I went back to London, the weeks went by, and I decided without a firm indication of success that the venture was too uncertain to continue. But on the 19th September another letter arrived from Fedoseev, asking again for a list of documents. Perhaps he forgot what he had written before? I made a telephone call to the Aleksinski household to ask whether the archive had been sold or not.

The son took the call, and told me, in his now familiar, slightly off-handed manner, that it was his father's business, and asked me to ring later. I presumed that the archive had not been sold (otherwise he would have told me outright) but they would not consider an offer from me to be serious. I decided not to waste my money, even on a telephone call. Early in October I had a card from them informing me (French fashion) that the old man had died. I wrote to Grégoire, expressing my condolences, and asking yet again for details of the holdings. He did not reply, so the whole matter was suspended.

★

With three unsuccessful attempts behind me, I thought I had reached the end of the paperchase, but I was wrong: another possibility came into view. Peter Reddaway was always on the lookout for people who might help, and in the early summer he wrote telling me that he could introduce me to a certain Russian lady, Irina Elkonina, who lived in Stockholm. She knew an émigré there who had helped people with relatives behind the Iron Curtain.

I dropped her a note, and on the 6th June she replied, telling me that she would be in Paris in July, when we could perhaps meet. This suited me, because I had to go there in connection with the Aleksinski papers, and it was much closer than Sweden. She would be seeing her brother, a member of the Leningrad Symphony Orchestra, which was giving concerts in the French capital. She would be staying at the Richter Hotel, so could I meet her there?

There was no question of my not doing so. I turned up at the hotel at the appointed hour and could not find her, but the Serb doorman said 'oui' when I asked whether she was in. Only later did I find out that he did not understand a word of anything except Serb, and answered 'oui' to all questions. When Irina eventually appeared in the vestibule I found her to be plump, fortyish, and very pleasant. She hopped about, birdlike, from one spot to another, looking around corners, and whispered to me, in conspiratorial fashion, that the Soviet party was under surveillance both by the French secret police and by couple of KGB operatives who played the violin (or violinists who worked for the KGB, no one was quite sure). The latter were supposed to inhibit contacts with foreigners, and although Irina was related to a member of the orchestra, she suspected that her presence was not welcome. In addition, there was a problem with the hotel manager, who believed all Russians to be capable of departing without paying their bill. So he was keeping an eye open as well.

In the end I got her into a quiet corner and revealed details of my case. She responded sympathetically, and gave me a very interesting piece of information: the Russian she knew in Stockholm, a certain Pavel Ivanovich Veselov (the surname means 'Cheery'), had enjoyed considerable success in actually getting people out of the Soviet Union, and had already extricated eleven. I pricked up my ears.

"Oh, Irina," I said, "do you know him very well?"

"Of course" she said, "I try to help him myself. But he is a very serious person and doesn't take on a case unless he thinks he can win it."

"How does he do it?"

"Mainly by paper – careful documentation of facts, campaigns in the Swedish press. It's all very legal, in fact he calls himself a juridical consultant. Once he starts something he never lets go. But he is a poor man, with no regular job, and he expects to be paid for his services."

"Do you think he could help me?"

"It's quite possible," said Irina. "If you want me to, I can ask him when I get back to Stockholm. But you must try and help me in turn: I'm looking for a temporary teaching job in England."

We struck a deal on the spot – each of us would make the relevant enquiries – and Irina dashed off, probably to dress for the evening concert. I left the hotel watched by French plain clothes men, a Russian (probably one of the violinists) and the manager. The Serb doorman smiled.

★

As the autumn approached, the Pimlico squares gradually lost their leafage and London became greyer. My discussions with Derek at our two beery venues became ever more despondent. Illicit travel to Russia was now too dangerous for me to consider, and I learned from Irina that the Finns had stopped their no-visa trips anyway. So far my paperchase had yielded nothing. Perhaps the best way forward was to put matters in the hands of Veselov, even if he was in the wrong country. In October Irina wrote to say that she had raised my case with him, and that he was expecting a letter from me. I wrote off on the 23rd, using her address, and got a reply within a week. It was not the sort of text you would get from a British solicitor, but I liked the precise wording and tough tone.

"Irina has graciously passed your letter on to me," he wrote. "Your case seems to me to be interesting and in principle winnable. Everything will depend on how it is conducted and the strength of character of the people involved. If you wish me to take charge of your efforts it is essential for us to meet. That can only happen if you come to Stockholm. I will want to know all the details of the case from the moment it started, and the people involved. My advice to you at the moment is not to do anything, anything at all, until we meet, that is, if you want me to help you.... Maintain contact with your fiancée as you have done before.... Please do not think that I will grab an axe and start hacking away, left, right and centre. I am a 'hunter', rather than a 'fighter'; a 'strangler', rather than a 'boxer'."

Pavel Veselov was obviously a man to be reckoned with. Had I at last found someone with the right mixture of experience, cunning and determination? As soon as I read his letter I knew I had to go and see him, the only problems being time and money. It was the middle of term, so I would have to wait until December. I told Derek all about it, of course, but decided not to involve him directly until I had found out more: his would be a separate case, anyway.

I took ship from Tilbury on the 10th December, sailing below the waterline. The smorgasbord supper cost 30 shillings – or the equivalent of two days' food in London – and once more I could not afford it. I was anxious to write my daily letter to Mila, but loath to let the Russians know that I was going to Stockholm: they might associate me with a well-known trouble-maker, and take it out on her. So I arranged to write to her through Jean-Michel in Brussels, keeping her abreast, in veiled terms, with what was happening. I got to Stockholm rather the worse for wear – the cheaper cabins on the ship had four bunks, so there was always someone moving around – and put up at the relatively cheap Salvation Army Hotel in the centre of town.

Irina was very welcoming. A day after my arrival Pavel Ivanovich indicated to her that he could see me. I was a little nervous, because he was not, to judge from his letter, very flexible or easy to deal with, but Irina took me around to effect the introductions. The street where he lived, Industrigatan, was as unprepossessing as its name, grey and absolutely characterless. The nameplate outside the flat bore the legend 'Elund' – the surname of his Swedish wife. We rang and the door was opened almost immediately by a big, balding man with high, Slavic cheekbones. He was aged fifty-odd, in his shirt-sleeves, and smelt slightly of tobacco. "I'm very pleased to meet you, Mervyn," he said in a nasal tone. "Come inside." We shook hands after I had crossed the threshold (to do otherwise is thought to bring bad luck in Russia). Irina adopted a slightly deferential air, and it was clear that despite his modest circumstances Pavel Ivanovich liked to be treated with respect.

"This is my wife," he said, turning to a woman many years his junior. A retiring creature, she knew no Russian, and clearly would not be involved in discussions. It seemed that she worked as a secretary and provided their only regular source of income. "And this is our cat Misha," Pavel Ivanovich added with more interest. A sleek black tom gazed at us from the top of a ramshackle bookcase. "He's very intelligent. I never let him out, so he can't get lost." I recalled Shura for a moment, and looked around. The flat was a cramped one-roomed affair, with a double divan bed and an excess of furniture. It was dusty, drab, and very Russian, rather like Pavel Ivanovich himself, I thought. The couple had no children. "Please sit down."

We got down to brass tacks immediately. "Perhaps you could start by telling me how you got into this business, and how you fight your cases," I said.

"Certainly. I work mainly through the Swedish press. I'll show you." He got up and rummaged in a drawer.

"The Soviet Embassy here dislikes Pavel Ivanovich," said Irina as he did so. "With all the fuss he's made they've changed two Consuls already."

At that moment Misha went berserk and ran up an old Turkmen carpet hanging on the wall. I tried to catch him, and got scratched.

"Misha!" cried Pavel Ivanovich. "Stop that at once!" And turning to me: "Is it bleeding? Wipe it with this." He handed me a none-too-clean tea cloth. Misha dashed off to the minuscule kitchen.

"I am told you got eleven people out," I said.

"I've only failed three times. In one of the cases the person died.

In another they did not have the courage to go on. The other is still outstanding."

"One of the people was actually in a prison camp," said Irina. "But Pavel Ivanovich got him released, even so."

At last Pavel Ivanovich found what he was looking for – not a folder, as I expected, but a large roll of what looked like wall-paper. Going to the far corner of the room, he paused dramatically.

"When I start a press campaign," he said, "it's no small matter."

And holding the free end of the roll with one hand, he propelled the rest across the floor. Stuck to one side of it, and now exposed, were dozens of articles from Swedish newspapers – *Expressen, Aftonbladet, Dagens Nyheter*.

"This is just one of my cases," he said. "All the press coverage I organised. It was successful."

There was silence as I admired his efforts, both at collage and extricating Soviet citizens from Russia.

"Pavel Ivanovich," I said reverently. "How magnificent! May I now tell you what happened to me?"

★

Discussions of my case in fact took up about thirty hours, spread over three days. Naturally, as we talked, I asked him about his background, but like many refugees he was unwilling to reveal much. He spoke with a colourful Volga accent, and was knowledgable about the great annual fair at Nizhni Novgorod (renamed Gorki in the Soviet period). He would have come to adulthood at the beginning of the Stalinist purges, and had, I imagine, never been anything but anti-Soviet. He was not only a Russian Orthodox Christian, but a conservative 'Old Believer'. His profound religiosity had prompted him to write and publish a pamphlet which proved, he claimed, the existence of God.

He told me that he had been a colonel in the Finnish Intelligence Service; possibly, he had been drafted for service in the Red Army during the Russo-Finnish War of 1939-1940 and had gone over to the Finns. He had a strong attachment to truth and honesty, without which, he said, any case could be lost. If he lied, and the press found out, his reports would never be accepted again.

He liked company, smoked strong cigarettes, and drank in moderation. He also liked a joke, particularly at Soviet expense. "One day, (he recounted) in a Lithuanian village, a peasant was standing by the well, shouting "Four ... four ... four ..." in Russian. A Russian soldier from a unit stationed nearby heard him, and came up, curious.

"Why are you shouting 'four'?" he asked. "Four what?"

The peasant pointed meaningfully down the well. The soldier leant over the parapet and peered into the depths, whereupon the peasant grabbed him by the seat of the pants and toppled him in.

"Five ... five ... five ..."

Apart from religion, Pavel Ivanovich's main source of solace was his unfinished historical novel about ancient Rome. Irina told me he spent a vast amount of time researching it, and one of his greatest pleasures was to read long passages to visitors. One evening I politely agreed to listen, but it soon was obvious, when he got into his stride, that the reading could go on into the early hours of the morning. His heroine was supposed to be a lively Roman courtesan, but she seemed more like a buxom whore from the Volga to me. Every so often her creator would pause and exclaim, "Oi, Mervyn, what a girl, what a girl!" After about half an hour I felt that really, fascinating though her antics might be, I could listen no more.

"Extremely interesting, Pavel Ivanovich," I said, as he paused at the end of a paragraph. "But I must be going. I'm sure it will be a big success when it's published."

"Oh, that's enough, is it?" he said, clearly disconcerted. I don't think he ever forgave me for not listening longer.

★

Pavel Ivanovich produced his own, quite genuine, news, by sending circular letters to every possible person and institution that might have even a marginal interest in a given case. It was the sort of thing I had been doing already, but much more aggressive, and on a bigger scale.

"What if none of them reply, or send a refusal?" I asked.

"If handled properly," said Pavel Ivanovich, "silence can be news as well. A brief refusal can make an excellent story."

"What about the risks for the people in Russia?"

"Well, no one has suffered so far. But someone might. It's a dangerous game. If you decide to go ahead, you must get over your fears before you start. For instance, Ludmila might get arrested; the KGB might organise an 'accident'; she might lose her job; they could start a press campaign against her, provoke trouble with her neighbours, and she could lose her Moscow residence permit; they might try and accuse her of breaking the law; they might disrupt contact between you, stop her invalid pension, or give her false information about you. I think that's about all."

"Enough, too."

"Publicity in the Western press is the best protection. If the authorities think their dirty deeds are going to attract public attention, they probably won't act."

"What about positive actions, like finding Lenin manuscripts?"

"That method should certainly be used also," said Pavel Ivanovich. "Any lever whatever. Keep it going if you can."

By the time he finished I had made twenty three pages of notes and firmly decided to cooperate with him. But there were two questions which awaited answers. How much money would he be asking for his services? And would Mila agree? The first question was the easier to answer. At our final meeting Mrs. Elund brought out a white table cloth and set the table for an elaborate meal. Clearly it was to be something of an occasion.

"I owe you a fee for consultations so far," I said to Pavel Ivanovich, a little apprehensively, as we started.

"Forty pounds," he replied without hesitation, slurping the scarlet borshch. He knew all about European currency rates and quoted in sterling. Forty pounds! I didn't have anything like that to hand – it equalled the entire cost of the trip.

"I haven't got much money left now," I said, "and I'm going back to England tomorrow. Would it be alright if I let you have it bit by bit, over the next month or so?"

Pavel Ivanovich agreed, for all his dealings were based on trust and honesty. Forty pounds, by professional standards, was a reasonable fee. Beyond that he evidently wanted his clients to place a high value on his services.

*

Mila's response took some time to obtain. Only on the the 22nd of December did I find someone who could take a confidential letter to her. I wrote an account of the conversations in Industrigatan and told her that if she wanted to comment on them in a normal letter she should refer to Pavel Ivanovich as the 'teacher of Irish'. So specific a term would leave no room for confusion.

"I asked the teacher," I wrote, "how he evaluates my efforts to get things moving, and yours, too. He thought our failures were to be expected and not significant. He is certain, that he can be successful, but only if we are both courageous and persistent..." There was no doubt in my mind as I wrote that which of us was most at risk. "If we go ahead with this... there may be unpleasantness for you at work, they might call you in for talks, but judging from the fact that you have not been called in so far, and you are not responsible for what is happening abroad, it is unlikely. In any case, if you need money I can transfer some to Russia for you. Are you prepared to do this? Are you ready for another struggle?... I am in favour of going for it, instead of waiting for years, begging without response...."

As I was finishing the letter I had another idea.

"In Moscow, at the moment, there lives a certain Englishman who worked for the KGB for many years and gave them a lot of valuable information. I think he lives in the large grey building on the south bank of the Moscow River, by the Bolshoi Kamenny Bridge. His name is Philby. He must have some influence in the KGB, at the top, and there may be a faint hope that he could help us. Perhaps it's worth your looking him up? I'll enclose a photograph of him, if I can find one. I haven't got the jam you sent me yet, but I know it has got to England. Is there a letter with it?"

I closed with second thoughts: "With regard to the Philby business, I don't know whether it would be wise or not... his flat is probably guarded and if the fools [goons] see you they might in their stupidity decide that you are up to no good. Also, Philby might refuse, or not be able to help. Apart from him there's George Blake. But I think the English spies are all very secondary. The main thing is the teacher of Irish."

Mila's response came through in her letter of the 22nd January, 1968, which was brought to London and posted by an unknown acquaintance. She was less enthusiastic than I had hoped. "With regard to Irish lessons," she wrote, "it's a very stressful and serious matter. It seems very difficult to me. What about trying for another visa?" In other words, the ball was still in my court.

*

I decided to press on. Pavel Ivanovich had made a deep impression on me. He seemed to have the virtues I admired most – honesty, intelligence and strength of character. His anger was admirable, too, in so far as it showed an emotional involvement in a good cause. In a peculiar way he had the air of a Sokolov, and thought like one, but in the interests of truth and righteousness. In the months that followed I conducted a hefty correspondence with him, sending off money and details about Derek. Irina wrote frequently, too. On Pavel Ivanovich's advice I wrote letters and appeals to an ever widening circle of people, including various women's organisations and all foreign embassies in London, with a more indignant and insistent tone.

It soon became evident, however, that this method was not going to produce quick results either. By now my French and Belgian initiatives were more or less dead, and nothing more had come through from Fedoseev. In April, 1968 Pavel Ivanovich wrote about quite another matter – he wanted to know if I could help him contact Greville Wynne, a British businessman who had once been jailed for spying behind the iron curtain, and might be able to help him, Pavel Ivanovich, locate a lost Swede. Wynne never replied to my letter.

After that Pavel Ivanovich stopped writing. He had no telephone (he said he was too poor to have one installed), and in the end, after weeks of silence, I got Irina to go and see him. The result was not very heartening. "Pavel Ivanovich," she wrote on the 20th May, "says that he has lost interest in your case, and does not consider it necessary to maintain a regular correspondence with you. He will write to you when he feels a desire, an inner urge, to do so." That was certainly the way he would have spoken.

I was fairly sure about what had happened. Pavel Ivanovich thought I was not paying enough for his advice, and was offended because (in his view) I had adopted his unique method without benefit to him. He was also annoyed by Mila's apparent unwillingness to make enquiries, as he occasionally suggested, in Moscow. But there was little I could do about that.

"Dear Pavel Ivanovich," I wrote on the 23rd May, 1968, "Mila and I are doing battle. We would like you to be with us, that will evidently not be possible. A pity. Yours, Mervyn."

★

Irina broke the news by letter: Aleksei Kosygin was to make a three-day official visit to Stockholm, starting on the 11th July. Pavel Ivanovich, sensing some excitement, had suddenly declared that he was ready to help. He believed it might be a good opportunity for me to hand the Soviet leader a letter. I was all too conscious of my failure to contact Kosygin in London, and thought it extremely unlikely that yet another missive would do any good – like so many others, it probably wouldn't even be read. But Kosygin might be more approachable in Stockholm, and the publicity could be useful. Term would be over, so I could get there without re-arranging my teaching.

The best way to start was to find a Swedish correspondent in London and obtain press backing in advance. The editors of *Expressen*, the paper I approached, were absolutely delighted: Kosygin was old, grey, and utterly uninteresting, the Ultimate Nightmare for any newspaper editor. He might be bringing his daughter with him, but (in accordance with Soviet practice) she would probably be kept out of sight. A love story was just what was needed to pep the visit up.

A cautious enquiry on my part elucidated that *Expressen* would make a contribution to my travel costs: as I wrote to Mila at the time, my expenses were running so far ahead of my income that I was seriously considering selling my flat in Pimlico and buying something cheaper in the suburbs. Yet when I put down the telephone after making the deal, I had the unpleasant feeling that I had sold my soul to the devil, something I had never done before. And it was all going to be rather bogus, a far cry from sparring with the KGB in Moscow. A correspondent called Jussi Anthal started the ball rolling a week in advance by interviewing me in London.

I flew to Stockholm on the 10th July, 1968, put up at the cheap Apolonia Hotel, and contacted Irina and Pavel Ivanovich. The *Expressen* journalists gave me a detailed programme covering every hour of Kosygin's stay, so that we could choose the best opportunity for a 'meeting'. The Soviet leader was to arrive by air next morning and go on to a government residence, the Haga Palace, for official talks. He would presumably be visible in the official car, and if the window were open, and the vehicle moving slowly enough, I could, perhaps, hand him a written appeal. It was all very contrived, but could be very eye-catching. On emerging from the hotel after breakfast, I found not just a car and a driver, but a reporter and two photographers as well. The paper wanted a larger pound of flesh than I had expected. Nonsensical, but it was too late to refuse.

I had time to spare at the palace before Kosygin came, so I decided to write to Mila, giving her some idea of what was going on.

"As you probably guessed," I wrote, "I've come to Stockholm to see Aleksei Nikolaevich and if possible give him a letter.... Just now I'm sitting in the quiet park surrounding the government residence. He should be here in about an hour. The residence is very large, with a beautiful lake in front. There's a police boat on it at the moment. A typical corner of Scandinavia, rather sad. I'm glad they don't charge you for sitting on the benches, but I am sure that the day is not far off when they will fit coin-boxes."

The *Expressen* news crew was hoping to create a dramatic situation, but it was soon clear that the massive police guard would thwart any attempt to get near Kosygin. In fact, when the moment came, his car passed quickly at some distance, and I could only glimpse his limp figure in the back. The newspapermen left as soon as they realised that no meeting was possible. My failure provided some sort of story, anyway.

Then, in the late afternoon, a newsworthy event did occur. Since the day was almost over, and I had got absolutely nowhere, I thought it might be a good idea to ask the Swedish police if they would allow me to hand Kosygin a letter personally. They did not have much to do, so their immediate response was to bundle me into a car and whisk me off to a police station at a place called Solna, where I was locked in a cell and not released until after eight p.m. There was no questioning, charge, or explanation. Tired and indignant, I made my way back to Pavel Ivanovich's, and told him what had happened. He was filled with joyous outrage.

"Terrible, and this is a so-called civilised country. But it's just what we needed. We might be able to win the case through this! Come on, we've got to get down to the *Expressen* office, perhaps they can still get something into tomorrow's edition." His jaw set hard, as it always did when he was in fighting mood. "The police officer will have to be disciplined, and we'll write to Minister Tag Erlander about it."

Expressen were delighted to get the story, and next morning it appeared not only in *Expressen* but in *Aftonbladet* and *Dagens Nyheter*: evidently the journalists passed some stories on. There was a picture of me speaking on the telephone, and looking suitably haggard. I was quoted somewhere as saying that Sweden was like a police state, and a solitary Swede wrote me an indignant letter saying that I had a lot to learn about behaviour in a foreign country.

Pavel Ivanovich drafted a complaint to the Minister, but it seemed rather pointless to me, so we did not send it. As for my appeal to Kosygin, none of the official bodies, Swedish or Soviet, would accept it, nor indeed the letter I wrote to his daughter. So I lamely dropped them into a post-box in Industrigatan, picked up my envelope with the cash at the *Expressen* office, and returned to England.

On arriving in London I found that about a dozen pieces had come out in the British press, all very small; and indeed, what else could one expect. As a result of the Swedes' efforts the German Sunday *Bild* – the equivalent of the London *Sunday Mirror* – ran an enormous two-page spread on us, with the old picture taken in the garden of the Palace of Weddings.

But I had to admit, in all truth, that the long months of effort had yielded little or nothing of benefit.

Eight. Success at Last

On New Year's Day, 1969, news in Swansea happened to be scarce, so the editor of the *Evening Post* decided to add a little sentimentality to the occasion (and do me a favour) by running another story on the case. 'Tale of Frustrated Love for Foreign Diplomats' ran the page-three headline.

> Life is indeed stranger than fiction and those who avidly follow the events at *Peyton Place* on television could more easily find drama and romance in the continuing story of Mr. Mervyn Matthews and his Russian fiancée, Ludmilla Bibikova. Just back in London after a visit to see his mother at Aberdyberthi Street, Hafod, Mr. Matthews, a university lecturer, has completed a mammoth task of writing his story of frustrated marriage plans to 110 heads of diplomatic missions in London.... Only a month ago I told exclusively in this column how Mr. Matthews had a chance meeting with the Russian Ambassador and his wife in London, and spoke to them, getting an immediate response from the ambassador.

In fact the 'immediate response' was entirely disappointing, and over in a few seconds. Some time in December Derek and I, on emerging from The Audley, noticed a Soviet Embassy car, registration number SU 1, standing outside the Mission of the United Arab Republic. The Russian driver was rather talkative and told us he had brought the Smirnovskys to a reception there. We waited until the distinguished couple emerged, and found they recognised us as soon as I opened my mouth.

"Mr. Smirnovsky," I said, "why cannot we get married?"

"We are well aware of the case," replied the Ambassador. "You must not create difficulties."

Poor Mrs. Smirnovsky looked genuinely alarmed, and they both dived into the vehicle as quickly as they could.

"It is one of the most heartening things that has happened for a very long time," Derek had told *The Post* bravely. "At least it proved that the Russians are well aware of our continuing fight to get married."

The truth of the matter was that despite the editor's encouraging comment, and all our efforts, very little of substance was happening.

The circular letters I replicated on a hand-driven rotoprinter brought no palpable result, except more mess in my bedroom. It became a sort of amateur printer's den filled with wax typing sheets and tubes of printers' ink which leaked onto the bedclothes. Early in April I designed a 'Three Soviet Women' leaflet with pictures of Mila, Eleonora and Mrs. Smirnovsky, together with an appeal for help, and I had it printed professionally. The police stopped Derek and me when we tried to affix copies to cars outside the Soviet Embassy. "Kensington Palace Gardens is a private road, you know. We'll arrest you if you keep doing this." The affair engendered only small articles in the *Daily Telegraph* and *The Times*.

Offering small items to the national papers and rushing down to Fleet Street at midnight to see whether they had been run in the morning editions was not without excitement. Even the Welsh language newspaper, *Y Cymro*, usually far removed from such concerns, published a forlorn little piece entitled 'Mewn cariad ond methu'n lan a chael priodi' (In love but failed to get married). Derek was doing his best with the papers out in Leytonstone, and one or two nationals as well. When he went on a package holiday to Tenerife he got himself a spread the local Spanish-language sheet, and he also managed an article in an Israeli paper, based on the fact that Eleonora was Jewish. But that was as far as it went.

At one point he told me that were it not for my persistence he would probably have given up long since. "Oh, Derek," I said. "Don't say that! I would not like to take the responsibility for someone else's life. Who knows what is going to happen? We might not get anywhere at all! Years of time and effort may be wasted." I will never forget his melancholy smile. "Oh, don't worry about that, Mervyn," he answered. "No, it wasn't you at all. I made my own decision." He was remarkably sensitive, and did not want me to feel guilty about anything.

From time to time, after so long a separation, petty frictions were arising with Mila. It was inevitable, I suppose, given the strains we were under. Late in December she wrote me rather a depressed letter, and on the same New Year's Day I replied: "The situation may seem hopeless to you, if you really think so you should either say so outright or believe in me even more.... In the course of the last nine months of 1968 about fifty articles have appeared in the newspapers of several countries on my attempts to sort things out. Apart from that please don't criticise things you don't understand, the point is you have hardly any facts by which to judge my activities. And remember that nothing could hurt me more than assertions that I am trying in vain. Today I was busy with our affairs, but I also started to prepare for term." On the 2nd January, as though she had read my thoughts, she sent a telegram: "Best new year greetings to my dear Celt, I love him faithfully, believe, and await our happiness, longing for you, kisses, Mila."

★

Occasionally I tried to cheer myself up by considering the positive elements in the situation. Mila was apparently safe, and not under threat from the Soviet authorities. The Foreign Office (now called the Foreign and Commonwealth Office) had at last realised the seriousness of our intentions and adopted a slightly more helpful attitude. They confirmed that our fiancées would be issued with official promises of British entry visas, should they be needed. In September, 1968 the new Ambassador, Sir Duncan Wilson had agreed to see me before leaving to take up his duties in Moscow. He was obviously more sympathetic than his predecessors.

As to the broader picture, the shadow of epilepsy, despite one or two queer moments, had not darkened over me, and I had acquired a very good friend in Derek. I had started to put my life together again, and was finding a little time for other things. Witness my letter to the General Manager of the Wimpey Bars chain: "Dear Sir, [I wrote] I have just purchased a cup of what you call coffee at Wimpey's in St. Mary's Street. Cardiff. It costs a shilling, but is TOTALLY DEVOID of taste. But totally. Would you kindly tell me how this has come about?" I had taken short holidays in Morocco, the Balkans and Turkey, though this meant delays in receiving Mila's letters.

More importantly, I restarted serious research work in the form of a book on contemporary Russian society. The writing would, I reckoned, take up to two years, and since there had been no reprisals against Mila so far, it was unlikely that the publication of a critical volume would provoke any. Starting this work, moreover, brought an unexpected bonus – I was offered a three-month Fellowship at Columbia University in New York to pursue it. New York is, of course, the home of the United Nations Organisation, and the campaign could be waged from there.

★

It was as I was making preparations to leave, in the middle of April, 1969, that the first, uncertain signs of movement came to my notice. Gerald Brooke had by then been in prison for four years, and his release was due in April, 1970. Meanwhile the Soviet spies Peter and

Helen Kroger still had a decade of incarceration before them. Suddenly, it was rumoured in Moscow that Gerald might not be released at all, but retried on new charges. There had already been a suggestion of the same order back in 1967, when *Izvestia* claimed that he had not only distributed anti-Soviet literature, but had also been "involved in espionage". The new rumour was ominous, but difficult for me to assess. And how would the British government react? As the Fellowship was all set up, with the necessary finance and leave from Surrey University, I decided to keep to my plan and go to New York.

Derek could be relied upon to keep a close eye on things in London. He had mastered most of my modest publicity techniques, and although he had little facility in writing, he invariably gave very sensible interviews. We arranged to write long letters to one another and exchange tapes: telephone contact was expensive. Back in Swansea, my poor mother would try to do something more with Neil McBride, the MP for Swansea East, and liaise with the *Evening Post*.

One of the things Derek was handling, incidentally, was a motion of support in the House of Commons. Over the years I had contacted many MPs, while Derek and my half-brother Jack knew others. Together Derek and I arranged to have a text drafted: "The House urges the Secretary of State for Foreign and Commonwealth Affairs to take up again the cases of Derek Deason and Mervyn Matthews both of whom wish to marry girls who cannot get a visa to leave the Soviet Union, both on humanitarian grounds and in order to remove what is becoming an increasing obstacle in the way of better Anglo-Soviet relations." We hoped we could get the motion signed by a goodly number of members, and that it would bear some fruit.

*

I arrived in New York at the crack of dawn on the 20th April, a bright, cloudless Sunday in the city. I never slept on planes, and there was a six-hour time-change, so I felt distinctly groggy. One of the great yellow taxi cabs delivered me to the Hotel Masters in Manhattan, where a one-room apartment had been reserved for me. I had spent very little time in New York before that, just the occasional weekend during my year at Harvard. The cab drove along the multiple traffic lanes, past huge apartment buildings which blocked out the sky. At that hour news-vendors were setting out veritable mountains of newsprint for sale. It was all so different from Moscow, and indeed, London.

When I got to the Hotel Masters I found I had been allocated a large room which was quite comfortable, but in sad need of decoration. Shabby lodging, however, did not worry me, I was long inured to it. My first concern, after setting down my suitcases, was to check the telephone system. I was disappointed to find that there was no direct line to the outside world, though contact could be maintained through the switch-board. When I went down to see who would be handling my all-important communications, I found a dear old lady called Grace who was much loved in the establishment but had little idea about the world outside America. I would probably be able to get through to Moscow, but it would not be easy.

After that I went out to explore the as yet empty streets. I had a cheap breakfast in a diner and saw a well-dressed negro couple slip out without paying, although the meal only cost 99 cents. New York had its sleazy side, too. On Monday I started my new existence – meeting the Director of the Institute, Marshal Shulman, settling in, finding a workplace, getting a library ticket, etcetera, etcetera. Marshal was a very eminent scholar, indeed he later advised the White House on its policy towards the USSR.

I had hardly been in New York a week when I received an interesting piece of news in the form of a small article which Derek had spotted in the *Guardian* just after I left England: "The Foreign and Commonwealth Office yesterday asked the Soviet Ambassador, Mr. Smirnovsky, if he could confirm reports that Gerald Brooke, aged 30, a lecturer, serving a five-year prison sentence in Russia for alleged subversive activities, was likely to be re-tried for espionage..." The F.C.O. action – summoning Smirnovsky – indicated that the rumour was well-founded. There was still no knowing how Harold Wilson's government would react, but obviously developments needed careful monitoring.

As for campaigning in New York, I wrote to U Thant of the United Nations, and sent him a separate appeal from Derek and Eleonora. The émigré Russian community could, I thought, be best approached through the *Novoe russkoe slovo,* the local Russian-language newspaper. I decided not to bother with the English-language dailies, as they would have little interest in a distant European love affair. The editor of the *Slovo* was Mark Weinbaum. When I visited him in his small, cramped office I found an affable, white-haired old gent, very cultured, and of the first, post-revolutionary, emigration. He listened with great sympathy and readily agreed to run an article on the case, with subsequent updates: but the stories, he said, would have to be interesting, because the paper's finances were dire, and he could not afford to lose readers. In fact two good articles resulted from our agreement.

A couple of weeks later the Brooke case developed further. On the 8th May the *New York Times* carried a story repeating the Soviet threat of a re-trial, but adding that in that event Great Britain would consider breaking off cultural relations with the USSR and cancelling a planned visit by the Bolshoi Ballet. This, I thought, would obviously cause consternation in the corps, but cut little ice in the KGB. Officers like Aleksei had an interest in ballet, and would probably prefer the dancers to stay in Moscow, anyway. The KGB enjoyed a good evening's entertainment as much as anyone else.

Some three weeks on, during one of my regular perusals of the European press shelf in the journalists' library, I found that the London *Times* dated 16th June carried an intriguing article. "Continued reports that the British government are preparing to negotiate an exchange of Peter and Helen Kroger for Mr. Gerald Brooke... have not been confirmed, [the article stated] but are placing the British Government in a difficult position ... a Foreign Office spokesman has said that negotiations on Mr. Brooke's case (not necessarily on a transfer with the Krogers) have been proceeding. There, it appears, the matter still rests. A spokesman did, however, yesterday deny reports of a visit to Britain by Herr Vogel, an East German lawyer, as being in any way part of the exchanges. Herr Vogel's name was connected with suggestions of a transfer in 1965."

A lot was obviously going on behind the scenes. If a spy exchange were to take place Derek and I still had no assurance that our fiancées would be included. The Foreign Office, in my view, might easily take the path of least resistance and leave them out. There would be just another flurry of words. As soon as I saw the report I sent telegrams to the Foreign Secretary and Brimelow, and also wrote to warn Derek. The telegrams were necessarily terse and to the point.

"Brooke-Kroger exchange must include Soviet fiancées Bibikova, Ginzburg. Watching developments closely. Considering public action. Letter follows", I telegraphed Michael Stewart. My telegram to Brimelow insisted that the "Brooke negotiations include Bibikova and Ginzburg, no other course acceptable". On the 18th June I followed the telegrams with parallel letters to the two men:

Dear Brimelow
    It has just come to my notice that you are engaged in negotiations with the Russians and... may be considering a Brooke-Kroger exchange. I wish to make it clear that... both Derek Deason and I will expect our long-suffering fiancées to be included in it.... The disastrous events of 1964 are still fresh in my memory, and it is not my

intention to allow the Foreign and Commonwealth Office to make more blunders at my expense; a Brooke-Kroger exchange [without the fiancées] would be another collapse on your part.... Frankly, we will require an undertaking... that any further exchange negotiations will also cover our fiancées.... Otherwise we shall have no alternative except to take every possible step, public and private, to prevent our interests being ignored.... May I add that the fact that our fiancées are Soviet citizens [and thus inaccessible to the F.O.] means nothing after so many tearful years.

Copies to the Prime Minister and the Director of Intelligence.

A cutting from the *Daily Telegraph* of the 2nd July which Derek sent on afterwards filled out the picture. Sir Denis Greenhill, Permanent Under-secretary at the Foreign and Commonwealth Office, had discussed the matter with Mr. Smirnovsky as long before as the 30th May. "The Foreign Office no longer denies that a deal is being considered," the article ran. "Arguments in Whitehall against submitting to blackmail are met by arguments that Brooke would suffer if Russia tries him on trumped-up charges." I was told much later that there had been a great row in the Cabinet, with Wilson adamantly opposed to the release of the Krogers on such outrageous terms. But he had allowed himself to be over-ruled on humanitarian grounds. Matters had been helped (from Gerald's point of view) by a British sailor called John Weatherly, who, while interned in Russia, had met Gerald. On getting back to England, he declared that Gerald's health was in a poor state and failing.

★

Certain things had to be done in New York, and quickly. The Foreign and Commonwealth Office was represented by the Consul, Sir Anthony Rouse. On the day I wrote to Brimelow I telephoned Rouse and asked if he would kindly help with official contacts. He gave me to understand, in beautifully cadenced English, that he had no intention of doing so. So I sat down and composed a pungent note to him as well.

Dear Sir Anthony

I have just sent a short telegram to Mr. Stewart explaining that Mr. Deason and I expect to have our fiancées included.... May I indicate to you now, as Her Majesty's representative here, that I intend to take all possible measures,... including public pressure and publicity... to see that the exchange (if it takes place) is broadened to include our most distressing cases.... Any publicity I organise will doubtlessly affect F.C.O.-Soviet negotiations and may be unwelcome to the Foreign Secretary. May I ask you to note my address and telephone number. Whether you pass on the purport of my letter is now your responsibility, though my own feeling is that it would be better for you to do so.

I got some press cuttings together, including the Russian ones, which he would probably not understand but might serve as a frightener. I took the envelope down to the Consulate and handed it in personally – sometimes one gets a sly pleasure from planting bombs under adversaries. I telephoned Derek to coordinate our efforts: we should not get anything into the papers, I said, so as not to complicate negotiations: but if Derek could manage it, he should go and see Brimelow and give him a full set of the circulars we had sent out. We wanted, within a fortnight, a firm assurance of inclusion in any agreement with the Russians.

★

The Moscow dimension had to be handled, too. What should I tell Mila? As it happened I was just preparing to telephone her. I decided it would be better not to dazzle her with any promise of progress. And strictly, there wasn't any: there were still too many bridges to cross. I ordered the call and eventually, thanks to Grace, the phone rang in my room. I heard the usual distant voice on the line.

"Mervusya!"

"Milochka, is that you? How are things in Moscow?"

"Just about the same."

"Did you get my parcel?"

"Yes, it was fine. How are things going in New York?"

I had a cautious phrase ready.

"Some positive elements seem to be creeping in to the picture, I can't say much at present. I've written to U Thant at the United Nations. I think it would be a good idea if you would make another formal application at the Palace of Weddings. Can you?"

Silence: would she or wouldn't she? Mila was always like that, she liked to retain some freedom of action.

"I'm planning to go back to England on the 19th of July," I said. "I'll ring you on the 15th or the 16th to confirm the date."

★

Early on the morning of Monday, 24th June, my telephone rang. On lifting the receiver I heard, to my immense satisfaction, the voice of

Sir Anthony Rouse. It was not only what he said, but also the fact that a Foreign Office finger had actually dialled my number. It must have done so at a behest from above! Yes, said Sir Anthony, he had been asked to ring me. Mr. Stewart had got my message and was taking a close personal interest in the outstanding Anglo-Soviet marriage cases. The Foreign Secretary would do everything to obtain a solution... I put the phone down in a daze. It seemed as though something really positive had happened at last.

A few days later I got Brimelow's own response (written on the 30th June).

> Dear Mr. Matthews
>
> I know you have already received certain assurances through Sir Anthony Rouse, which we sent in reply to your earlier telegrams.... I would like to repeat the message from the Secretary of State.... There are no further developments which I can report to you at present. But I can certainly undertake to keep you informed.

My Fellowship at the Institute was coming to an end, and the new developments made me anxious to return to England. I arrived in London on the 20th July: the motion had just gone down in the House, with no less than 32 signatures. I telephoned the Foreign and Commonwealth Office: Brimelow wanted to see me quickly, and an appointment was arranged for the 22nd.

On arriving at King Charles Street, I found that Sir Thomas had acquired a large office, but personally had not changed in the slightest. Of course, since he had, in Foreign Office terms, assumed an optimum image many years before, there was no need for him to do so. He greeted me with his usual business-like, but slightly distant smile. It was soon apparent that he intended to reveal as little as possible. No, the solution might not be entirely satisfactory, but he hoped to see us married by the end of the year. I knew about Certificates of No Impediment, didn't I? No, he was not aware of the motion in the House, or that the KGB had tried to recruit me. In the negotiations so far, my case had given most trouble and the Russians had wanted to exclude it from the agreement. Now it would be a question of Soviet entry visas being issued on a certain date. The F.C.O. wanted all questions solved. Many incidentals were involved, and all the F.C.O. could get from the Russians would be 'consent' for us to marry: whether marriage actually took place was an entirely different matter.

I asked about the date when Derek and I could expect to get our long-awaited visas. At that point Brimelow showed that he could be a master of insult, as well as of diplomatic nicety. I suppose he had to get his own back for my unconcealed lack of confidence in him in the past. "You can go away on holiday in September," he said, "but be here after that. If I gave you a date now you would rush down to the *Daily Express* office and sell it." I was so taken aback I omitted to ask, in the same vein, why he had not done so himself.

It was not the first time I had left those pretentious corridors with mixed feelings. As I walked down Downing Street my head was buzzing with questions. Had the Russians really made a genuine attempt to stop the marriage, or was it just a ploy to register their disapproval of my press campaign? Had all my efforts over the last five years actually been counter-productive? I wondered, too, whether the objections had originated in Moscow, or in the distinguished brain of Shishkin, my arch-enemy in London. I had done my best to publicise his KGB status in letters I sent to his colleagues at the Embassy and people elsewhere. That must have rankled. Beyond that, I was concerned about the actual marriage arrangements: the agreement seemed to be extremely vague – recalcitrant officials in Moscow might still be able to delay or torpedo things. Impossible to know, of course.

When I got back to Pimlico I made a note of all that Brimelow had said, should it be needed later. I had arranged to telephone Mila that evening, and now I was a little more specific. "There is really a bit of movement," I told her. "Whatever your holiday plans, keep a few days in hand for the autumn." She did not ask for details, but as she told me later, she had already guessed that something might be afoot. She had met the ubiquitous Victor Louis when making another futile enquiry at the OVIR office, and he had been most anxious to get a 'lovelorn' story out of her. She was frightened of publicity, and had refused to say anything.

In London, however, things were moving a little more quickly than the good knight had revealed. A day or so after I met him Mr. C.S.R. Giffard, his subordinate, wrote to me: "You may find that the wording of the agreement means that you will be granted the [Soviet entry] visa on the 24th October." This peculiar formulation was perhaps intended to inhibit publicity, but it was the most explicit I could get. Derek and I would have liked a much earlier date.

★

Gerald Brooke arrived back to England on the 24th July, and news of his arrival took up most of the front page of the *London Evening News*. The handsome young man returning home after a long, undeserved ordeal in a Russian prison camp was a top-class story.

The proposed marriages were covered briefly, with the picture of Mila and myself taken at the Palace of Weddings in 1964.

I telephoned Mila and told her, at last, that the spy exchange had started, and we were to be part of it. She was preparing to set off for a motoring holiday in Northern Russia with her friends who had a tiny car, so I was lucky to catch her. I had not expected exclamations of delight, nor tears of joy, and there were none. We had both gone through too much, and had been disappointed too often. Moreover, the issue of the visas was still two months off, and the long interval basically unexplained. Even when Derek and I got to Moscow, the Palace of Weddings might raise technical difficulties: a month's notice was still required for registration. So it was not surprising if I sensed a hint of sadness in Mila's voice. Apart from all the unanswered questions, she realised too well that she would be leaving her family and her country, possibly for ever, to dwell in an unknown land. This would be no ordinary marriage.

On the following day – which happened to be my thirty seventh birthday – the story of Gerald Brooke's arrival dominated all the national dailies, and even the return of the American astronauts from the moon did not push it off the front pages. Just before she left Moscow, Mila wrote to me describing what had happened there – I got her letter about a week later.

> Mervusik, my dear, today, the 25th, is your birthday, sincere congratulations, I wish you good health, success at work, personal happiness. And I love you very much. I am in a spin. Victor Louis started looking for me from the morning onwards. I didn't say anything, but they'll make things up, anyway. He wanted me to say something for his readers. Perhaps I should have, but I refused. He uttered some banalities about us being brave, heroes, and lucky. Then my sister Lena, who's on holiday in the Baltic, rang. Valerii [Golovitser] and my friend Rima called in. Journalists rang from the *Daily Express*, but I put them off as well. Friends rang and congratulated me, they're all overwhelmed. I've had so many telephone calls, and I'm trying to pack for the holiday. I can hardly stand up.

Michael Stewart was due to make a statement in the House the same afternoon. I contacted John Smith, my M.P., to try and get a ticket to the visitor's gallery, but he could not help. Somehow I managed to gain admittance to a diplomatic gallery. It must be the most cramped seating in the world – I found I had to sit bolt upright, with very little room for my legs, under the eagle eye of an attendant – but it was wonderful to be there. Although I could not see very much (except, as it happens, Mr. Smith) I could hear everything loud and clear. Derek had managed to get into the Strangers' Gallery, so, appropriately, we were in the House together. Not many MPs were present.

After announcing that the Krogers were to be released on the 24th October Mr. Stewart continued: "It has been arranged, as a separate matter, that three British subjects who have for some years been endeavouring without success to marry Soviet citizens, will, not later than the 24th October, be granted visas to enter the Soviet Union to register their marriages...." A small cheer was raised.

Next day full details of the exchange were carried prominently on the front page of *The Times*. The other couple mentioned in Mr. Stewart's statement were Camilla Grey, an English art historian who had lived in Russia, and her fiancé Oleg Prokofiev, son of the great composer. Included also were one or two more shadowy figures – two Britons jailed for drug offences, and two British spies involved in the Portland spy ring (who were now to be paroled early). In future there was to be improved access to British citizens imprisoned in the USSR. Of all the people involved, the only ones I had ever heard of were Camilla and Oleg; but Camilla had always been very discreet and had not wished to be associated with our campaign.

The papers carried a lot of editorial comment, much of it negative: "The higher value you put on human life, the more vulnerable you are to inhuman blackmail" ran the editorial in the *Daily Sketch*. "There is nothing but contempt and very great concern for future relations after this example of blackmail, applied to a man who had obviously committed no offence that would be regarded as an offence or crime in a democratic society."

"Mr. Stewart was asked in the Commons," stated the *Daily Express,* "what is to prevent an innocent British tourist being seized in Moscow to set up a sinister package deal for a Russian spy? Mr. Stewart's reply: 'I think one can say with reasonable confidence that a British citizen who goes to the Soviet Union and who carefully observes their laws while he is there is not at risk'. This is obviously true at the moment while the Red spies Peter and Helen Kroger are still held in Britain. But once they are freed in October?"

To tell the truth, although I benefited from the arrangement, and had long fought for it, I thought these comments well justified. Britain had had a terrible deal.

★

Later in the day I sent Mila a letter. "I am writing to you on my birthday. I knew approximately from the middle of June that the

Foreign Office had a heightened interest in our marriage plans: and I had some further indications a few days ago. But I decided not to tell you until everything was publicly announced. I have been very nervous, and running about. I was in the House of Commons today when Stewart announced the deal. The papers were after me. But Thank God, everything is getting quieter now."

The *Evening Post* suggested that the population of Swansea – or at least its readers – would be delighted. Certainly, my mother was foremost amongst them. "I am very happy that things seem to be going well with you," she wrote to me, "I hope there will be no further hitches and that everything goes smoothly. My advice to you would be to abide by the plans of the Foreign Office. Don't be difficult in any way.... Everyone down here in Swansea sends their good wishes. Please let me know what is happening.... Ask Mila to write to me, or I would write to her if you gave me her Moscow address."

In Pimlico congratulations came rolling in by telephone and letter. Newspaper correspondents started calling at the flat, and on occasion had to be refused entry. There was a very nice telegram from Des Zwar, who was still keeping in touch with me. And some income tax forms which arrived a day or two later bore the terse inscription, in an unknown hand: "Glad to hear the good news yesterday."

★

Derek and I met in The Albert to discuss the developments. As far as we could make out, this was not only the end of one thorny path, but also the beginning of another, though hopefully shorter. The Foreign Office been unwilling (or unable) to commit itself regarding the actual marriage arrangements, and we found the Soviet Consulate less than helpful.

We had gone along there and spoken to an official called (I believe) Kutuzov, as Shishkin, we were told, was 'out'. Kutuzov asked us to call back next day, which seemed to be a hopeful sign: but when we did so, he would say only that the visas would not be granted until October. The Russians clearly wanted to synchronise this with the release of the Krogers, though even so the reason for the choice of the 24th was never explained. We would be getting only tourist visas, as private ones took six months to process. The wedding date would be arranged after we arrived in Moscow.

With regard to the one-month waiting period for registration, Kutuzov said, we could return to England and would be permitted to re-enter Russia for the wedding. Our Russian fiancées would make their applications for exit permits in the normal way, after the marriages. There was nothing more to be added, (Kutuzov cut us short) so please come back early in October for all the necessary arrangements to be made. Meanwhile, at the Palace of Weddings, Efremova had confirmed the need to observe the waiting period when Mila called on her a few days earlier.

Derek and I agreed, after considering the matter, that I should write another letter to Michael Stewart setting out our concerns, and asking for more specific assurances. There was also the problem of handling the press: several papers were desperate to cover the marriages, but would any of them be prepared to meet the rather considerable cost of the air tickets (two returns and two singles, plus incidentals) without distasteful publicity?

A day or two later, with this in mind, we telephoned the *Daily Express* and asked for a confidential meeting with one of the news editors. We went to the office by appointment, and found him to be a mild-mannered, middle-aged man who seemed completely out of place in his imposing, high-backed editorial chair. Then we moved to a pub outside for a more detailed discussion. The editor seemed rather puzzled by our secretiveness – he knew better than we that the concept of 'confidentiality' has a short life in Fleet Street. He said that financial assistance would be available, but proposed, naturally enough, that The *Express* handle all arrangements after the marriages, including our return to England, with secret hotel accommodation and exclusive interviews.

At this point Derek and I decided, very amicably, to follow different paths. Derek accepted the offer, while I resolved to play everything off my own bat, regardless of the cost. If the battle was indeed won I had no further interest in public exposure. My main desire was to get Mila back to England as quietly as possible, pack all the files away – and sell the damned rotary printer. My book on Soviet society might even help me to get a job at one of the country's two venerable universities. Everybody enjoys being famous, but my own public image, in so far as I had one, was too coloured by misfortune and failure. I appeared to be more of a victim than a hero.

★

A last adventure awaited us: the return to Moscow. It would be pleasant to relate that we viewed it with warm anticipation, savouring images of white snow, gilded cupolas, warm furs, the smiling faces of beloved ones. Alas, our thoughts mainly centred on the daunting bureaucratic problems. We ordered plane tickets for the 24th of October, so as to depart for Leningrad in the afternoon, and fly on from there. This was to avoid journalists who might be waiting for us if we boarded the direct Moscow flight.

On the morning of the great day, tickets in hand, we went to the Soviet Consulate to pick up our visas. The Krogers were due to leave the country on a Warsaw flight at 11.15 a.m. Kutuzov greeted us behind a broad official smile, and somewhat to our relief there was again no sign of Shishkin.

"Ah, yes," said the Soviet official effusively, when we were shown into his office. "You've come for your visas. But I'll have to ask you to wait for a while." He disappeared, leaving us, as I recall, alone.

We exchanged glances: my God, what were they up to now? Had something gone wrong? By this hour the Krogers must certainly have left Heathrow. After a few very unpleasant moments we tumbled to a likely explanation: the Consulate was probably waiting until the plane carrying them had not only taken off, but was actually outside British air space.... Had we but known it, their release from Parkhurst provoked a patriotic demonstration among the inmates. Eventually Kutuzov reappeared with the small, familiar blue pages in his hand.

"Here you are, gentlemen, your visas," he said. "Have a good trip!"

"But they're only for ten days," said Derek. "Registration takes a month."

"Ten days is long enough to get married and divorced," Kutuzov answered with a laugh.

★

We got to Leningrad and changed planes, arriving at Vnukovo airport in Moscow well after midnight. How strange it felt to be back on Soviet soil! The airport was virtually deserted, but we managed to get a taxi to take us to the centre: I had a little Soviet money for the fare. Glancing out of the back window of the vehicle as we sped along the dark, frosty road, I was gratified to note that we were not being followed. We looked forward to arriving: the girls knew approximately when we would come, and should be waiting. The plan was to go to Mila's first and then get Derek off to Eleonora's new flat out in Kuzminki.

The taxi stopped in Starokonyushenny pereulok. We alighted and walked through the two dimly-lit archways of Mila's block. It was not snowing, yet bitterly cold, many degrees below freezing. We pushed open the creaky house door and went up the few steps to Mila's communal flat. At that hour the house was very silent, nothing stirred. I don't know how Derek felt, but I was more tired than excited. I had telephoned Mila before leaving London, and there was no doubt about the welcome we would receive. Surely there could be no surprises now.

I rang the doorbell, and we stood there for a moment, expecting to hear steps inside. There were none. We rang again, and again. Nothing.

"What's up now, do you think?" Derek asked, nervously. "Surely she hasn't been taken away?"

I shared his apprehension, but there was no point in jumping to dark conclusions.

"No idea. She should be waiting. I think the best thing to do is try and phone the flat from the street, the phone may be louder than the doorbell, and someone else may answer. Perhaps they're all asleep."

Unfortunately, as I well knew, the Moscow public telephone system ran solely on two-kopek pieces, which people collected and treasured precisely for that purpose. If I could not find one we faced a cold, uncomfortable night on the pavement, wondering what had happened. Eleonora had no telephone, and could not be reached by that means. At that point Providence intervened with three small miracles. Firstly, I found a two-kopek coin in my pocket. Secondly, the phone in the street worked, and did not swallow the money without connecting, which happened very often. And thirdly, the receiver was picked up at the other end. It was Mila's voice, sounding hardly nearer than when I phoned her from England.

"Hello, Mila?"

"Yes, yes. Mervusya? Is that you?

"Is everything all right?"

"Yes."

"Why didn't you answer the doorbell, then?"

"I didn't hear it. I was afraid I wouldn't sleep, so I took a sleeping tablet".

"Oh, my God. A sleeping tablet? Tonight of all nights? Anyway, Derek and I are here, on the Arbat. We'll be around in two minutes."

Mila opened the door, a small figure in a colourful Russian dressing gown, sleepy, but with an expectant look on her face. We embraced warmly, an embrace awaited for three years, ever since my brief sojourn in the National Hotel in 1966. There was no great romantic surge, only a deep contentment that at last we were together. For a few moments the remaining hurdles receded from our thoughts. Derek was there, anyway, and we our first task was to get him off to Eleonora's. That was my job. Somehow we found another taxi, and after another long ride I delivered him to Kuzminki: we found Eleonora's flat without much difficulty, and she, plump, excited, and bright-eyed, threw herself into Derek's arms. I had not met her before.

When I got back to Mila's it was well after midnight by British time. I took off my outer garments and sank onto the divan, Mila beside me. What a day! Fancy taking a sleeping tablet the very night Derek and I were supposed to arrive! Frailty thy name is woman. This was one detail which should not be allowed to get into the press.

★

Despite our misgivings we hoped that the actual marriage arrangements would go smoothly, thanks possibly to some sort of fiat from the KGB. As it was, the process creaked and juddered to the very last.

The next morning all four of us met at the Palace of Weddings, clutching our passports and new Certificates of No Impediment. We asked the middle-aged matron who was on duty (the place was always full of them) whether she could give us an early registration date. Clearly she had received no instructions about these strange couples, and was terrified. She looked at the translations of the certificates and (desperate for a pretext to put things off) declared them to be inadequate. We should get the documents properly translated and notarized in Moscow, and re-present them in a day or so.

It was the beginning of a new bureaucratic round. Derek and I contacted the Embassy and asked them to intervene. Then we made the obligatory visit to OVIR to get our temporary residence permits. The problem at the Palace was indeed sorted out after a day or two, and we were asked to attend for the registration at 10 a.m. on Thursday, 30th October. We decided not to have any celebration in their hall (champagne parties were common) or indeed afterwards. Derek and Eleonora would quietly go off on their own.

Mila and I got up early on Thursday morning. It was to be another wedding day, but we had few pleasurable expectations: would anything go wrong again? While we were having breakfast we decided, rather unexpectedly, that all the misery of the last five years did not justify dressing up. So instead of donning my suit, I put on the old tweed jacket and trousers I usually wore in the lecture room. Mila set aside the dress I had brought from England, and wore an ordinary, workaday skirt and blouse. We took the gold ring which had been bought in such tearful circumstances five years earlier, and found a taxi.

It did not take our two wedding parties long to assemble at Griboedov Street, because there were so few of us – Mila, myself,

Mila's grown-up niece Nadya and her husband Yurii (to act as witnesses), together with one or two of Mila's friends whom I hardly knew. Derek and Eleonora brought only Eleonora's sister. Although I was expecting some press presence (it could hardly have been otherwise), I was disconcerted to find a whole bevy of journalists waiting outside, rather as before Victor Louis was among them.

Once inside the building, the formalities (to our relief) went according to plan. We were invited to surrender our passports, and we were led, first Mila and I, then Derek and Eleonora, into a hall decorated with red drapes and an austere white bust of Lenin. A portly matron read the Soviet marriage statement, asked us to kiss, and then declared that in Soviet law we were married. At long last the gold ring was placed on Mila's finger. It had taken us five years and just under five months of unremitting effort.

In the corridor outside another matron returned our passports, open at the page where the marriage stamps had been placed. Glancing down at Mila's skirt, she exclaimed: "And you are our least attractive bride!" I was glad our gesture of protest had been noticed. We had a few photographs taken in the corridor, though when we were through Eleonora exclaimed that we had inadvertently used the entrance to the gents' lavatory as a backdrop.

Outside in the street the correspondents asked us for comment, but none of us were in a mood to say anything – Mila and I because we were tired of the fuss, Derek and Eleonora because they had their agreement with the *Express*. We walked briskly down the street, the press close on our heels. Yurii found this troublesome, and although I did not myself see it, took a swing at one of them. He did not know much English, but I distinctly heard him shout "Bastard", probably without realising how offensive the word can be.

Thence, by invitation, to the British Embassy, where the atmosphere was more relaxed. Officialdom had decided that it would be nice if we all celebrated with a glass of wine, and received the Embassy's good wishes. A few minutes more, and we were back in the real Moscow on Sofiiskaya naberezhnaya. We photographed one another standing against the parapet of the Moscow River, with the Kremlin in the background.

After the wedding I hoped to stay in Moscow, safe and sound, for several days, to browse in the bookshops, and perhaps work at the Lenin Library. For someone involved in Russian studies it was a valuable opportunity. I had no intention of contacting Vadim or Aleksei – Mila was against it, and they would probably have refused to see me, anyway. But the pleasure of a few days' work and relaxation was also to be denied me. Word quickly came through from

OVIR that we would all have to leave Russia quickly. Mila and I went along to the office, where a silent, sour-faced official took away her Soviet internal passport, and issued a foreign passport. It was the only document which permitted a Soviet citizen to cross the frontier.

Our last evening in Moscow was, in a way, the saddest of all. Dozens of Mila's friends came to her room to say goodbye. The Russians, like the Welsh, savour endless adieus, and they sat in slow relays on the little stools. Only Valerii Golovitser remained throughout, a silent and mournful figure in the corner, overwhelmed at the loss, probably life-long, of his good friend Mila. To make things worse, she was being taken off by a Britisher he had once befriended. In the end the crush got too much for me, and I went out for a solitary walk along the Arbat, deserted and quiet at midnight.

On the 3rd November Derek and Eleonora went straight back to London to fulfil their obligations to the *Daily Express*, and take up residence in Leytonstone. There was a lot of sentimental press coverage. I decided that in order to avoid the same fate Mila and I would fly out to Vienna, spend an entire afternoon and evening honeymooning there, and proceed to London the next day.

Over the previous few months many small steps had been taken to getting married and extricating Mila from her inhospitable homeland, each step bringing the solution a little nearer. But I think the moment I actually felt that it was really 'all over' came only when we walked into the arrival hall at Vienna airport. At last we were both off the aircraft and safely in the West, well and truly out of the reach of the KGB. Mila's eyes widened with surprise at the neatly-uniformed bag handlers, so different from the drab porters at Vnukovo.

*

There was a small contretemps at London airport when we found that Mila's documents would not admit her to the UK, perhaps because we had come unexpectedly via Vienna. For a few minutes, while smiling officials sorted things out, we stood on different sides of the barrier. But of course, we were on British soil and really had nothing to fear. We reached my little flat in Pimlico, our ultimate goal, an hour or so later. Waiting for me was a cutting from the *Evening News*, dateline 30th October, 1969, which Jack had sent on. It was not quite what I would have wanted.

Britons Marry in Moscow
From Victor Louis, Moscow

Dr. Mervyn Matthews and his Russian fiancée of five years, Ludmilla Bibikova, were married today at Moscow's main register office, the

Palace of Weddings. They were accompanied by eight close friends but no one from the British Embassy.

After the ceremony, which is surprisingly short, taking about five minutes, they realised they had been unwise to dismiss the taxi in which they had arrived. While waiting for another... Dr. Matthews and his bride were photographed by a newsman.

In fact the couple had been doing their best to avoid the Press, and tried to hide their faces behind the bride's bouquet of white chrysanthemums.

The bridegroom tried to discourage the photographer with shouts of 'Bastard'....

The word, of course, was not mine – and I was very distressed by Louis' having attributed it to me. What a way to depict such an occasion! When I called at the *Evening News* office a few days later, to try and get a correction published, the paper's lawyer brushed the matter off as inconsequential. Wearily, I decided not to pursue it further.

But even so I wondered what was behind it. Victor Louis saw and heard all that happened, and was well aware of the unfortunate impression that his report would make. He had confined his remarks to me, not mentioning Derek and Eleonora. My first thought was that this was a dig per favour of the KGB: but later I came to a less sinister conclusion. The press had, on the whole, stood by us magnificently, and were doubtlessly entitled to a sugary double-wedding scene, with hugs, kisses, and lots of flowers. The newspapermen on the spot were disappointed when they did not get it. Maybe Victor Louis was only voicing, in his own way, their general discontent without understanding the force of the word. Had Mila and I treated them unfairly? Perhaps. Derek, I thought, may have acted more properly in coming to an agreement with at least one major British daily.

*

On the 10th November we sent a joint letter to Michael Stewart.

The years of separation are over. May we thank you for the major part which you played in bringing this about. The decision which you had to make in this sad affair was a difficult one, but there is no doubt that in the circumstances you acted in the most humane and liberal manner. That is something that we and our wives will always gratefully remember.

Yours sincerely,
Mervyn Matthews, Derek Deason.

A few days later Mr. Stewart replied:

Thank you for your letter of the 10th November. I am glad it has now
been possible for your marriages to take place after so many years of
waiting, and I should like to take this opportunity of wishing you and
your wives every happiness in the future.

Yours sincerely,
Michael Stewart.

Epilogue

Grow old along with me!
The best is yet to be,
The last of life, for which the first was made.

Thus spoke Rabbi Ben Ezra in Robert Browning's famous poem.
But he was wrong, of course; growing old is a sad experience, and I,
for one, have never been able to reconcile myself to it. I do, however,
gain a mite of satisfaction from recalling memorable moments of the
past, and considering the lives of people who played a part in my
own.

★

It was the summer of 1972, a warm sunny afternoon in Leningrad. I
had just spent a morning at the famous Publichka, or public library,
and was walking back to the Astoria hotel, where I was staying.
Although I believed I was still *persona non grata* in Russia, the Soviet
Embassy had for some reason issued a visa for a short tourist trip.
Mila was safely in London, with our son Owen, now one year old,
so there was nothing to fear on that front. I had seized the opportunity and returned to Russia.

Suddenly a car drew up alongside the pavement and a couple of
plain clothes men jumped out. In a moment I had been bundled into
the vehicle, while a young man who happened to be sitting on a
bench nearby looked on in horror. He realised, no doubt, that he had
just witnessed a small KGB operation – the arrest of a hapless
foreigner. Obviously, my visa had been issued in error. The KGB
must have got onto my tracks after I had telephoned Mila's niece
Nadya in Moscow, to tell her I was coming: a few days in the Soviet
capital were included in the tour.

The KGB car took me straight to the Leningrad office of OVIR,
and I was questioned about where I had been. The obdurate officials
could not digest the fact that as a tourist I had actually spent the
morning reading books. In any case, they said, I was *persona non
grata*, my visa was being annulled, and I would have to give an
undertaking to leave the country as soon as possible. Otherwise I

200

would be escorted out by the military. The Intourist desk at the hotel would arrange the travel, at my expense. I agreed to sign their document, because by doing so I would be free for a few hours more, and could warn Nadya that I would not be coming. Brezhnev's Russia had changed little.

Being arrested again was an exceedingly unpleasant experience, but no disaster – my near and dear were ensconced in Pimlico. I went for a walk through the gardens of Marsovo Pole to calm my nerves, and then made my way back to the hotel. By now it was early evening. No sooner had I got to my room than the telephone rang – the KGB service in the hotel had been waiting for me.

"Would you come to the Intourist desk immediately, please."

I made my way down the ornate staircase, with the merry strains of 'Kalinka', the well-known Russian folk song, audible in the background. A folk orchestra was regaling a group of American tourists in the restaurant, all of them oblivious to unpleasant realities outside. A KGB man was waiting for me. He had already spoken to the Intourist staff.

"You wish to change your travel arrangements?" asked the beautifully dressed lady behind the counter. "What has happened?"

I looked at the man beside me. "You had better ask this dreadful creature," I replied.

"We have prepared a ticket for you to travel to Helsinki by the night train."

I returned to my room, packed my case and took a taxi to the Finland Station. I spent the few minutes left before departure looking at the locomotive which Lenin was said to have used on his clandestine return to Russia in 1917. When I boarded the Helsinki train I found there was hardly anyone on it. The customs formalities at the frontier were rigorous, and the official stole the little Soviet money which I still had. The border guard, on seeing my cancelled visa, was almost threatening, and I feared for moment that he would intern me. But I was still in the carriage as it was shunted over the little bridge into Finland. Next day, after a tussle with British Airways about paying for the Helsinki-London flight, I returned to London.

It was about two o'clock when I opened the front door of our house in Pimlico, and walked into our living room. Mila was sitting at the telephone, waiting for my call from Russia. I had promised I would ring just then.

★

Come July, 1979, and the Matthews family of four, including seven-year old Owen and little Emily, aged two, stepped off the plane at Vnukovo airport. The Soviet government had unexpectedly informed the Foreign Office in London that a family visa would be available for me and the children to enter the USSR. Mila, as a Soviet citizen, did not need one. I insisted that the children travel on my British passport: if they were registered in their mother's, their citizenship could be questioned, and they might (in the worst case) not be let out of Russia.

We spent a month living with Sasha and Lena in their flat on Frunzenskaya naberezhnaya. It was still highly unusual for foreigners to reside privately in Moscow, and many of the Vasin visitors were embarrassed to find me there. One of them told us coyly that a review of my new (anti-Soviet!) book about privilege in Russia had just been broadcast on Radio Liberty, which was still mostly jammed in the USSR. On the streets outside there was the old-style goon supervision, but that did not bother me much: there was little to be feared, now. We spent a lot of time out at the dacha, showed the children the Moscow sights, and visited Mila's friends – that is, those who did not mind opening their door to a foreigner.

Valerii Golovitser had married and become a father himself. He was still trying to get a visa for them all to emigrate. One evening I telephoned him at his new flat near the Moscow film studios, and he responded by inviting me over.

"I'll meet you at the metro station," he said, "the block is not easy to find. It'll be dark and you don't know the way."

When I got to the station a familiar figure was waiting for me, elegantly dressed, as always. It was rather like our meeting at the Kroptkinskaya station in 1963. We exchanged greetings, and walked slowly to his block, chatting about our families. We entered the hallway, and stepped into the lift.

"It's on the sixth floor," said Valerii, pressing the button.

The lift doors closed, and we were suddenly alone, both (I am sure) thinking about the passage of time since we had met in his room on Ryleev Street. I looked at his pale, fine features, and he smiled gently, as he had done years before. We were in Russia, and there was only one way to respond: I put my arms gently around his neck and kissed him.

"Over fifteen years!" I said.

"Yes, fifteen."

A moment later the lift doors opened, and we were being greeted on the landing by his wife Tanya and their little son Alesha.

When I tried to return to Russia in the following December, I was again refused a visa. Perhaps the Radio Liberty book review did it.

★

December, 1988, perestroika. The USSR, as I had known it, was on the verge of collapse. The Soviet throne was now occupied by Gorbachev, a benign, smiling figure. On this occasion I got a visa through the good offices of the British Council, and went to Moscow for a month to research social problems. I was lodged in the University Hotel, not far from the Lenin Hills. The plane had arrived late the night before, and I saw little except dark streets after my arrival. I left the hotel after breakfast to go and register at the faculty. The scene outside was familiar Moscow: a broad suburban highway, blocks of austere, Khrushchev-style flats. Though there was little snow, the temperature was way below zero, and everybody (including myself) was muffled in heavy clothing, furs and boots, Russian fashion.

I walked a couple of hundred yards to the nearest trolley bus stop and looked carefully around. As far as I could see, nobody was following me. No KGB goons!

I boarded the trolley bus and went into the centre of town, keeping a careful eye on my fellow-passengers and, as best I could, on the road behind the vehicle. The window was dirty and ice-encrusted. But it did not take me long to determine that there was no surveillance of any kind. Unbelievable! For the first time ever I felt free on the streets of Moscow. A miracle had occurred – Russia really had changed.

★

On an afternoon in February, 1992, at precisely 12.30, I pushed open the heavy door of one of the side entrances to the Russian State Security building on Dzerzhinski Square – formerly the citadel of the KGB and the most feared edifice in the Soviet Union. The security guards at a desk inside were expecting me, and asked for my passport.

"I have an appointment with Mr. Kondaurov," I said.

The guards took a quick look at a list and checked the document I had handed them. Then they telephoned on an internal line. A moment later a young and attractive secretary appeared.

"This way, please."

We went down a corridor lined with closed bookcases, and came to an anteroom.

"Aleksei Petrovich is expecting you. Would you like to go in?"

She opened the door of the inner office and ushered me in. It was just the kind of room you would have found in one of the privileged Soviet institutions in the old days, high ceiling, parquet floor, carpeting, and an imposing desk. Its occupant, Aleksei Petrovich Kondaurov, was tall, dark, and welcoming. He took his seat behind the desk which had no less than six telephones on it. The new State Security administration had opened a public relations section, and I was there, believe it or not, by invitation. Russian Security (whatever its other functions) was now ready to greet former sovietologists, and was even curious about what they did. Aleksei Petrovich showered me with questions.

"How did you study Russia?" he asked. "And the KGB? What materials did you use? Let me give you a copy of our new magazine [he handed me an expensively-produced journal entitled *SB, Sluzhba bezopasnosti,* or 'Security Service' in English]. Of course, we are looking for material, and we might consider printing an article from you, as a former sovietologist. You say you may be writing a memoir about those years? You want to contact Aleksei Suntsov, a KGB officer? Well, I'm not sure, it's a long time, of course, nearly thirty years or more.... Would you like a cup of coffee while we talk?"

Nothing was decided, except that I might call again. But isn't life amazing, I thought, as I retrieved my passport, and pushed my way back out into the street.

★

Death of a Party Man
by Owen Matthews

The Moscow Times, 27th January, 1996

On an October morning in 1937, Boris Bibikov was shot in Stalin's purges as an enemy of the people. Nearly sixty years later his grandson Owen Matthews went to Kiev to look at the secret files.

My mother Ludmilla's earliest memory is of a December night in 1937 when she, aged three and a half, and her 12-year old sister Lenina were woken by the sound of their Mother, Marfa Platonovna, bursting into the room screaming. She snatched Ludmilla out of her bed. Armed men in uniform pushed them both to the ground, wrested the child away, and dragged the Mother into the hall. As Ludmilla ran out after them she was knocked down by a soldier's rifle butt. Marfa and her children were carried down to the street and put in separate police cars.

As their Mother was driven away, Lenina and Ludmilla struggled free, and vainly ran after the departing car. The soldiers caught them and drove them to the Simferopl childrens' prison.... The children were not to see their Mother again for eleven years. Their father, unknown to them, was executed on the 14th October, 1937....

It had been five months since my grandfather, Boris Lvovich Bibikov, party secretary of the Chernigov region of the Ukraine, had been arrested while on holiday. (A true communist, Bibikov had been a party member since the age of 21 and had received the Order of Lenin for his part in building the Kharkov Tractor Works.) The day after his arrest the NKVD came in the middle of the night to search his four-roomed flat in Chernigov.... Lenina [went to Moscow, and accompanied by her uncle] saw Beria, a small bald-headed man, in the Lubyanka. [Lavrenti Beria was Stalin's chief henchman and for years ran the programme of mass arrests.] He said, "We'll look into it" and sent them away. In fact he did nothing.

Lenina lost contact with Ludmilla, and found her only by chance, bloated with hunger and crippled by tuberculosis of the bones, in the Urals town of Solikamsk in 1943. In the same year she got engaged, after two weeks of courtship, to Aleksandr Vasin, a young tank captain. On his way back to Moscow to get married his car ran over a land mine, and his left leg had to be amputated with a wood saw.

Ludmilla, after 14 years in orphanages, won a place in Moscow State University, concealing the fact that her parents had been purged. Marfa Platonovna went partially insane in the labour camp of Karlager in Kazakhstan: she was released from the camp in 1948 but spent the next year in exile. She married a fellow exile, a priest, and had a child by him, but the child died on the train as she was returning to Moscow. Until her death in 1983 in her native Crimea she called her children 'orphanage urchins'. She visited the family in London in 1976....

It was only in 1956, when their father was officially rehabilitated, that the family was informed of his death, and only in 1990 did the authorities issue a genuine death certificate. And it was only in December, 1995 that the Ukrainian Security Service finally allowed me access to the secret files.

The file in Kiev consisted of 260 pages, a combination of absurdly petty items and the starkly shocking, long confessions written in microscopic crabbed writing, certainly under torture. The formal accusation was signed by Stalin's chief prosecutor, Andrei Vyshinski. More than half of the file consisted of the rehabilitation investigation instigated in 1955.

(Slightly abridged and edited by his Father)

*

It was only in 1998, as I was writing these pages, that I tried to find

Vadim and Aleksei. Both of them would have been in their early or mid-seventies: no great age, though statistics show that Russian men die young.

"Adventures," I had said to Vadim in the fraught spring of 1964, "can be fascinating things."

"Yes," he said, with his slightly twisted smile, "especially when they're over!"

That was about the last thing he ever said to me. When my life began to fall apart in Moscow I thought it was pointless meeting him – indeed I had no time, and he made no effort to maintain contact with me. The Institute for Oriental Studies, where he said he worked, was dissolved and amalgamated with other institutions. When I looked him up in the worn catalogue of the Lenin Library in 1998 I was unable to find any publication in his name subsequent to his candidate dissertation, or any evidence of further involvement in Korean studies.

Aleksei did not disappear quite so effectively. I had obtained his surname – Suntsov – from MI5 soon after I returned to England: it was all they ever told me about him. Someone (it may have been Sokolov), mentioned that his patronymic was Vasilievich. In the 1970s, while reading John Barron's well-known book on the KGB, I ran into Aleksei again, as a reference in the index. He was a high flier in the KGB, with top connections in the foreign diplomatic community.

The story Barron tells is interesting in its own right. The French Ambassador in Moscow at that time, a certain Maurice Dejean, had amorous proclivities, and laid himself open to blackmail by bedding an all-too-willing Soviet chambermaid in the Embassy. He was, however, under the surveillance of a senior KGB general called Gribanov, without appreciating Gribanov's subversive role. In any case, Dejean knew him only as Gorbunov. Contact between them was easy, as the Ambassador was encouraged to maintain social relations with prominent Soviet officials. On the other hand, the KGB, had they but realised it, were on to a dead duck, because Dejean's horizontal posturing was already known where it mattered in Paris, and would have precluded him from access to the most sensitive material. According to Barron, de Gaulle himself had once greeted the Ambassador with the words "On couche, Dejean?"

And Aleksei? He was Gribanov's back-up. "Because Gribanov could not devote himself entirely to Dejean [wrote Barron] he chose a polished and handsome KGB officer, Aleksei Suntsov, to help tend the Ambassador. When Dejean flew to Paris to attend Big Four conferences in 1960, Suntsov went along also, and he turned up at Moscow functions Gribanov could not attend, to take care of the

Ambassador." Had I then known of Aleksei's social connections, I would have been most flattered by his attention. In 1998 the press office of the Russian internal security service grudgingly revealed that he had died, but they added that they could not, by law, provide further information.

And that was as far as I could take matters for the time being.

⋆

I remained in touch with most of my true Moscow friends. Valerii Golovitser's ninth or tenth application to leave Russia was successful and in 1980 he took his family to the United States. It meant giving up his Soviet citizenship and possibly never going back. But eventually he got a responsible job organising U.S. tours for Russian ballet, and returned to Moscow frequently. Valerii Shein stayed in theatre administration in Moscow, and, highly unusual though it was, married an English girl, a Russophile and friend of Mila's in London. After perestroika he was able to hire out theatres himself, and became quite affluent.

In 1998 Igor Vail' was still in the Moscow telephone listing, albeit at another address, so of course I gave him a ring. He was delighted to hear from me, though he had not lost sight of me completely, having read some of my articles in the Russian press. He had, it appeared, been waiting for more than thirty years to apologise for his role in the red sweater affair. He confirmed that the provocation had been organised by the KGB directly, just as I had suspected.

On the morning of the fateful day the KGB had urgently summoned him to the Lubyanka and threatened him for two hours. They seemed to know things that had been said when he visited me at MGU, so they must have had listening devices in my room. They told Igor (as I had long suspected) that if he did not assist in their operation to entrap me they would have him expelled from Moscow University. Thus he was subjected to much more specific pressure than Valerii Golovitser. Naturally, the poor fellow had little alternative but to cooperate – hence his nervous response to my telephone call, urging me to come to his flat. Afterwards, while waiting in the militia station, Igor had seen Aleksei, "a well-dressed, handsome man" go to the commandant's office. Subsequently the KGB had called him in just once, *pro forma*, and then left him in peace. By 1998 he had retired from a life-time of teaching in Moscow schools.

Irina Ivinskaya married a former well-known dissident, and eventually settled in Paris, but she never lost her profound affection for her homeland, blemishes and all. Her book of memoirs sold very well in

Russia. In the early seventies Pavel Ivanovich Veselov came over to London to attend to one of his cases, and stayed with us in Pimlico: I found he had not changed in the slightest. His horizons were very modest, and he kept saying he could hardly believe he was in London. He died of cancer in Stockholm in December, 1979, and his friend Irina organised his funeral. His real name was apparently Volyakhov. For all his good works, he died as poor as a church mouse.

Victor Louis continued to live in Moscow with his English wife, and his son, on reaching adulthood, ran the popular English-language *Moscow Tribune*. Ironically, it was considered to be a competitor of the *Moscow Times* for which my son Owen worked. "My father," Mr. Louis junior told me during another of my telephone conversations, "was not the only Soviet journalist to work for a Western paper, there were one or two others. Many colleagues were envious, and ready to malign him in any way possible."

★

Mila's departure seemed to unsettle the Vasin family. Although they were by Soviet standards privileged, both daughters married foreigners and went to live in Germany. When Nadya left, her father Sasha was distraught, the chances of her returning, even for a family visit, being negligible. As she was being driven off to the airport he ran down the snowy street, limping on his artificial leg, shouting "I'll never see her again." Thus did Soviet Russia treat her most faithful sons. Had he only but known the strange path his country would follow! In 1976 Marfa Platonovna got an exit visa, and came to see us in Pimlico. She told friends, on her return to Russia, that she had been in 'fairyland'. After Sasha's death in 1980 Lena visited both her children in Germany, and also our family in London.

★

Derek, dear Derek, lived with Eleonora in Leytonstone. I did not maintain close contact with him, because I had no idea how his marriage would go, and I feared there might be a painful culture clash. I decided that if there were any unhappiness there, I would rather not know about it. But as I discovered later, my apprehensions were quite unfounded, and the couple lived together in great amity. When, in his fifty-sixth year, Derek died suddenly of a heart attack, his wife was distraught, for she loved him dearly.

Other non-Russian friends, Martin Dewhirst, Peter Reddaway,

Gerald Brooke, Georges Nivat, were all to pursue respectable and successful academic careers. Martin, it turned out, had been more involved in the Brooke affair than I realised, in so far as it was he who had introduced Gerald Brooke to Georgii Miller in Oxford. Security in the NTS may have been much better than many people thought, because Aleksei never asked me about Miller.

★

That the Foreign and Commonwealth Office improved a little is evident from my story. In the course of four decades the organisation did eventually produce one fine Ambassador for the Moscow post, and although distinctions may raise eyebrows, I hasten to name him as Sir Roderic Braithwaite. I had no further contact with Brimelow or any of his colleagues: I did, indeed, write to him, about 1981, when the Russian section at Surrey University was under threat of closure, as I thought he might help. By then he had floated even higher, and acquired a seat in the House of Lords. He did not reply, and I much regretted having written. Although I found his conduct unacceptable I did, over the years, meet people who knew about his apparently modest background, and who had a good word to say for him. When the East German regime collapsed, Wolfgang Vogel, the Berlin lawyer, was accused of breaches of the law, and (I believe) detained for a time, but to judge from subsequent photographs in the German press he never lost his enigmatic smile.

★

"Just a short note to wish you a safe and pleasant journey to Moscow and a safe return," my mother had written to me on the 20th October, 1969, before I left to get married. "I hope and pray that you and Mila will be very happy together, but remember Mervyn you can't expect to have it all your own way as you always have.... I also pray that Mila will settle happily in this country. I would like to give you both a good wedding present of about £50. You need have no fear of me forcing myself on you, but it would be etiquette for me to meet Mila as soon as possible. God bless you and guide you always. Fondest Love, Mother."

At that time of our arrival in London my mother happened to be in Cardiff Hospital, where she went periodically for asthma treatment. So I took Mila down, and the two main female players in my life met at a hospital bedside. It was a lovely meeting, second only to the momentous moment when I had proposed in the kitchen at

Starokonyushenny pereulok. Both women glowed with pleasure. My Mother was to die of cancer only two years later, but there was never the slightest hint of tension between them. She was captivated by Mila's radiant smile and a respect for her which never waned. Mila could be very good with people of the older generation.

My spouse quickly came to appreciate the advantages of living in London, and got a job teaching Russian, which over the years enabled her to introduce hundreds of Britishers to her convoluted native tongue. Soon after our arrival in England, incidentally, Lord Brockway invited us to have tea at the House of Lords, having arranged to be photographed with us afterwards. Somehow he envisaged our case as an example of his successful relationship with the Russians. Mila and I moved, a little regretfully, from the flat in Belgrave Road to a house in one of Pimlico's less attractive streets. It seemed only natural that the language of the household should be Russian, and that our son and daughter should grow up with the imprint of that distant land upon them.

*

On the 6th January, 1999, just before three o'clock, I arrived at the KGB Veterans' Club near October Square in Moscow. "You're a little early for the appointment," said Vadim Leonidovich, the deputy manager. "But no matter, you can wait in my office until the lady arrives."

And indeed a few minutes later a lively seventy-year old, rather overweight, like most Russians, but with a pleasant, welcoming face, bustled in. Vadim Leonidovich rose respectfully to his feet. They seemed to know one another well.

"I'm Ina Vadimovna Suntsova," she said, turning to me. "And you're Mervyn Matthews? I must admit I wouldn't have recognised you. When was it we last met, 1959 or 1960? When Aleksei Vasilievich took us to a restaurant."

"Was it the Ararat?"

"No, I think it was the Budapest. They had a new cook, and offered a selection of pastries. In fact we met twice. On another occasion we all went up to the Lenin Hills together, near the university, in Aleksei Vasilievich's car, to look at the lights of Moscow."

"I think I can just remember that, though I have not included it in my book. I've brought the typescript along, to show you what I wrote about Aleksei. I shall ask you for his photograph in return. I never had a chance to photograph him."

"Well," she said meaningfully, "we'll talk about photographs later."

When I was writing the book the thought that Aleksei's widow might read even a few sentences never entered my head: and had she, at that moment, suggested any changes, I would have been hard-pressed to respond. I described Aleksei as accurately and objectively as I could, and suppression of the truth was out of the question. But Ina Vadimovna turned out to be a reasonable woman, and having heard most of what I wrote about her late husband, she did not ask for a word to be changed. In fact, she was flattered by a few of my phrases, and confirmed possession of the solid gold watch which had so impressed me when we first met. I uttered a thought that had long been in my mind.

"Was Aleksei from a noble Russian family?"

Ina Vadimovna smiled. "Yes, he was, but I would prefer not to name it."

"That explains an awful lot," I said, thinking of his smooth demeanour. But I decided not to pursue the point, because there were obviously things she was not prepared to reveal.

"Please tell me as much as you can about him."

"We were both twenty-two when we married, and I was profoundly distressed when he died in 1994, after a long illness. No, I won't say what it was. The Committee for Interdepartmental Information? What he told you about working for it was correct, but the Committee was transferred from the Ministry of Foreign Affairs to the KGB under Foreign Minister Gromyko. Yes, Aleksei was attached to the United Nations, and served in New York and Washington in 1955. He went on to head an English Department in the KGB, and rose to the rank of colonel. This is his photograph in uniform."

She rummaged in her bag for a moment and pulled it out. Although I knew all too well that Aleksei was a KGB officer, seeing a picture of him in military attire, albeit decades later, was something of shock. But his face was exactly as I remembered it: it had been indelibly imprinted in my memory. Ina Vadimovna would not tell me which 'English Department' he headed, presumably because she thought it might still be secret. It may have been part of the Second KGB Directorate, which was thought to handle foreigners resident in Moscow.

"Did you, incidentally, ever meet the French Ambassador Maurice Dejean?" I asked.

"Of course."

"You knew that Aleksei was handling my case. Did he ever tell you anything about it? The trips to Siberia and Gagry, for example?"

"I knew that he took you to Siberia, but I knew nothing of Gagry.

He went away from time to time. I know that he was bitterly disappointed in you, and complained. 'Matthews,' he would say, 'the nasty boy, he let me down, after all I've done for him.' You know, he meant the 'nasty boy' in the Chekhov story, who deliberately annoyed every one. When things didn't work out with you, it definitely had a negative effect on Aleksei's position in the service. But tell me, why did you have dealings with him in the first place?"

"Mutual misunderstanding, I suppose. I was twenty-seven and regarded it as a sort of game. He thought he could recruit me, and to begin with did not reveal his intentions. He seemed quite happy to entertain me in good restaurants, so I just let things float. We both thought we would win."

"Yes, young people do rash things. But later you were involved in some sort of scandal, weren't you?"

"The KGB stopped me from getting married and soon after expelled me from Russia. They organised a 'provocation', a trap. I was accused of 'speculation' because I sold a red sweater to a friend. The idea was to blackmail me into working for Soviet security."

Ina Vadimovna seemed genuinely taken aback. "A speculation charge just for selling a red sweater!"

I thought for a moment of asking her who in the KGB had controlled my case, and kept me apart from Mila for so long: somehow I doubted that it was Aleksei himself, though he could have been involved in some decision-making. Even so, the Brooke case, and any association with it, would have precluded an easy solution. Was Aleksei was more of an enemy than I suspected? Ina Vadimovna would scarcely have known anything of such matters, and would not have revealed them if she did. So I did not enquire.

"Did you know Aleksandr Fedorovich Sokolov?" I asked. "Aleksei once told me Sokolov was his boss. A very peasanty type."

Again the knowing smile. "Rather a thick-set man with thinning hair and a kind face? Yes, I met him. He worked in Aleksei's department of the KGB, under Aleksei, of course. Perhaps he pretended to be more of a peasant than he was? Perhaps Aleksei handed you over to him when he realised that you were not worth his time."

"And did you know Vadim Popov, or his 'uncle'?"

"Vadim's uncle?" She laughed dismissively, feeding my suspicion that no such uncle had ever existed. "I knew Vadim very well, he was a close friend of Aleksei's. He lived near Novoslobodskaya Street, not far from us. He got married late in life, in his mid-forties.

"He specialised in Korean studies for a time, didn't he?"

"Yes, but he did lots of other things as well. He certainly took a full-time job in the KGB under Aleksei, and they used to meet very

often. They were friends. Later, when Aleksei fell ill and was transferred to a teaching post, they rather drifted apart. I think Vadim took
some sort of job in analysis."

"What did Aleksei teach?"

"His work experience, of course."

I wondered whether I had figured as a cautionary tale in his lectures.

"I used to have Vadim's telephone number," she continued, "but
he moved when he changed his job. I imagine he's still alive, though
I have lost contact with him. A lot of the people have moved out of
the organisation, and I know the wives, mostly."

"If Vadim became a full-time KGB officer, I doubt whether he
would speak to me about these matters, even now."

"What happened after your wife left Russia?"

I explained the family situation in London, and told her our son
Owen was currently working as a journalist in Moscow.

"So you'll let me have a photograph of Aleksei for the book?" I
concluded.

She hesitated for what seemed an age, then, to my delight, drew
more photographs from her bag. "I hope publishing any of these
won't have political consequences for us. But you weren't involved in
politics, were you? Or intelligence?"

"No," I said. "But in any case a thirty-year old photograph of a
deceased KGB officer could not possibly cause any problems today."

"Will the book be published in Russia?"

"Who knows!"

"Well, have this one then. It was taken about the time you knew
him. Better not have the one showing him in uniform. The strip of
grey hair on his temple started very narrow, when he was young, and
got wider as the years passed. But now I have a favour to ask you."

"If I can help you, I will."

"Aleksei Vasilievich's grand-daughter Marina is studying business
at a university in Moscow, this is her photograph." Ina Vadimovna
showed me yet another print, this time of an attractive young Russian
girl at a party table. "She is supposed to do work practice in an
English-speaking office in Moscow, but we cannot find anywhere.
Do you think you, or Owen could help? We would be most grateful."

"I'll give you his telephone number," I said. "I'm sure he'll do
what he can. And I'll ask one or two friends myself."

The interview was clearly coming to an end.

"Thank you for the photograph," I added. "I'll have it copied and
see that you get the original back through the Veterans' Club. And
thank you for talking to me."